By Invitation Only

By Invitation Only

THE RISE OF EXCLUSIVE POLITICS

IN THE UNITED STATES

Steven E. Schier

UNIVERSITY OF PITTSBURGH PRESS

Published by the University of Pittsburgh Press, Pittsburgh, Pa. 15261

Copyright © 2000, University of Pittsburgh Press

Manufactured in the United States of America

Printed on acid-free paper

10 9 8 7 6 5 4 3 2 1

LIBRARY OF CONGRESS CATALOGING-IN-PUBLICATION DATA

Schier, Steven E.

  By invitation only : the rise of exclusive politics in the United
States / Steven E. Schier.

     p. cm.

  Includes bibliographical references and index.

   ISBN 0-8229-5712-4 (pbk. : acid-free paper) — ISBN 0-8229-4109-0
(cloth : acid-free paper)

  1. Political particpation—United States. 2. Political
parties—United States. 3. Pressure groups—United States.
4. Lobbying—United States. 5. Electioneering—United States. I. Title.

JK1764.S36 2000

324'0973'09049—dc21   99–050620

for Mary

Contents

Acknowledgments   ix

Introduction   1

1. The Rise of Activation Strategies   7

2. The Great Disintegration: From Partisan
   Mobilization to Activation   42

3. Candidates, Parties, and Electoral Activation   89

4. Interest Organizations and Electoral Activation   125

5. Interest Organizations and Government:
   Lobbying by Activation   155

6. From Activation to Inclusion   194

Bibliography   223
Index   239

Acknowledgments

Two scholars deserve praise for clarifying this book's purpose. John Green of the Ray Bliss Center at the University of Akron first suggested the term *activation* as a contrast to *mobilization* and helped me sharpen the conceptual differences between the two terms. My colleague Norman Vig at Carleton College drew my attention to the ubiquity of activation strategies in contemporary American politics. The thesis of this book emerged from their seminal contributions. I must also thank John J. Coleman of the University of Wisconsin—Madison, G. Calvin Mackenzie and L. Sandy Maisel of Colby College, Burdett Loomis of the University of Kansas, Rich Keiser at Carleton College, and several anonymous reviewers for also helping me develop my argument. During my time directing Carleton's Washington program in the fall of 1997, I was able personally to interview many leading national lobbyists, who shared many insights into their part of the activation game. Carleton students helped me at every step of the way as well. My two research assistants, Justin Magouirk and Tonya Mykleby, provided extraordinary assistance. Justin researched the scholarly literature on turnout with an acumen usually demonstrated only by the very best graduate students. Tonya's very thoughtful and substantive comments on each chapter significantly improved their contents. Both will have outstanding careers as political scientists, should they care to join the discipline. (Message to both: political science needs you!) Thanks also to Niels Aaboe of the University of Pittsburgh Press for his unfailing support along the way.

Mary, Anna, and Teresa endured my months of preoccupation with this project and gave me the best possible recreation when I was away from it. Their love and support provided the most important element in my completion of this book.

Northfield, Minnesota
August 1999

By Invitation Only

Introduction

American politics has become a politics of exclusive invitations. Political parties, organized interests, and candidates for office all strive to prevail in elections and policy-making by motivating carefully targeted segments of the public to vote or press demands upon elected officials. In the process, a large segment of the public—about half—receive little invitation or inducement to participate in our politics. Despite our public reverence for democratic participation, the bleak reality of American politics falls far short of the ideal. What brought us to this point? The causes are many. The decay of political parties, the rise of new political technologies, and the evolution of an increasingly user-unfriendly electoral system created perverse incentives for political elites. In recent decades, parties, interests, and campaigns have discovered what has become the most efficient way to succeed in elections and policy making. That way involves activation—identifying and activating the small segments of citizens most likely to "get their message" and vote or lobby government. The cost and risk of reaching out to all citizens is increasingly irrational for these elites. Providing exclusive invitations is the rational way to political success.

This book addresses three audiences. One is the professional audience of political scientists. They will find here a review of a broad literature concerning political parties, interest groups, campaigns and elections, political behavior, and normative and empirical democratic theory. It is organized around a theoretical argument about how and why activation, the politics of exclusive targeting, differs from the inclusive partisan mobilization practiced by American parties in the nineteenth century. Political elites' contemporary use of activation strategies results from the advent of new incentives for them as rational actors, a central insight of the "new institutionalism" in the study of American politics. As the incentives changed for these actors, so did American politics. Elite interviews and documentary research concerning the activities of five major interest groups supplement the literature review and theoretical argument throughout this book.

Students of political science make up a second audience for the book. Many learn about particular problems in electoral politics and lobbying but may not be aware of their common roots. Many citizens don't vote because no one invites them to participate. Candidates and parties conduct boring campaigns because they address their appeals to a small segment of the adult population. Money grows in political importance because it is essential to successful activation by parties, candidates, and interests. Groups proliferate because of the competitive threat of rival interests. Parties matter less because they have little claim on voters beyond that exercised by candidates and, increasingly, organized groups. These particular problems derive from the politics of activation. Teachers will find this book a useful addition to courses in parties, interest groups, elections, political behavior, empirical democratic theory, and American politics.

The broader group of politically aware citizens constitutes a third audience for the book. Here they can find an underlying explanation of several of the problems of America's democratic politics, along with an assessment of possible reforms. Without an accurate diagnosis, attempted remedies are futile. Many voguish reforms, aimed at improving electoral and governmental politics, lack that accurate diagnosis. My final chapter, described below, assesses which reforms might actually create a more inclusive American politics.

THE ARGUMENT

Chapter 1 presents the main argument of the book. It first distinguishes activation, the finely targeted, exclusive method contemporary parties, interests, and campaigns employ to cultivate popular support, from the more inclusive electoral mobilization undertaken by political parties during the partisan era of the last century. Activation's traits are revealed through reference to recent political science literature. The legitimating arguments of activation come from participatory democratic theory, which is oblivious to the problems of activation. At its root, activation arose as a rational response to a political environment characterized by party decline, a proliferation of organized interests, and new efficiencies in communication and campaign technologies. The result is a contemporary politics "by invitation only."

Chapter 2 explains the disintegration of inclusive electoral politics resulting from the shift from partisan mobilization to contemporary activation. Old-style mobilization was inclusive because it involved simple partisan messages, communication by personal contact, social networks with strong voting norms, and adequate time for citizens to absorb the partisan message. Party strength in American politics declined due to a combination of structural reforms pressed by the progressive movement and changes in the national policy environment. As presidents gained power at the expense of Congress and as Congress made economic policy more automatic and less discretionary, voters came to view partisan control of government as less consequential to their personal livelihoods. The rise of television and new campaign technologies encouraged a further individualization of electoral campaigns.

Chapter 3 portrays the "state of the art" activation practiced by contemporary political campaigns. In contrast to the era of partisan mobilization, candidates operate more individualistic campaigns with more expensive techniques and target the electorate much more carefully. Careful targeting becomes a strategic imperative for campaigns, given their limited financial resources. The chapter explains the central role of campaign consultants, the importance of negative advertising, and the variety of firms involved in selling candidates to voters. Political parties, once at the heart of election campaigns, now primarily supply money to help candidate-centered campaigns disseminate their individualistic messages. The chapter concludes by examining the crucial "swing voters" that contemporary campaigns target for activation. The Clinton reelection campaign's careful targeting of suburban swing voters reveals how activation biases its appeals toward relatively affluent citizens. The narrow focus of candidate messages in 1996 contrasts markedly with the broad-brush partisan messages of the last century.

Chapters 4 and 5 detail how the burgeoning number of interest organizations energetically employ activation techniques in political campaigns and governmental lobbying. Chapter 4 portrays the many avenues of interest influence in the electoral arena. Interest organizations are defined and their campaign strategies identified. These include gathering information, raising funds, contributing money to candidates and parties, and activating grassroots membership. The successful grassroots mobilization of the Christian Coalition in 1994 receives particular attention, as does initiative politics in California. The initiative, once touted as a hallmark of participatory democracy, has decayed into an arena dominated by well-funded interests that try to direct public policy through clever advertising.

Chapter 5, the second chapter focusing on activation by interest organizations, examines their activities in lobbying government. The increasing use of "outside" lobbying strategies, in which interests activate fragments of the public to put direct pressure on legislatures, receives attention. Interests also use a variety of activation tactics to recruit and keep members. The chapter concludes with several case studies of successful interest organizations that explain how the organizations successfully recruit members, activate them for lobbying, and influence election campaigns. The grand result of interest lobbying is a proliferation of narrow, particular demands on the governmental agenda rather than consistent governmental attention to identify and address majority preferences.

Chapter 6 assesses reforms that might produce more mobilization and less activation in American politics. Electoral rules seem a more promising means of reform than do changes in national economic policy. Dramatic changes in economic policy that will make parties and elections more important to the public seem highly unlikely. The goal of reform must be simpler and more decisive elections, requiring a stronger party role in elections and more incentives for citizens to vote. Recent campaign finance reform measures threaten a counterproductive result by weakening the ability of parties to raise and spend funds in elections. Ultimately, only more sweeping changes can restore mobilization. Mandatory voting and a partisan ballot are most likely to bring forth a fresh form of partisan mobilization. Other nations with these procedures have more decisive and inclusive elections than does the United States. We can learn from their examples and bring the entire public back into electoral politics.

CHAPTER I

The Rise of Activation Strategies

The critical element for the health of a democratic order consists in the beliefs, standards and competence of those who constitute the influentials, the opinion-leaders, the political activists in the order. . . . If a democracy tends toward indecision, decay and disorder, the responsibility rests here, not with the mass of the people.

V. O. Key, *Public Opinion and American Democracy*

This book is about the distinction between two words. Their different meanings explain how America's popular politics has changed for the worse over the last one hundred years. The first word is *mobilization,* defined here as the partisan method of stimulating very high turnout in elections during the period of peak party power that lasted from 1876 to 1892. The second word is *activation,* meaning the more contemporary methods that parties, interest groups, and candidates employ to induce particular, finely targeted portions of the public to become active in elections, demonstrations, and lobbying.

The two terms reveal very differing processes by which political elites engage the public. First, the two processes differ in their *focus*. The partisan mobilization of the past was inclusive, seeking to arouse all possible voters to vote in response to a direct partisan message. Activation, conversely, is exclusive by design. Candidates, interests, and consultants carefully identify those in the public most likely to become active on their behalf and then employ a variety of inducements to stimulate the action. New communication technology makes such microtargeting possible and allows elites to expend resources in arousing the public far more efficiently—and narrowly—than in the days of mobilization.

The two processes also differ in their *agents,* or sources of stimulation of the public. Mobilization was a heavily partisan process, dominated by strong party organizations and party messages. Politics centered on elections, and most voters viewed electoral choice as a partisan choice. In contrast, thousands of different organizations and individuals attempt activation today. Individual candidates now make their own personal appeals to an electorate uninterested in parties. A dizzying array of interest groups seeks to impart selective information and activism expertise to their potential supporters in the public. Parties still get out a message during elections, but it often gets lost in the competitive din of activation appeals.

The processes also differ in their *method.* Partisan mobilization involved broad appeals often carried through personal conversation with local party workers, or through America's then highly partisan press. In contrast, activation is research-driven by polling and focus groups, allowing the activators to target precisely those most likely to respond to appeals. Activation employs telephones, direct mail, and Internet communication in a way that allows distinctively phrased messages of maximum possible impact. It does not seek to get most potential voters to participate in an election, as does mobilization, but instead fires up a small but potentially effective segment of the public to help a particular candidate at the polls or a particular interest as it lobbies government.

Finally, the processes differ in their *impact on popular rule in America*. Partisan mobilization encouraged heavy turnouts of eligible voters, most of whom cast a clear and decisive ballot for one of the two major parties in an election. A simple, direct, electoral verdict allowed for a relatively clear correspondence between the views of voters and the actions of government. Activation has no such representative function. It works to further the purposes of particular political elites during elections and when they lobby government, regardless of what most citizens think or desire. It is now possible for candidates, parties, and interests to rule without serious regard to majority preferences as expressed at the polls. Mobilization encouraged popular rule. Activation impedes it. Sadly, the rise of activation destroyed the prospects for majority rule in American politics.

The distinction between these two words is not helped by the indiscriminate use of the term *mobilization* by scholars of popular politics. They commonly label the partisan era of 1876–1892 as characterized by a very intense "mobilization of the electorate" (Silbey 1998, 8). Yet, scholars also use *mobilization* to describe the contemporary politics of exclusive targeting. For example, Steven Rosenstone and John Mark Hansen assert, "Intent on creating the greatest effect with the least effort, politicians, parties, interest groups, and activists mobilize people who are known to them, who are well placed in social networks, whose actions are effective, and who are likely to act"

(Rosenstone and Hansen 1993, 33). This analysis perfectly describes the logic of contemporary *activation*, not the inclusive partisan *mobilization* of over a century ago.

By using the term *mobilization* indiscriminately, scholars miss the important distinctions, discussed above, between politics during the peak of the partisan era and politics today. The relationship of political elites to the public has shifted greatly in its focus, agency, method, and impact on popular politics. We need to recognize this more explicitly in the way we describe that relationship. Hence the need for the distinction between the two words, and the purpose of this book.

EXPLAINING PARADOXES

The decline of mobilization and the rise of activation explain many contemporary paradoxes of American politics. It is paradoxical that in an era when direct, participatory democracy seems ever more popular, the public is dismayed at its consequences. The popularity of what James Madison termed "direct rule by the people" is everywhere evident. Polls reveal the public supports abolition of the undemocratic electoral college in selecting presidents. Direct policy-making by initiative and referendum thrives in many states (Cronin 1989, 51). Interest groups enjoy a great vogue as a means of popular participation, their number mushrooming in recent decades (Baumgartner and Leech 1998, 103). One might expect this wave of participation would produce greater popular content with government and its operations.

Not so. Certain forms of direct popular participation in government have become more fashionable, while popular disaffection from government has grown as well. Figure 1.1 charts the rise of interest groups in Washington and the growing number of Americans who believe government is "controlled by a few large interests." Why would this perception grow as the number of interest groups rose greatly and the number of Americans joining and active in groups grew as well? The interest group world of Washington in the mid-twentieth century indeed featured "a few large interests"—big business, big labor, veterans' organizations, and farm groups had far fewer rivals for access and influence than they have now (Baumgartner and Leech 1998, 110–11). Times have changed. A national survey in 1989 found that 79 percent of Americans are members of groups and 48 percent reported affiliation with a group that takes political stands (Verba, Scholzman, and Brady 1995, 63, 50). Today, "groups 'r' us" (Rauch 1994, 48). Over a thousand corporate trade organizations, representing businesses ranging from the American Bankers Association to the Association of Dressings and Sauces, now have Washington headquarters. Environmental groups, virtually nonexistent in D.C. in 1950, are numerous and influential, including organizations such as the Friends of the Earth and the Sierra Club. The largest membership group represented in Washington today, the American Association of Retired Persons with thirty million members, did not even exist in 1950. The 1970s witnessed the proliferation of many public interest and social justice groups and movements, many still very active in Washington. In 1959, political scientist Charles Lindblom claimed that "every important interest has its watchdog" in policy making (Lindblom 1959, 85). That is truer now than when he wrote it. Yet the public emphatically does not see it that way.

Figure 1.1 illustrates another paradox of our politics. Despite all this participatory effort, increasing proportions of Americans believe that elected officials do not care what they think. This perception collides with the scholarly picture of officeholders continually "running

Figure 1.1 Increase in Groups and Public Alienation

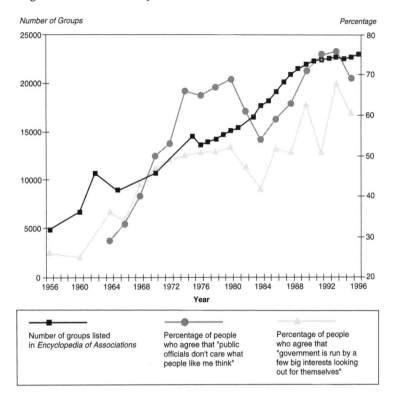

scared" of popular opinion and attempting to be as responsive as possible (King 1997). Figure 1.2 adds a further dimension to this curious situation. Alongside the growth in groups and rising level of public education is a drooping trend in voter turnout. Political scientists have long held that higher education promotes a person's likelihood of voting (Campbell et al. 1960; Nie, Junn, and Stehlik-Barry 1996). Rising education levels may stimulate group activity, but certainly not voting. Political scientists have sound explanations for the rise of interest groups and the decline of voting despite rising education levels, as future chapters make clear (Nie, Junn, and Stehlik-Barry 1996).

The rise of activation strategies spawned the advent of these paradoxes. Although the American public has more political resources—in terms of education, at least—that should yield high electoral participation, citizens do not receive inclusive invitations to participate. Instead, an exclusive, invitation-only sort of targeting dominates American politics. The result: a more educated public that participates less, and the rise of popular alienation.

Political activists and operatives efficiently stimulate participation

Figure 1.2 Voting as a Percentage of Voting Age Population and Increase in Education

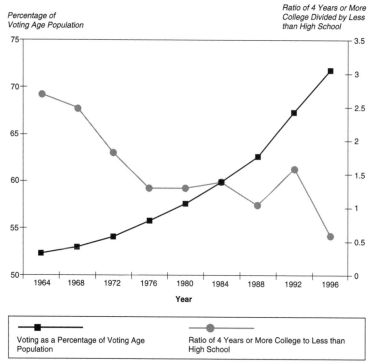

by the parts of the public most likely to become active for them given an appropriate stimulus. Campaigns target the undecided and less than firmly committed voters with ads and phone calls in the final weeks of an election campaign. Interest groups through phone and mail contact those members most likely to respond with activism. The message delivered through these strategies seeks to influence an incentive held dear by a political decision maker: reelection, or power over legislation, budgets, and policy implementation. The result is a complex and frequently tawdry battle among a multitude of national groups and officeholders. Richard Neustadt describes current Washington policy making as

Warfare among elites, waged since the 1960s in the name of causes, not com-promises, fueled by technology, manned by consultants, rousing supporters by damning opponents, while serving the separate interests of particular candi-dates and groups at times. . . . They try incessantly to win a given election, to promote or to stop a given legislative provision, regulation, appointment, con-tract, or executive decision in diplomacy and defense. (Neustadt 1997, 187)

Activation strategies occur because elites—officeholders, campaign consultants, interest group operatives—have limited resources. They cannot contact everyone in the nation about their agendas. Given lim-ited time, money, and expertise, it is only rational to identify likely supporters as accurately as possible and stimulate them to help you as efficiently as you can. Much of our national politics results from acti-vation strategy. It is the political variant of "niche marketing" found throughout our economy. In Washington, everyone is doing it. Who does it best greatly determines who governs.

Activation strategies contrast starkly with electoral mass mobiliza-tion by political parties. Mobilization predominated during election campaigns during the late nineteenth and early twentieth centuries, declining greatly in presence and effectiveness after 1950. Party mobilization involved geographically based, partisan appeals for voters. Party organizations sought power through elections and offered voters a variety of material, social, and issue benefits in return (Wilson 1995, 30–56). Traditional partisan mobilization was a crude tool, operating via personal and print communication. Precise targeting technologies were not yet invented. Unable to efficiently identify those most likely to become active, party leaders blanketed entire neighborhoods with partisan appeals. Instead of narrowcasting to the active, parties broadcast to the masses. Parties sought to lower information costs for low-knowledge voters by advocating a simple party-line vote. Many voters willingly obliged, producing higher turnout than strategic activation has produced in recent decades (Ginsberg and Shefter 1990, 3). Party elites had to encourage rule by popular majorities in order to gain power.

Activation strategies, in contrast, mobilize strategic minorities while cloaking the effort in a misleading guise of popular rule. The "legitimating arguments" come, as we will see, from the proponents of participatory democracy. Washington operatives use strategic activation of *their* people as an example of direct rule by *the* people, conflating a faction of the public mobilized by an elite with majority opinion. This is not misleading if *their* people in the aggregate resemble *the* people. They usually do not.

PATTERNS OF ACTIVATION STRATEGIES

The citizens who respond to activation strategies are often an unrepresentative lot. Only a small fraction of the public makes up America's activist population. For many interest groups, strategic activation simply involves "rounding up the usual suspects" who by making their views heard in government give the illusion of widespread popular sentiment. Most of these activists come from an elite stratum of the public whose members are far more politically sophisticated than the average citizen. Activists have much more knowledge of and interest in politics than their fellow citizens.

W. Russell Neuman found the public divides into three groups with varying degrees of political sophistication. Twenty percent of the public are "a self-consistent and unabashedly apolitical lot" (Neuman 1986, 170). The apoliticals very seldom vote and are not ashamed of their apathy. Most citizens are found among the 75 percent comprising Neuman's "mass public" who are "marginally attentive to politics and mildly cynical about the behavior of politicians, but they accept the duty to vote, and do so with fair regularity" (1986, 170). Those most likely the targets of activation strategies are the activists, comprising only 5 percent of the adult population with uniquely high levels of political involvement and sophistication (170).

Other recent studies reveal the unrepresentative characteristics of political activists. Steven Rosenstone and John Mark Hansen find that "the pool of political activists is enormously unrepresentative of the population, no matter how many people are involved" (1993, 235). The authors identify "governmental activists," those who attempt to influence governmental officials, and "electoral activists," those who are active in elections beyond voting. Both groups are much more educated and affluent than those who are less active. The political activity with by far the lowest education and income skew is voting, much less unequal in its incidence than attending meetings, writing legislators, working on campaigns, or attempting to influence the voting of others (1993, 234–37). A landmark study of political participation by Sidney Verba, Kay Lehman Schlozman, and Henry Brady found a similar pattern. The authors create a measure of "participatory distortion" for a variety of activities. This compares average characteristics of activists who engage in various political activities with the average of the public at large (1995, 468). Corroborating Rosenstone and Hansen, the authors discover that voting produces the least distortion, but campaign contributions the most.

The evidence is clear. No other political activity is as representative of the public will as voting. One reason why other activities— writing letters, attending protests, joining groups, giving money—are less representative is that they result from strategic activation. Verba, Schlozman, and Brady find that whites and high-income individuals report many more invitations to participate in politics than blacks, Latinos, and low-income individuals (1995, 150–53). Although America has a profusion of interest groups, the pattern of activism skews the resources of groups toward advantaged individuals, whatever their issue agenda.

Rosenstone and Hansen present the underlying logic for this pattern of strategic activation. One must understand the costs and benefits individuals perceive when deciding whether to participate. All of us are members of social networks involving friends, family, neighbors, and co-workers. Since all of us seek acceptance from fellow network members, we are inclined to take cues from them. Social networks share the cost of acquiring political information and create social expectations for political participation or nonparticipation. Groups and campaigns try to spur activism directly through contacting individuals and indirectly by encouraging network members to encourage participation among fellow networkers. Groups and campaigns, given their limited resources, try to induce activism as efficiently as possible.[1]

Given this drive for efficiency, Rosenstone and Hansen list the tendencies of activation strategies. First, campaigns and groups are most likely to contact people they know. The cost is low, and probability of success is high. Second, people at the center of social networks are more likely strategic targets. They are easier to identify and more likely to be effective. Third, those most effective at producing political outcomes are more likely strategic targets. Fourth, those likely to respond by participating are also likely targets (1993, 30–31). This logic produces the skew in activism revealed in the preceding paragraphs. The logic of strategic activation produces a self-sustaining stratification of political activity in which a small proportion of the public is effectively and constantly induced to participate directly in politics. The current vogue of participatory democracy is both a consequence and a cause of this activation syndrome.

THE PARTICIPATORY JUSTIFICATION

The term *participatory democracy* can encompass a variety of political arrangements. A more participatory democracy can result from increased use of reforms such as initiative, referendum, and recall and

1. Rosenstone and Hansen (1993) and many other political scientists use the term *mobilization* to denote activities to induce political participation. Here I use the term *activation* instead in order to contrast it with wider-scale mobilization efforts of political parties in the nineteenth and early twentieth centuries. Thus activation strategies commonly seek to spur activity in a small, carefully targeted fraction of the public. The distinction between activation and mobilization has great consequences for empirical democratic theory and the possibility of majority rule, as subsequent chapters reveal. I am indebted to John Green, director of the Ray Bliss Center at the University of Akron, for the distinction.

through more "grassroots" political activity. Some go further and argue that new technology permits direct popular voting on policy as the norm in government (Budge 1996). Both incremental and radical participatory reformers draw inspiration from Jean Jacques Rousseau, a prominent early participatory theorist. In his famous *Social Contract,* Rousseau argued that the people as a whole are sovereign and all laws must flow ultimately from assembled meetings of the people. "The sovereign, having no other force than the legislative power, acts only by laws; and since the laws are only authentic acts of the general will, the sovereign can only act when the people is assembled" (Rousseau 1978, 98).

Rousseau has more in common with incremental rather than radical participatory reformers. He favored daily rule by an elected "aristocracy" with occasional popular meetings to ratify the results (1978, 86). Current advocates of participatory democracy tend to share Rousseau's aversion to representative government, which he termed an inadequate substitute for the sovereign "general will" of the people (101–04). Representatives cannot represent the general will, because that only resides in the people and sovereignty cannot be transferred (102–04). A similar critique of representative government informed the thinking of another major source of current participatory thinking, the progressive movement of early twentieth-century America.

Progressives argued that the corrupt behavior of elected representatives in certain cities and states amounted to an abuse of sovereignty. The source of corruption lay in the party machines that used control of government as a means to enrich their supporters (Mackenzie 1996; Ginsburg and Shefter 1990). The progressive movement created a new electoral regime to weaken party control and strengthen participatory democracy. Civil service reform ended government employment through partisan patronage. The secret ballot and registration requirements lessened party-sponsored fraud and coercion at the polls. Primary elections weakened party organization control of nominations. Replacing party column ballots with office-bloc and nonpartisan ballots increased the difficulty of following partisan cues in the voting booth. The initiative, referendum, and recall allowed for popular, participatory circumvention of party-controlled legislatures (Cronin 1989, 38–59). The widespread adoption of these reforms lessened partisan mobilization and boosted participatory mechanisms that would encourage the advent of activation strategies.

Leading progressive reformers justified their actions in the name of direct, participatory democracy. Governor Robert M. La Follette of Wisconsin advocated the direct primary based on a simple normative principle. "Go back to the first principle of democracy. Go back to the people" (Lovejoy 1941, 36). Governor Hiram Johnson of California claimed that the initiative, referendum, and recall "give to the electorate the power of action when desired, and they do place in the hands of the people the means by which they may protect themselves" (Lee and Berg 1976, 98). Individual voters could protect themselves from the predations of corrupt parties and interests that can flourish in representative institutions. By making participation more complex and difficult, however, progressive reformers increased the cost of mobilizing popular majorities and made rule by activated minorities more possible and thus more widely attempted. Chapter 2 develops this point further.

The turbulence of the 1960s brought another wave of participatory fervor into American politics with the rise of many "movements" of aggrieved citizens—women, gays and lesbians, Christian conservatives, African Americans, and opponents of the Vietnam War. Many political theorists, sympathetic to these movements, wrote in support of participatory democracy. Jack Walker argued that such movements help society in many ways; they "break society's log jams . . . prevent ossification of the political system . . . prompt and justify major innovations in social policy and economic organization" (Walker 1970, 244). Carol Pateman, a leading participatory theorist of the time, admitted that participatory democracy asks much of individual citizens, but that the results of participation can be grand. "One might characterize the participatory model as one where maximum input (participation) is required and where output includes not just policies (decisions) but also the development of the social and political capacities of each individual, so that there is 'feedback' from output to input" (Pateman 1970, 43). Participation produces more able, better citizens, an argument Pateman shares with John Stuart Mill and other earlier democratic theorists (Mill 1910, 217). Pateman's study of worker self-management in Yugoslavia led her to conclude that participatory mechanisms increase citizen knowledge and efficacy. Since participation makes better citizens without threatening regime stability, more participatory democracy is needed (Pateman 1970, 49).

Benjamin Barber continued the theoretical defense of participatory democracy into the late twentieth century. Barber argued that American citizens were apathetic because they were powerless, not powerless because they were apathetic. Our "thin democracy" of representative institutions and elite interest groups produced this powerlessness (Barber 1984, 3–26). The antidote is "strong democracy" incorporating progressive participatory structures and more: national town meetings, neighborhood assemblies, office holding by lottery, national initiative and referendum, and other reforms (273–98). The goal is to create more knowledgeable, active, and public-spirited citizens. "Only in a strong democratic community are individuals transformed. Their autonomy is preserved because their vision of their own freedom and interest has been enlarged to include others; and their obedience to the common force is rendered legitimate because their enlarged vision enables them to perceive in the common force the working of their own wills" (Barber 1984, 232).

Barber's vision is indeed beguiling, but it must be examined in light of the realities of America's current system of strategic activation. Participatory theorists ask more of citizens in order that citizens might contribute more to the quality of our collective political life. Participatory contributions require time and information-gathering and processing costs. For a minority of more educated and informed citizens, the information-gathering costs of participation are lower. Further, the benefits of participation will not be valued equally by citizens. More educated and informed—"properly socialized"—citizens will value the personal benefits of participation more than those who have been less inculcated with civic virtues. The market for participation is very cost-sensitive. This sensitivity gives rise to activation strategies. These strategies don't aim at the improvement of the commons as a primary goal (and as participatory theorists would wish) but instead serve to further narrow group or campaign goals. The arguments of participatory theorists, however, give a grand normative justification to the pursuit of meaner goals through strategic activation.

Jeremy Richardson explains some broader implications of the market specialization resulting from political activation:

Just as consumer products and services have become more differentiated and specialized in response to more sophisticated consumer demands, . . . participation in the political process is increasingly linked to specialized or "attentive" publics, specialized issues and specialized participatory organizations. This trend may not be solely due to a more sophisticated and better-educated citizenry. Just as with products and services in the marketplace, there are entrepreneurs who seek market opportunities for political participation. New issue-related organizations emerge, not just because of existing public concern about an issue, but also because organizational entrepreneurs emerge who see opportunities to create new organizations (and careers for themselves) by mobilizing public support and funding for interest groups around new issues which they place on the political agenda. . . . These new "entrepreneur-driven" organizations are increasingly important in setting the political agenda to which political parties, as well as governments and legislatures, have to respond. (Richardson 1995, 124)

These are not the results foreseen or desired by participatory advocates. The current plethora of entrepreneurs and issue-based organizations exists alongside a larger group of passive citizens. Entrepreneurs carve up the public into targets of activation opportunity, rather than mobilizing most citizens into a fully participatory democracy. Only inclusive electoral participation spawns majority rule. Partisan mobilization passed this test, but contemporary activation does not. Participatory theory that fails to acknowledge and address the shortcomings of activation hardly furthers inclusive popular rule in America. We now have political participation without a popularly inclusive government. The shortcomings of participatory theory become obvious once the origins of activation strategies come into focus. Its sweeping endorsement of participation in an era of activation reveals a disastrous incomprehension of the reasons for the decline of popular government in America.

ORIGINS OF ACTIVATION STRATEGIES

Why the widespread use of activation strategies at the end of the twentieth century? Their onset is not a mysterious dispensation of fate. Instead, it became rational and efficient for individuals to pursue opportunities for political influence through the narrow scope of activation instead of the broader framework of traditional partisan mobilization. Three large phenomena account for the shift: (1) the decline of party influence in the electoral process and among voters, (2) the proliferation of interest groups since 1960, and (3) transformations in the technology of politics that greatly contributed to (1) and (2). Together they created an environment in which entrepreneurial politicians and group leaders relentlessly activate fragments of the public to vote and press demands upon government. *For parties, campaigns, and interests, activation is the rational response to a political environment transformed by these forces.*

Over the last hundred years, elections in America gradually converted from party-dominated to candidate-dominated competitions. Old-style party mobilization grew from party dominance over the key campaign resource of the time: labor. Government patronage delivered armies of party workers during the election season. "The capacity of party chairmen to offer government jobs in return for party support was a major resource relied upon by party organizations" (Rose 1997, 53). The passage of civil service reform at the national, state, and local levels, beginning with the national Pendleton Act in 1883, gradually drained away from parties the control of labor essential for organizational muscle in pre-electronic election campaigns. The advent of the direct primary, a participatory reform mentioned above, was another major blow to party electoral power. By losing the power to bestow nominations, party organizations lost control over their candidates. Candidates, in turn, found themselves individually responsible for attracting voters. "The introduction of the direct primary encouraged candidates to develop their own campaign organizations, or pseudo-parties, for contesting primary elections" (Herrnson 1988, 26). By midcentury, primaries were ubiquitous in elections for state and national office. Party organizations found themselves possessing few of the desirable resources for electoral competition and no controlling authority over the identity of their candidates. The national campaign finance legislation of the 1970s reinforced this pattern by sharply limiting party spending on behalf of candidates and structuring legal fund-raising and accounting for contributions around the campaigns of individual candidates (Sabato 1984, 276–86).

In addition to declining power in the electoral process, parties also suffered in the hearts and minds of voters. Beginning in midcentury, voters began to split partisan tickets more frequently. The percentage of self-identified independents rose from 23 percent in 1952 to 33 percent in 1996 (Center for Political Studies 1996). Further, the proportion of Americans having no views about either of the major parties grew steadily in the late twentieth century (Wattenberg 1996, 50–73). With depleted resources, parties also found voters less willing to consider or accept partisan messages. Individual candidates, ever sensitive to voter preferences, responded by running campaigns with less partisan and more individualist themes.

In the 1980s, national and state parties adapted to their reduced circumstances by enhancing their role as service providers for their candidates (Coleman 1996b, 371). Party organizations raised money and subcontracted for polling and advertising on behalf of their candidates. By targeting money and services strategically, the national parties could maximize their impact on elections. They now help most in the small group of hotly competitive House and Senate races, while remaining only minimally involved in other races (Herrnson

1988, 109). Such activities keep party organizations relevant, but hardly dominant, in electoral competition. State and national parties provide a far smaller share of campaign resources to their candidates than they did one hundred years ago, and they have far less control over who runs under their party labels.

One major consequence is the steady decline in the number of people who report being contacted by a party during an election campaign (Rosenstone and Hansen 1993, 162–77). This contributed to declining turnout in elections. At the same time, however, increasing numbers of Americans reported contacting governmental officials. While electoral politics shrivels, governmental politics thrives (Rosenstone and Hansen 71–125). We can solve this puzzle by examining the second force behind the rise of activation strategies, the proliferation of interest groups.

To understand the group proliferation displayed in figure 1.1 of this chapter, it helps to comprehend the reasons why groups form. Any explanation must begin with Mancur Olson's landmark work, *The Logic of Collective Action* (1965). Olson argued that when individuals seek material benefits in the form of collective (nondivisible) goods from government, group organization is often difficult because of the "free rider" problem. That is, individuals may choose not to join the group because they will receive the collective good anyway if the group forms and succeeds. This spawns entrepreneurial activity by group leaders to provide selective benefits for joiners (or impose selective costs upon those who don't join). Hence the abundance of large membership interest groups offering special benefits (travel tours, magazines, insurance) for members. Group entrepreneurs also often attract a smaller group of individuals motivated to express their views about ideology or particular issues. Satisfying the "expressive" goal of "voicing deeply felt value commitments" has become an entrepreneurial activity of recent decades (Salisbury 1990, 210). The rise of many movement and cause groups in myriad issue areas attests to the success of entrepreneurs offering expressive benefits.

But why now? What prompted the burgeoning of entrepreneurial group formation in recent decades? G. Calvin Mackenzie (1996, 59–60) provides a roster of likely reasons. Three major structural transformations of society and politics in the mid-twentieth century helped to create the more proximate causes of group formation. First, the rise of an educated and affluent middle class created a huge set of consumers of group benefits. Activating more knowledgeable and affluent citizens is easier because they get the message more readily and have more resources to devote to supporting the message. The costs of activation became lower, contributing to its proliferation.

Second, party decline, discussed above, provided new opportunities for entrepreneurial activity. With weakened party identification, entrepreneurs could more readily create commitments for group-based goals and find more resources to do so with the decline of party dominance of electoral resources. Third, new technologies made communication with prospective members less costly—quicker and more efficient. While print and personal conversation dominated during the early partisan era, multiple communication and targeting technologies now allow entrepreneurs to efficiently locate potential supporters and make the pitch to them. Technological change is such a major force propelling activation that it receives extended treatment below.

Given party decline, widespread education and affluence, and new technology, more specific political circumstances helped to drive group growth. National government involvement in domestic problems expanded in the 1960s, creating new issue areas ripe for group formation—environmental, urban, cultural, and poverty issues among them. Concurrently, and in part because of governmental expansion (Walker 1991; Costain 1992), new movements of previously marginalized groups—African Americans, Latinos, women, Christian conservatives, and gays and lesbians—further broadened the issue agenda of national politics. With more issues gaining popular currency, additional group formation became possible. This wave of entrepreneurial activity among group and movement leaders lowered the information costs for future entrepreneurs by showing them how group formation was done—how to target and with which technology and message. Mackenzie calls this the effect of "contagion" (Mackenzie 1996, 60). The spiral of group organization, once begun, fed on itself.

Under this onslaught, some established, large organizations began to suffer fragmentation. Heinz, Laumann, Nelson, and Salisbury (1993) find that farm groups fragmented in the 1970s and 1980s into more specialized organizations. Why? "Larger associations tend to take positions that minimize internal conflict, thus encouraging specialized interests to develop independent strategies" (1993, 376). "Peak" business organizations such as the National Organization of Manufacturers and the Chamber of Commerce found themselves advocating alongside over a thousand specialized trade associations by the 1990s. As larger, established groups sought to avoid internal conflict, demand for more specialized interest organizations rose. Potential members found the political stakes great enough to support new groups. Entrepreneurs discovered they could command sufficient resources to influence politics with narrower groups. Concurrently, policy-making became less dominated by exclusive "iron triangles" of groups, bureaucracies, and congressional committees (Heclo 1978). The cost of entry into policy competition declined as more groups formed. The motives, means, and opportunities for new groups grew together.

By the end of the century, an issue-oriented citizen desiring to participate in national politics had no shortage of interest group options. And groups might seem a more appealing venue than political parties. "Parties offer a wide-ranging program of policies which may include some policies to which the individual is opposed or at least unsympathetic. An alternative is to join or donate resources to a pressure group . . . espousing either a single-issue or a related set of issues—thus avoiding the need to accept policies and programs to which one is opposed" (Richardson 1995, 126). Group entrepreneurs perfected a variety of grassroots recruitment and activation strategies—employing material and expressive incentives—to identify and utilize potential supporters (Faucheux 1994).

Changes in technology, a third big structural change, shaped the particular activation behaviors by entrepreneurs in the less partisan, more group dominated environment. Partisan politics of decades ago thrived on the military-style mobilization of party workers in election campaigns. Reformers took this control of labor in elections away from party organizations, and new technologies arose that could be widely dispersed and employed in elections and in lobbying government. Technology made money more important than labor in elections, and primary nominations made individual candidates the central money-raisers of the new campaign system (Lowi and Ginsburg 1998, 289–301). As independent entrepreneurs, candidates began hiring their own pollsters, direct mail firms, and advertising consultants with the money they raised. The primary campaign expense became

TV time for ads tailored carefully to the sensibilities of "swing" voters.

The "few large interests" that dominated Washington in midcentury suffered a similar fate to that of party organizations. Traditional lobbying (Hrebnar 1997, 79–117) involved personal contact between established Washington interest representatives—usually lawyers—and lawmakers, bureaucrats, and administration officials. This highly skilled labor was in relatively short supply and expensive to purchase. New technology changed dramatically the arts of advocacy in Washington and greatly lessened the advantages of traditional lobbying. Direct mail could target possible members and communicate with supporters, as could satellite television, phone calls, e-mail, web pages, and faxes. Activating loyal members to contact their legislators proved more effective than merely hiring traditional Washington lawyers. Washington law firms had to adapt to the new technology and grassroots tactics it spawned. Many now use grassroots tactics (Plebani 1997).

The new technology lowers the costs of activation. Identifying supporters and communicating with them is easier than ever before in national politics. The technology is also widely available and transportable. One can arrange state-of-the-art communication from anywhere in the country. All this should stimulate group formation and the uses of activation. With ever more activators operating, competitively successful activation becomes more difficult, particularly when each individual candidate or organization has limited resources. Hence activation involves narrow, precise targeting of the public in order to be successful. Gone are the days when large partisan organizations could monopolize resources for mobilization and engage the general public broadly at election time. The new modus operandi involves slicing surgically into the public to bring out just the right segment to vote in an election or make a spiel to government. The content of such messages is crucial. That content has changed in recent decades as public attitudes have altered.

CAMPAIGN AND INTEREST GROUP MESSAGES

Successful activation turns mainly on accurate identification of the appropriate audience and the appropriate tone and content for that audience. Candidates and interests use messages that they estimate are most likely to succeed with their targeted segments of the public. Hitting the right target with limited resources involves differentiation between those more or less likely to become active. Activation thus serves to reinforce the stratification of public activity and knowledge about politics. The intended audience also must find the tone and content of the message persuasive. Activation also reflects the configuration of attitudes about politics, politicians, and the political system among the target audience. Those attitudes are often postpartisan, cynical, and critical of established authority.

The core logic of activation involves nudging those with the greatest marginal propensity to become active into motion. This is the part of the public with the greatest motivation to learn about politics. Motivation to learn results from a constellation of traits: interest in politics, a personal sense of political efficacy (a belief that activism is worthwhile and produces benefits), and a sense of civic duty (Delli Carpini and Keeter 1996, 214). Education is the key facilitator of such motivation. Education reduces the costs of gaining and processing political information in several ways. More educated people can sort through relevant information with less effort and receive socialization that inculcates in them a sense of the benefits of political knowledge (190).

Another key effect of education is its placing of individuals in social networks of similarly educated individuals (Nye 1996, 11–39). Some networks are closer to political life than others. Norman Nie, Jane Junn, and Kenneth Stehlik-Barry identified a measure of "network centrality," a simple additive scale of how many political leaders and members of the media are known by individuals questioned in a national survey. They found 48 percent of the public knew none, but 19 percent know three or more (1996, 48). Education correlated positively with network centrality (1996, 49), and voting and other forms of political participation were stimulated by network centrality (1996, 67–68).

By this evidence, about one-half of all members of the public are difficult candidates for activation. They rank lower in education and occupy social networks far from politics and power. Any activation strategy with such a group is likely to be high in cost and involve modest results. Within the 19 percent in more central networks, activation can work much more effectively. Careful targeting, however, is crucial with this elite group because they are likely to have fixed views on a number of issues—only a fraction of them may be susceptible to a particular activation message from a candidate or interest group. Interest groups use grassroots strategies to hit those in networks most inclined to participate. Campaigns are more likely to target moderate-knowledge voters who are undecided. One cannot understand the messages without examining the precise part of the stratification pyramid of political interest and motivation targeted by them.

A broader aspect of activation entails the political atmosphere surrounding the creation of appropriate messages. The "political environment" helps to shape the substance of activation (Delli Carpini and Keeter 1996, 216). At century's end, certain attitudinal tendencies of the American public structure that environment. Partisanship among the public is weak. Voters split tickets frequently, the number of strong partisans in the electorate has declined, and a growing proportion of Americans has no feelings—positive or negative—about political parties (Wattenberg 1996, 58–72). Parties are losing their association with candidates and major public issues in the public mind (89). Partisan appeals are far less useful for candidates than in the past, and interests have little incentive to couch their message in explicitly partisan terms. The precise targeting of activation permits campaigns and interests to tap other targets of motivation than the broad and increasingly weak labels of partisan affiliation.

The public also evidences high levels of political alienation, lacking trust in politicians and political institutions. Joseph Nye, Philip Zelikow, and David King suggest several reasons for the rise of citizen distrust: Vietnam and Watergate, the ideological polarization of partisan elites, the rise of adversarial national media, and television's contribution to declining partisanship and its negative political advertising (1997, 269–70). The authors also credit the rise of "post-materialist" political values with increasing popular alienation.

Post-materialist values, identified and tracked in forty-three nations by political scientist Ronald Inglehart over several decades, include "elite challenging" political values (Inglehart 1997a, 221). As more citizens begin to take prosperity for granted, attitudes critical of conventional political authority arise. Individuals look beyond immediate material concerns and seek self-expression and self-realization as personal goals. They become critical of the traditional participatory forms of partisanship and voting and seek newer participatory venues. This is particularly the case with highly educated, high-income individuals—those most prone to hear the siren song of activation in the first place. They have higher incomes but not higher perceptions of subjective well-being, making them a receptive audience for negative political ads and grassroots activation by interest groups. Inglehart finds rising levels of political interest and newer forms of political participation across many advanced democracies in recent decades, evidence of a growing post-materialist political style (1997b, 293–323).

Audience characteristics, then, dictate the substance of activation messages. Political motivation is clearly stratified, making identification of target publics possible at the middle (by candidates) and high end (by interests) of the motivation continuum. Among those likely to vote or participate beyond voting, partisan messages are less useful. Alienation from government makes negative messages about candidates and government more successful. Rising post-materialist attitudes offer rich opportunities for those who seek to activate higher income and education individuals for participation beyond mere voting. Activation has come into its own not just because of improved techniques by those who would induce it, but also because the public increasingly looks beyond conventional political participation to make its points with governments. Group proliferation and grassroots participatory politics occur as an increasingly alienated public seeks new modes of participation to challenge suspect governmental elites.

In this environment, candidates traffic in advertising that is highly personal or carefully targeted to particular issues resonant with swing voters (Sabato 1984, 111–97). The 1996 reelection campaign of

President Clinton was a state-of-the-art effort aimed at activating key groups of swing voters with carefully scripted issue messages (Stengel and Pooley 1996; Morris 1997). Partisanship had little to do with it. A cynical public frequently is receptive to negative advertising during campaigns, as the early Clinton ads attacking Dole revealed. Negative ads, however, have the unfortunate effect of discouraging voting (Ansolabehere and Iyengar 1995, 99–115). Those with lower information and education also rely most heavily on television for information about politics. The negative tone of political advertising and news sharpens their disaffection with politics (Robinson 1975, 101). Strategic activation, in its message and tone, often drives away those already at the margins of civic life. Many contemporary activation strategies actually increase political stratification and popular alienation.

CONSEQUENCES OF ACTIVATION

The implications of ubiquitous activation strategies, hinted at above, are multiple and disquieting. Activation flourishes because the politically sophisticated find it an efficient means to influence what government does. Since this perception is widespread, activation exists throughout America's political system. The frequency of activation means its effects upon American politics are pervasive. With activation comes advocacy of more participatory forms of citizen activity. In assessing activation's consequences, we must also consider those of the participatory ethos it spawns.

Groups and campaigns must target well to activate effectively. That means carefully separating the wheat from the chaff. The wheat are those who are likely to act in response to the right mix of messages and inducements. The chaff are those who won't respond unless more drastic and expensive activation measures occur. Activation, through its lack of emphasis on those who don't participate in politics, reinforces and worsens political stratification in America. Americans vary greatly in political knowledge (Delli Carpini and Keeter 1996) and sophistication (Neuman 1986). Activation perpetuates and reinforces these differences within the public. By preaching to potential converts, campaigns and groups help to set limits on mass involvement in politics.

The narrow strategic focus of activation makes majority rule at best an incidental byproduct of this system. Candidates gain election by targeting a small group of swing voters, in search of a plurality of those who vote, not a majority of all citizens. Groups and parties have little incentive to command majority opinion if they can prevail without it—and they often can. Elected officials pay particular attention to "attentive publics," the minorities actively engaged in issues of the moment (Arnold 1990, 60–68). The power of attentive publics lies in their ability to get the message out to larger numbers of their fellow citizens comprising the "inattentive public" about what government is doing. Additional activation can make life difficult for incumbents. R. Douglas Arnold notes that lawmakers only have to consider the larger group of the inattentive public under two circumstances: if an issue might rouse the inattentive public and if a faction of the attentive public stands ready as "instigators" to activate them (Arnold 1990, 70).

Even if instigators must activate broadly to succeed, majority opinion is not necessarily brought to bear on the decision. Efficient activation often avoids targeted minorities "appealing to elected officials over the heads of the public" (Baer and Bositis 1993, 55).

Another consequence of participatory activation is the hyperpluralism evident in the corridors of government. Jonathan Rauch explains how the incentives for group organization and activation have grown in recent decades. "The interest group industry pays rising returns on investment and enjoys falling costs; its potential base [includes] a practically unlimited pool of capital; its technological base grows ever more sophisticated; it is supported and staffed by an expanding infrastructure of professionals who know the business" (Rauch 1994, 58). As activation becomes more efficient for more entrepreneurs, the national political system gets clogged and public alienation mounts. Groups "begin to choke the system that bred them, to undermine confidence in politics. . . . The system might begin to defeat the purpose for which it exists, namely, to make reasonable social decisions quickly" (61).

As groups swamp the system, and participatory forms grow in popularity—in great part because of the rhetoric of successful activation—the representative and deliberative functions of legislatures weaken. America's founders envisioned a deliberative national government, dominated by the Congress. By this theory, "there are two kinds of public voice in a democracy—one immediate and spontaneous, less well informed, and less reflective; the other more deliberative, taking longer to develop, and resting on a fuller consideration of information and arguments—and that only the latter is fit to rule" (Bessette 1994, 212). Activation engenders a seemingly "spontaneous" voice in fact produced by elite, entrepreneurial calculation. The goal of activation is results, not discussion as an end in itself. Inevitably, the vogue of activation weakens the deliberative norms of government. Myriad groups put on grassroots pressure for action, making it more difficult for lawmakers to act intelligently. Robert Dahl summarizes the syndrome: "the number and diversity of interests have increased without any corresponding increase in the strength of the process for integrating interests; and plebiscitary techniques have gained ground without a corresponding increase in representativeness and deliberation" (Dahl 1994, 100).

The paradoxes displayed in figures 1.1 and 1.2 reveal another disturbing consequence of activation strategies. A theory of individual representation through participation underlies activation. However, this participation occurs in a political structure that places heavy demands on the citizen:

In the world of American politics, citizens are asked to undertake a wide array of civic activities: select qualified representatives (both within parties and in general elections) for local, state and national offices . . . vote directly on policy issues through initiatives and referenda; fill the thousands of voluntary, appointed and bureaucratic civic roles required for the machinery of campaigns, elections and government to work effectively; help shape local, state and national political agendas through numerous outlets from public opinion polls to public demonstrations to direct contact with public officials . . . navigate government bureaucracies for information, goods and services, attend local government and civic meetings, and more. (Delli Carpini and Keeter 1996, 3)

These myriad participatory venues give entrepreneurs many opportunities to activate effectively. Most activation efforts distinguish the activist few from the passive many. Hence diverse groups of active citizens besiege government while most Americans feel no connection to the political system. The system's complexity discourages many citizens, creating even more benefits for successful activation. The large scale of citizen responsibilities, created through the participatory theories inherent in the progressive reforms, makes activation a particularly valuable strategy for candidates and groups. Since the task of the citizen can be quite demanding, the prize goes to those best able to convince a targeted group of fellow citizens to do just a bit more.

James Bryce almost one hundred years ago identified three intractable impediments to the realization of successful participatory democracy: severe time constraints for citizens, competing demands for leisure time, and the complexity of many policy issues (Bryce 1909, 237, 240, 331, 356). The complexity of the political system creates yet another great barrier. One solution, in practice when Bryce wrote, was party mobilization of the mass public to overcome these impediments. Mobilization has given way to activation, a system by which minority interests manipulate the complex electoral and governmental system in the misleading garb of participatory democracy.

We have every evidence that the era of activation is here to stay. Rising education levels and economic security create steadily greater numbers of citizens with post-materialist values, including belief in participatory democracy and "elite challenging" political tactics (Inglehart 1997a, 220–21). Political entrepreneurs can activate them at relatively low cost. Ever more activation strategies result, creating a dense crowding of vocal, segmented, and relatively elite Americans around the governmental stage (Nie, Junn, and Stehlik-Barry 1996, 131–32). Governmental participation grows, while, due to declining party contact, electoral participation withers (Rosenstone and Hansen 1993, 56–70). Changes in voting turnout from year to year become the byproducts of the activation strategies of elites, decline in party attachment and contact, and the disappearance of person-to-person political conversation (Nie, Junn, and Stehlik-Barry 1996, 132).

Today, neither parties, interests, nor candidates need concern themselves with the harmful system-level consequences of their activation strategies in elections. It is not, as they see it, their problem. Should they give up their effective tactics because of a concern for system-level effects, they will lose their ability to compete with their rivals. Our electoral politics have become one great "tragedy of the commons" in which what is good for the powerful electoral actors despoils our politics in disquieting ways. America lost much more than expected when it abandoned party-based popular mobilization as its model for electoral politics. Although popular inclusion proved a practical imperative in the mobilization era, it is not in today's electoral politics.

The complex political system in the United States provides manifold avenues for participation, and millions of Americans use those avenues every year; but most Americans do not and probably will not. The vogue of participation holds that all should "get involved." The process in fact encourages only a strategically selected few to vote in elections and petition government for their interests. This is a particularly grand example of unintended consequences. The decline of our popular politics proceeded in several steps. First, progressive reforms that extolled popular participation weakened parties, thus causing the electorate to shrink. As chapter 2 makes clear, the progressive attack on parties and veneration of direct, popular participation became the crucial legitimating arguments for the rise of activation strategies. Second, the proliferation of narrow interests in recent decades made interests less well loved in the public mind, fueling popular alienation. Third, new communication and campaign technologies made it possible to prevail in elections and lobbying by activating only a small fragment of the public. Attempts to engage fellow citizens in political activity decayed into narrow strategies to divide the public into activist factions. Thus the inclusive electoral mobilization of the partisan era shriveled into a much more exclusive contest of politics "by invitation only," driven by the imperatives of activation.

America's era of activation is ultimately an era of self-delusion. We trumpet popular participation, yet we have raised the costs of participation and reward those who overcome these costs by activating fragments of the public. The following chapters examine the activation phenomenon in more detail. Chapter 2 explains the decline of partisan mass mobilization and the rise of activation strategies. The impressive ability of candidates, interests, and parties to activate selected parts of the electorate receives analysis in chapters 3 and 4. Chapter 5 explains how various interests and movements employ the arts of activation, illustrated through case studies of state-of-the-art activation by five major national interest groups. The concluding chapter summarizes the problems of activation and considers several reforms that might revive majority rule in American politics.

CHAPTER 2

The Great Disintegration
From Partisan Mobilization to Activation

The key point is not that the parties declined over the last
century—although they did. It is that eventually it became
possible for an ambitious politician to win nomination and
election without relying on the party.

John Aldrich, *Why Parties? The Origin and Transformation of
Party Politics in America*

America's complex politics of activation is a late twentieth-century
phenomenon. For most of the nation's history, parties played a
more dominant role in linking public opinion to government
than they do now. Odd as it may seem at the end of the twentieth
century, there was a time when a much less educated electorate par-
ticipated in elections in greater proportions and with greater exuber-
ance than citizens do today. Party influence over government's electoral system and policy environment is weaker than in those times. A
more educated electorate now pays less attention to cues from parties
and votes less. Nonelectoral activation, involving grassroots participation induced by group entrepreneurs, has grown far more frequent in

recent decades. Myriad group pleas often supplant election results as a guide for governance. The link between electoral results and governmental action thus is less clear (Ginsburg and Shefter 1990).

The linkage began to loosen with the political consequences of the 1896 presidential election and progressive reforms of the electoral system in the early twentieth century. Recent empirical trends also combined to weaken it further. A steadily larger proportion of Americans hold post-materialist values, involving less faith in the efficacy of parties and voting and supporting more "elite-challenging" forms of participation (Inglehart 1997b). Rising education levels have increased the importance of relative years of education and decreased the importance of absolute years of education in stimulating political participation (Nie, Junn, and Stehlik-Barry 1996). While entrepreneurs unrelentingly activate those who are relatively highly educated, those with lower education vote less. Voting participation thus declines, and much participation—with an elitist skew—has nothing to do with elections.

It was not always thus. The following chapter examines the transformation of America's popular politics from the party-dominated era of the late nineteenth century to our current age of activation. The transformation reveals the difference between contemporary activation and the mobilization practiced by political parties over one hundred years ago. At first glance, the difference between activation and mobilization may seem slight. Both seek to lower the costs of participation so sympathetic citizens can be induced to participate on behalf of a candidate, party, cause, or group. Activation, however, is an unsavory offspring of earlier mobilization strategies. Parties in the nineteenth century crafted wholesale messages during election campaigns in order to broaden their appeal among the mass public. Activation, in contrast, involves retailing a message to a carefully selected target audience. Parties in the past broadcast their messages throughout the nation in contrast to the frequent narrowcasting of activation strategies.

Broadcasting was inefficient, but rational, given the limited means of mass communication available at the time—newspapers and personal contact—and the importance of labor in campaigning. Today, technology is more important than labor in campaigns. Targeting likely supporters during the partisan era involved a labor-intensive shoeleather effort by party workers, canvassing neighborhoods door-to-door. This proved efficient, given the technology of the time. New technologies now permit even more efficient targeting that omits many in the public previously reached through partisan mobilization. Scientific polling can identify the subgroups most in need of an activation message, which can then arrive via mail or electronic means. Newspapers in the past provided partisan public messages, to a large audience; today phone and direct mail can provide private, finely targeted candidate- and issue-specific messages to potential supporters. Communication technology during the partisan era encouraged mass mobilization; now it does not.

Traditional party mobilization involved four participation-maximizing characteristics that contemporary activation does not. First, the party message was conceptually simple, involving an argument for voting for a particular slate of candidates with common partisan traits. Today, voters are showered at election time with a blizzard of candidate and issue messages that makes their choices more demanding and complex. This serves to reduce turnout; the simpler party message facilitated turnout. Second, personal contact by party workers made mobilization particularly effective. The decline of party contact contributed to lower turnout in recent decades (Rosenstone and Hansen 1993, 214–27). Third, those targeted for contact need time to absorb and act on the message. Today, that time is harder to come by, particularly when voters are beset by a plethora of activation messages at election time. Fourth, party mobilization worked because many citizens with low education nevertheless inhabited social networks with strong voting norms. Nie, Junn, and Stehlik-Barry (1996, 131–66) find that such norms are weaker today, even in social networks of much more highly educated individuals.

Weaker voting norms make activation an effective strategy. Effectiveness requires an accurate assessment of who will participate on your behalf and who will not. Since participation norms now vary more widely than before, activation efforts must be precise to be efficient and effective. Traditional mobilization was less efficient for the partisan goals of those doing the mobilization, but a happy consequence of its broad reach was high popular participation in elections. New technology permits rational and efficient behavior by groups, campaigns, and parties that weakens mass participation in elections. By activating only the more politically sophisticated, they contribute to declining turnout in elections. And when groups activate citizens to influence government between elections, they often make elections less decisive for the consequent actions of government. Traditional partisan mobilization reinforced the link between mass electoral verdicts and government actions; activation is largely destructive of this linkage.

This chapter explains the disintegration of partisan mobilization into activation in American politics. Changes in America's electoral structure and policy environment decreased the importance of parties in the electoral system. Weaker parties encouraged the rise of activation strategies. A clear definition of party strength in elections and policy making is necessary before any ebbing of that strength can be shown. The following section sets forth definitions of party strength upon which later claims of party decline are based.

DEFINING PARTY STRENGTH

Political scientists usually discuss parties as agents within America's electoral structure (Epstein 1986; Herrnson 1988; Wattenberg 1996; Schattschneider 1977; Key 1961). Parties owe their origins and development to the imperative of electoral competition. They structure electoral choice and competition, facilitate popular participation in government, disseminate political information, and help to recruit candidates and define the national agenda. Parties lie at the heart of democratic politics; as E. E. Schattschneider claimed, democratic politics is inconceivable without them (1977, 1). Any definition of party strength must include an assessment of how well they perform their electoral role.

Alan Ware defines party strength in a way that incorporates the essential aspects of parties' electoral duties: "A strong party organization is one which, at the very least, can determine who will be the party's candidates, can decide (broadly) the issues on which electoral campaigns will be fought by its candidates, contributes the 'lion's share' of resources to the candidates' election campaigns, and has influence over appointments made by elected public officials" (1988, x). By this definition, party strength depends upon control of nominations, politically important resources (money, volunteers, polling and advertising expertise), and influence over the agenda of the election and the appointments made by its public officeholders.

All of these aspects of party strength have declined since the late

nineteenth century. Primaries greatly weakened control over nominations and party organizations now control a smaller share of the
politically important resources in electoral competition. Because of
this loss of control, party influence over the issues at play in elections
and the appointments in government has also shriveled (Ginsberg and
Shefter 1990; Crotty 1984). Some recent scholars argue that parties
are resurgent after their nadir during the 1970s (Herrnson 1988,
1996a; Frendreis 1996), commanding a greater share of politically
important resources. This may be true, but it is easily overstated. The
political and structural changes related in this chapter reveal that any
uptick in party power in elections can only be incremental.

A related, crucially important role for parties involves their impact
upon governmental policy making. Although electorally strong parties may influence governmental action, parties' power depends on
how they affect what government does. The broader policy environment can boost or depress party power. John J. Coleman defines party
strength in terms of the governmental policy environment: "The periods of party strength in the United States are notable for three factors. First, the parties had control over a policy domain; second, that
policy served to divide the parties consistently over time; and third, it
was an area about which voters and elites cared" (Coleman 1996a, 15).
For a party to be strong, its actions must affect many citizens on an
important, lasting issue. Coleman finds that the debate over the tariff
during the late nineteenth century, discussed later in this chapter, satisfied his definition of party strength far more than national policy
debates do now (1996a, 33–170). The two major parties differed
clearly over the tariff, had control over the issue in Congress, and the
issue seemed of premier importance to many voters. Today, parties
have little comparable control over their candidates and officeholders

and do not diverge so clearly on any issue of decisive importance in elections and governance. The agenda is more crowded and complex than in the late nineteenth century, and individualistic candidates and officeholders fudge many potentially important partisan differences.

Coleman argues that party strength in the electoral system may facilitate party power in governmental policy making, but that electoral power does not "substitute for nor guarantee" power in policymaking (1996a, 15). Since parties are both electoral and governing institutions, the analysis here assesses the trends in party electoral and policy power from the period of peak party strength to the present. It examines control over nominations and electoral resources, the election agenda and governmental appointments, as Ware suggests, along with the evolution of partisan control over policy domains of crucial importance to elites and the broader public, following Coleman. As Coleman finds, party electoral strength has covaried with party strength in government since the late nineteenth century.

WHY PARTIES FORM

Why did party strength increase during the nineteenth century? To answer this, we first need an understanding of the origins and early development of parties. John Aldrich in *Why Parties?* provides a theoretical framework useful for understanding party beginnings and evolution. Aldrich argues that major parties are instruments fashioned by politicians seeking to fulfill their ambitions: "My basic argument is that the major political party is the creature of the politicians, the ambitious office seeker and officeholder. They have created and maintained, used or abused, reformed or ignored the political party when doing so has furthered their goals and ambitions" (Aldrich 1995, 4). What goals do politicians pursue through parties? Essentially three:

reelection, the pursuit of good public policy as they define it, and influence and prestige in government (Fenno 1973). Aldrich argues that "ambitious politicians turn to the political party to achieve such goals only when parties are useful vehicles for solving problems that cannot be solved effectively, if at all, by other means" (1995, 5).

Although politicians influence greatly the power of parties, so do other factors, according to Aldrich. Parties seek power through the extant rules of the political regime. In America, that means the constitutions and laws structuring and regulating the legislative, executive, and judicial branches of local, state, and national government (1995, 5). These "rules of the game" determine what parties can do and how politicians can use them to get and maintain power. The dramatic decline in party power over the last hundred years was in part propelled by changes in election laws. Changing the rules changes what parties can do, and how useful parties can be in satisfying the ambitions of politicians.

Aldrich also notes a third factor affecting the operation of parties, the "historical setting" (1995, 5). The term encompasses a variety of influences on party power and behavior. Each historical period has its particular ideas, values, technological possibilities, and partisan alignments. These give substance to the ambitions of politicians and help to set the institutional rules of party competition. As history alters, so does the utility of parties for politicians, the substantive issues at play in politics, the means of political communication, and the competitive situation of the parties in the electoral arena. Such historical changes contributed to the decline of once powerful parties in the United States. Politicians found other, more useful means of achieving their goals, and the power of parties in the American political system shrank.

What problems can politicians solve by forming and maintaining parties? Aldrich points to three essential problems of free government that parties can help solve. First, it is difficult for politicians to work together collectively when making policy. Governments regularly provide public goods, such as national defense, which provide benefits that are nonrival and nonexcludable.[1] That is, they are equally provided for all and no citizen can be deprived of them. Why should an individual politician expend effort to create public goods, however, when he or she can enjoy them without acting? The result is that politicians will provide fewer of these goods than may be necessary, leaving everyone worse off. To serve the nation and their collective policy goals better, politicians need binding partisan commitments to cooperate to provide public goods. Agreeing to a partisan affiliation lowers the cost of governing among like-minded politicians and allows public goods to be provided. Simply put, parties allow politicians to cooperate and share credit for providing goods that individually they have little incentive to secure for the public.

Second, parties allow coherent majorities to form in legislatures where otherwise chaos might reign. When hundreds of lawmakers convene, they are very unlikely to agree spontaneously to a common agenda. On most issues, there is no obvious majority preference among a majority of legislators, but rather a variety of policy options, each of which, under certain circumstances, might become the majority preference (Aldrich 1995, 38–39). Parties provide a means for structuring stable majorities around particular policy options in leg-

1. Nonrival and nonexcludable traits are shared by public and collective goods, mentioned in my discussion of Mancur Olson (1965) in chapter 1. In this case, public goods are provided by government and are available universally, making them a particular type of collective good.

islative bodies. This aids lawmakers in pursuing reelection, making policy, and gaining political influence. Without partisan structure, the instability and uncertainty of the legislative agenda would obstruct most legislators' pursuit of their goals.

Third, parties can be a very effective means of satisfying the reelection goals of politicians. To win an election, politicians must encourage the participation of their supporters. This means lowering the costs of voting and acquiring necessary information among those citizens who might support a particular politician. Parties are a means to this end. They provide a "brand name" that "provides a lot of information cheaply" to voters who have limited time and education (1995, 49). Partisan "get out the vote" efforts can encourage turnout of supporters less expensively than if each candidate created his or her own turnout effort. This "economy of scale" lowers the cost of reelection for politicians (1995, 50).

The story of American party development is that of ambitious politicians using parties to solve the above problems within a structure of institutions and laws and over varying historical periods. In the late nineteenth century, politicians found parties supremely useful in solving these problems. Today, they find them less useful. This chapter particularly focuses upon the declining utility of parties for politicians in popular elections. Changing institutional rules and historical circumstances led to a century-long partisan decline and the rise of activation strategies.

Aldrich explains how the problem of unstable majorities in the first Congress spurred the ambitious Alexander Hamilton to form a stable voting bloc favoring the Washington administration's economic policies. His goal was a lasting "long" coalition of supporters. Hamilton's organizing prompted counterorganizing by his policy oppo-

nents James Madison and Thomas Jefferson. In pursuit of stable legislative majorities, the first two-party system was born in the American republic (1995, 78). Hamilton's Federalists opposed Jefferson's
and Madison's Democratic-Republicans (later known as Democrats).
The "great principle" separating the two parties concerned the scale
of national power. Without stable parties, the question would receive
erratic treatment from a legislature dominated by shifting sectional
interests (1995, 93).

Changing electoral rules prompted the next major alteration in the
American party system. As states expanded the franchise to all white
male citizens in the early nineteenth century, the problem of mobilizing the public in elections grew for the parties. Although the parties continued to divide on the question of national power—with
Democrats against and Whigs, replacing the Federalists, for—the
problem of securing stable support from the public grew. Legislative
leaders of each party marshaled resources to create mass-based parties to overcome Aldrich's problem of collective action. The Democratic and Whig "brand labels" lowered information costs for voters
and parties made voting easier by printing party ballots, canvassing
the citizenry to notify them of the election, and creating a booming
partisan press. The parties were very decentralized, with state and
local political clubs holding much power—a characteristic of American parties persisting throughout the nineteenth and early twentieth
centuries.

Aldrich cites three reasons for the decentralized character of the
parties. First, since political clubs had formed at the state and local
levels, it was less costly for leading national politicians to draft them
into the party than to start up clubs from scratch. Second, local organization allowed the parties to respond flexibly to diverse local and

regional issues. Through this localism, both the Whigs and Democrats for decades straddled the slavery issue dividing the North and
South. Third, a local focus made mobilization most effective, since it
depended on personal contact and local newspaper appeals, the dominant mobilization techniques of the time (1995, 112). Parties also
mobilized many workers with the promise of material gain. Government employment for the party faithful through the patronage of the
"spoils" system created under the Jackson presidency provided jobs
for partisans, often regardless of their qualifications. Although local
in structure, the parties satisfied all of Alan Ware's criteria of party
strength: they controlled the nomination of party candidates
(through the storied "smoke-filled rooms"), directed the agenda of
campaigns, contributed most of the resources for the campaigns (volunteers and partisan press coverage), and secured appointments of
their members to office.

The slavery issue eventually split the Whigs and led to the creation
of the Republican Party in the 1850s. After the Civil War removed the
issue from the agenda, the two major parties entered an era of peak
influence in American politics. Why did their influence crest then? The
following section identifies aspects of the institutional environment,
particularly the electoral structure and method of gaining government
employment, that spurred party power. In addition, a very competitive
partisan alignment promoted party strength, as did the dominant
means of communication, newspapers and word of mouth. The ideas
and values on the national agenda, particularly the rise of the tariff
issue, also aided the parties. A partisan "golden age" had arrived.

The following sections explain the periods of party strength and
weakness since the Civil War in reference to two major influences.
First, electoral laws and institutions served to structure party compe-

tition, define party power, and shape the particular utility of parties for politicians. Second, the national policy environment reveals the role of parties in articulating the dominant ideas and values in each historical period. In the later 1800s, parties dominated both the electoral structure and national policy environment. In 2000, they dominate neither. A careful examination of the period of peak strength demonstrates just how far they have fallen.

THE PARTISAN GOLDEN AGE: 1876–1892

Early one evening in October 1876 groups of young men wearing military-style caps and capes and carrying kerosene torches in the shape of rifles gathered in the sixth ward of the city of New Haven, Connecticut. The men were members of the "York Escort," the "Shelton Escort," the "Bradley Guard," and the "H. G. Lewis Guard," marching companies formed for the presidential campaign that year and named in honor of four of the city's leading Democrats.

. . . All four of these successful, middle-aged men belonged to the city's Protestant, Yankee upper-middle class. The members of the marching companies, mostly Irish immigrants and the sons of immigrants, lived and worked as day-laborers and factory operatives in the poorest sections of New Haven's fifth, sixth and eighth wards.

By seven o'clock, the companies had formed into line and lit their torches. On orders from the commanding officers, the men set off, a brass band at their head, through the darkening streets of their city. Several blocks away, the procession was joined by the "Deutsche Feuer" or "German Sweepers" carrying brooms "symbolical" of the coming "sweeping clean of corruption from the land."

In the third ward, the parade met two more companies of the "Shelton Escort" and the "Young Democracy," the latter with a banner that read "A clean sweep for our next mayor—William R. Shelton." At city Democratic headquarters, the procession, now numbering about five hundred uniformed, torch-bearing marchers, offered an escort to several politicians, the orators for the evening.

Returning to the sixth ward at eight o'clock, the companies found three or four thousand people filling the streets around a temporary platform at a main intersection in a working-class neighborhood. Gas lights and Chinese lanterns brilliantly illuminated the surrounding buildings. As the companies marched and counter-marched, the band played and fireworks lit the sky. "The windows near," a reporter noted, "were filled with the fair faces of ladies, who smiled down upon the enthusiastic crowd below their sympathy with the meeting and its objects." While the band blared "The Star-Spangled Banner," a huge flag bearing the names and portraits of Samuel J. Tilden and Thomas A. Hendricks, the Democratic presidential ticket, was "flung to the breeze" from the roof of a building. "The cheering and applause was deafening and continued," the reporter wrote, "the audience being so worked up by the occasion that it was with great difficulty that they could be called to sufficient order to allow the speakers to proceed." From the platform, six orators in turn denounced the corruption of the Republican party, praised Tilden and the American flag, and urged men to vote a straight Democratic ticket. Because the audience was so large, politicians also left the stand to speak from two points in the crowd. After more music and fireworks, the meeting ended at 10:30 "with cheers for Tilden and Hendricks, and William R. Shelton for Mayor." (McGerr 1986, 3–4)

So it went at one of thousands of spectacular Democratic and Republican rallies during the very partisan presidential campaign of 1876. Sheer pageantry aside, the above example explains much about the impact of strong parties upon the politics of the era. They generated mass enthusiasm of a sort seldom seen today. They also educated young voters (in this example, many of the marchers) on the importance of politics and party affiliation. The process of acquiring attitudes, opinions, and beliefs about politics, known as political socialization, had a far stronger partisan component back then. Rallies also provided a mode of political participation equally available to all citizens, unlike the segmented and stratified modes of participation today (McGerr 1986, 41). They linked partisans of diverse class and ethnic backgrounds to one common cause.

It is hardly surprising that such an inclusive, enthusiastic, partisan politics stimulated "as full a mobilization of the mass electorate as this country has ever experienced" (Kleppner 1982, 33). Over three-quarters of eligible voters cast ballots in presidential elections from 1876 to 1892; over half voted in off-year congressional elections (1982, 33). This high turnout is particularly remarkable given that the electorate was young (in 1870, 48.5 percent of voters were under thirty-five) and, by today's standards, uneducated (in 1890, only 5.5 percent of the electorate had graduated from high school and less than 2 percent were college graduates) (1982, 36). The high turnout occurred across class, ethnic, and religious lines (1982, 38).

In the parlance of contemporary political science, more eligible voters occupied social networks in which voting norms were strong. That strength grew from the activities of political parties and the local level. Through personal contact and support for a highly partisan local press, parties whipped up enthusiasm for politics. Historian Richard L. McCormick explains how parties could be so effective:

Party loyalties were strong and voting behavior stable in nineteenth-century America because partisan attachments—like religious affiliations—had deep roots in family and community life. Party leaders voiced the same values that voters learned in their homes and churches, and when leaders discussed national issues they related them to cultural and communal concerns of greatest importance to most people. (McCormick 1986, 10)

In such a situation, parties became invaluable to politicians. Strong emphasis on the "brand label" through party appeals proved a useful way to stimulate turnout, and direct personal contact with voters through a partisan canvass of households conveyed the message in a memorable way. Spectacle and the enticement of patronage jobs and material assistance from party leaders spurred party supporters to action. Partisan papers were the major means of receiving news. Parties themselves printed the partisan straight-ticket ballots used in elections. No organization could rival the political party for effective communication between politicians and voters for the purpose of popular mobilization in elections.

The key to party effectiveness was their strong local organization, a trait that has vanished today. This was the heyday of partisan machines, dominating urban politics (most notoriously in New York City's famously corrupt "Tweed Ring") and statewide politics as well. In such organizations, power over candidate selection rested in private meetings of local party leaders (Herrnson 1988, 11). Each local party organization sought to maximize the vote for the party's ticket, but national party organization was weak and had relatively little influence on the outcome of elections (McGerr 1986, 34).

Local rallies got the party message out in a spectacular way. They raised voter knowledge about the party ticket and strengthened the voting norms within social networks of party supporters. Direct personal contact through local canvassing by party workers also enhanced knowledge and voting norms. For those who were particularly helpful during elections, the prospect of local government employment or favorable treatment at the hands of the party's elected official beckoned (Herrnson 1988, 13).

National parties, in contrast, had few resources to deploy in elections. After the national convention selected the party's ticket through a prolonged deliberative exercise involving many ballots, most electioneering occurred at the state and local level. The national party committees seldom met between presidential elections, maintained headquarters only during presidential campaigns, and exercised no control over state and local nominations. National party chairs had small staffs and limited help from the congressional campaign committees charged with working on House elections.[2] During presidential campaigns, the national committee subsidized friendly newspaper editors, scheduled leading orators for rallies around the country, and paid for free distribution of local partisan papers. The congressional committees usually handled production and distribution of campaign literature (McGerr 1986, 33–35).

Throughout the nation, the press coverage had a strongly partisan flavor on a daily basis. As a journalist observed in 1871: "No political paper in the United States can be independent and live. It may, in some cases, be independent of persons, but never of party principles and party fealty" (Lesperance 1871, 176). Newspapers then were not highly profitable enterprises and needed printing business on the side to keep the paper running. A successful political party had many printing needs. Politicians needed papers equally badly, as they were the only mass medium available at the local level. In the 1870s and 1880s, the vast majority of newspapers, all of which were local in their circulation, were also partisan (McGerr 1986, 15–16).

Local parties also dominated the machinery of elections. Voting regulations were matters of state and local law, and parties arranged them to their advantage. At the polling place, voters had to publicly select ballots printed by the parties. Thus voting was a public act, and voters received strong encouragement to choose between competing tickets. Local parties could reliably offer material benefits to voters with the certain knowledge of how they actually voted. This allowed parties to allocate benefits efficiently for the purpose of staying in

2. State legislatures chose senators until the adoption of the seventeenth amendment to the Constitution in 1913.

power. Party leaders chose election officials, a patronage plum helpful at election time (McGerr 1986, 63–64). This led to frequent charges of corruption at the polls. The scale of corruption is difficult to assess, given the murky circumstances in which it might have occurred. Historians tend to agree, however, that corruption did not inflate turnout greatly with phony votes. It is equally possible that the corrupt practices resulted in lower turnout numbers than actually occurred. After all, a party may want to inflate some vote counts and depress those likely to benefit the rival party (Argersinger 1985–1986).

The policy environment of the era also contributed to the dominance of political parties. Parties organized around issues that "were deeply meaningful to most workers" (Shefter 1994, 145). The tariff issue occupied the center of the national agenda throughout the late nineteenth century. Republicans favored high tariffs to stimulate industrial growth and national prosperity. Democrats attacked the tariff as a tax on working people so that corporate leaders could reap greater profits.

Trade policy, according to John J. Coleman, had four distinct benefits for political parties in this era. First, control over trade policy was centered in Congress. Since parties organized the business of Congress, trade policy became very much a partisan issue in national politics. Second, trade issues had a direct and comprehensible effect on the livelihoods of voters. Tariffs raised prices of imported goods for consumers; reducing them cut into business profit margins. Third, trade policy opinions tended to be stable, and rivalries existed among the public. Either one endorsed tariffs to stimulate local business or opposed them as a tax on consumers. Fourth, opinions on the tariff tended to overlap with existing regional and ethnic divisions (Coleman 1996a, 12–21). Southerners and many immigrants gained little from tariffs but paid higher prices for imported goods as a result. Both tended toward the Democratic Party for ethnic and regional reasons, making the Democrats an antitariff party. Republicans were concentrated among the business community and more skilled workers, both of which were heavily Protestant and northern. Skilled workers and businesspeople facing stiff foreign competition for manufactured goods saw the benefits of protective tariffs. It meant higher wages and profits for newly developing American industries.

The golden age of parties featured a national policy environment in which partisan differences over the tariff proved strongly important to most voters. Parties differed clearly on the major policy issue of the time, and those issue differences reinforced regional and ethnic partisan divisions. With such strong public support, parties could dominate the electoral system and governing institutions. Ambitious politicians found parties the essential tool in winning reelection, making good policy, and gaining personal influence in government. Governing elites and the mass public strongly believed that the best form of government was party government.

The experience of my great-grandfather, Stephen E. Schier (after whom I am named), illustrates the effect of this system on the individual voter. Stephen grew up a German Catholic in the small Iowa town of Fort Madison, located in the southeastern corner of the state on the Mississippi River. Educated at Catholic schools where instruction was in German, he developed a strong allegiance to the Democratic Party.

In Fort Madison, practically all Catholics, the large majority of whom were of German extraction, held Democratic loyalties. Earlier, Protestant settlers of British and Scottish ancestry, several of whom ran local manufacturing companies, were equally strong Republicans.

Stephen worked in a local haberdashery and encountered tariffs primarily as they raised prices for himself and his family. He read the local partisan paper, the *Evening Democrat*. His brother Henry, also a Democrat, served as county sheriff. On election day in 1884, Stephen's vote for Grover Cleveland and the entire Democratic ticket was a natural result of his concern over the tariff and partisan identification rooted in his membership in ethnic and religious communities, reinforced by his regular reading of a partisan press. For the original Stephen E. Schier, as for Americans of his era, electoral politics was most emphatically partisan politics.

At the end of the twentieth century, few, if any, Americans inhabit a partisan environment resembling that of Stephen E. Schier. Increased mobility broke up many ethnically homogeneous communities. Electoral reform made voting private and readily permitted split ticket voting. Partisan newspapers of the sort Stephen read have vanished. Public policy now involves complex discussion by experts, shifting interest group coalitions, and frequent fuzzing of differences by individualistic politicians. Party organizations have minimal presence in the daily lives of Americans. This great transformation caused popular mobilization in elections to wither and spurred the rise of activation strategies. Its origins lie in the complaints of reformers about the excesses of the partisan era. The progressive movement arose to reform the electoral system and create new means of policy making immune from partisan control. Policy innovations during the New Deal of the 1930s further limited the role of parties. American politics at the end of the twentieth century is very much a politics created by reformers (Mackenzie 1996). The root of these changes, however, lay in the many shortcomings of the ascendant parties of the late nineteenth century.

LESS THAN GOLDEN: FLAWS OF THE PARTISAN ERA

The apex of party power produced political practices that would spawn widespread public revulsion today. Corruption at the polls was widespread; patronage hiring and graft in office became commonplace. The partisan press distorted public understanding of politics and the demands of the emerging working class only gradually entered public debate through the parties. All of these practices boosted party power. All, appropriately, have vanished due to subsequent reforms. Many of them derived from the flourishing of political machines throughout the country, a trend that mushroomed during the heyday of the parties in the 1870s and 1880s.

The prerequisite for party rule was electoral victory. Since voting was public, making it costly for voters to deviate from the party line, parties could coerce and downright bribe voters to win office. Payment for voting became widespread during the partisan era. As many as one in five New Jersey voters, for example, received election day payments during the 1880s; Indiana politicians paid as much as $15 a vote in 1888 (Schudson 1998, 163–64). In addition to bribes, vote fraud proved common. Election officials falsified returns in Michigan and Indiana (Jensen 1971, 38–41). Boss Tweed in New York, after the fall of his notoriously venal machine, admitted that in New York City during his reign, "the ballots made no result, the counters made the result" (Board of Aldermen 1878, 133). Winning office was expensive, yet the spoils of office were alluring. At times, candidates purchased party nominations from party committees with cash payments (Schudson 1998, 152).

Machines dominated city and state governments by handing out jobs to party workers and corruptly rewarding important party members and kindred interests with public money. Widespread graft involved kickbacks from favored contracts or by the sale of land to government at inflated prices. When parties controlled state and local governments, they made thousands of patronage appointments that were seldom based on the merit of the applicant for the job. Patronage in national government centered in the postal service with its boodle of jobs, numbering 78,500 by 1896 (Skowronek 1982, 72). Patronage employees often gained their jobs in return for kicking back a percentage of their annual income to the party that secured their employment.

Although all this seems the stuff of sensational press exposés, few were forthcoming during the height of the partisan era. The newspapers, many financially supported by the parties, had little interest in biting the hands that fed. Partisan papers also gave the news a "spin" by not mentioning or greatly downplaying news that was bad for the party, while trumpeting the ill tidings that befell their opponents. All this impeded the ability of citizens to comprehend just what the parties and the government were actually doing. The norm of "press objectivity" seldom appeared and did not receive its first major voice until the *New York Times* in 1896 vowed to "give the news impartially, without fear or favor, regardless of any party, sect or interest involved" (Emery and Emery 1988, 274).

Political parties during their golden era often sought to incorporate new immigrants into the political system. For example, New York's Tammany Hall naturalized thousands of new citizens in the 1870s and 1880s. Most of the naturalizations were illegal, as Tammany ignored the legal waiting period before citizenship could be granted. They needed the votes immediately. This sort of aggressive political incorporation empowered parties and gave them the ability to exclude interests and viewpoints that were uncongenial to the party's agenda (Shefter 1994, 200). Many machines sought to aid the working class through aid or employment for individuals but remained cool to broader class appeals and agendas from socialists and labor militants. The American Federation of Labor, led by the conservative Samuel Gompers, reached frequent accommodations with local machines at the expense of more radical labor activists. Machines tended to emphasize community and ethnic politics and appeals; they accommodated "reasonable" labor demands when necessary. However, as America industrialized in the late nineteenth century, many machines became fiscally conservative regarding financial assistance for the working class and the poor. Why? To win the competition among jurisdictions for economic development, taxes had to be kept low. Since graft was frequently expensive, that left few funds for mass relief of the poor (Erie 1988, 46–47). Machine voters did receive assistance, but only in forms that machines could control and in amounts that did little to alter the distribution of income in America.

As parties grew in power in the late nineteenth century, they limited the issues, controversies, and alternatives at the center of American politics. More visionary options often faded due to party opposition. Parties obstructed investigative journalism and frequently defrauded the polls. They often trafficked in corrupt practices when in control of state and local governments. All of these pathologies of party rule created a strong reaction among the more educated, idealistic residents of machine-dominated jurisdictions. Try as they might, parties could not squelch demands for more honest and efficient elections and governance.

PROMPTING PARTY DECLINE: PROGRESSIVISM'S RISE

Many Americans today, looking back on the partisan era, can find much fault with it. Party power limited voter choice and spawned public corruption. The party system received similar criticism in its heyday. A group of highly educated, urban Republicans, called "Mugwumps," decried the shortcomings of the partisan system and urged structural reform in the 1870s and 1880s. Fashionable journals of the time, such as the *Atlantic Monthly, North American Review, Harper's Weekly,* and the *Nation,* served as platforms for reformist agitation. The reformers wanted to replace the politics of partisan spectacle with campaigns that sought to educate the public about the major issues before the nation. "In place of emotional party spirit, they offered a cool, social scientific politics of education. In place of parades and rallies, they relied on factual pamphlets and tracts. In place of the doctrine of party loyalty, they elevated the ideals of individual conscience, independency and business methods" (McGerr 1986, 66).

Mugwumps were often outspokenly antidemocratic, denouncing the power of immigrant votes in elections that sustained corrupt political machines. For example, in 1878, historian Francis Parkman decried "an invasion of peasants" from abroad and pronounced universal suffrage a "questionable blessing" (Parkman 1878, 7). The progressive movement of 1890–1925 grew from such criticisms of the political system.

Progressives fundamentally restructured the electoral system in ways sympathetic with the earlier Mugwump critique. Like the Mugwumps, progressives were highly educated, native stock business and professional people appalled by the excesses of party rule. Many lived in cities dominated by immigrant-dominated machines and shared Parkman's skepticism about the virtues of the newer American citizens. "All the great problems," declared reformer Robert DeCourcy Ward, "are tied up with the one great problem of foreign immigration" (Wiebe 1967, 62).

Badly outnumbered by partisans in the 1870s, the views of the Mugwump reformers did eventually prevail. In response to reformist criticism, the partisan flavor of campaigns receded in the 1890s. The national parties, heeding the call of reform, adopted more educational and less spectacular campaign tactics during the presidential election of 1892. The number of torchlight parades dwindled and the number of informative pamphlets increased. Turnout in 1892 dropped to 75 percent of eligible voters, the lowest since 1876 (Kleppner 1982, 176). The 1896 election, following a similar educational and less spectacular style, witnessed lower turnout still. The candidates, Republican William McKinley and Democrat William Jennings Bryan, aggressively educated the electorate about the major issue of the moment, whether to base the dollar on a gold or silver standard. A silver standard meant a weaker currency, making it easier to repay debts; a gold standard meant sounder money, a position backed by creditors. Bryan, speaking for the agricultural areas of the country in the south and west, argued for silver; McKinley, backed by business, espoused gold.

The battle over this issue produced a partisan realignment of the electorate. In place of a closely competitive party system of the 1870s and 1880s, the new alignment of partisan affiliations after 1896 produced noncompetitive regions throughout the country. While the south and west were solidly Democratic, Republicans dominated the northeast and middle west. This produced lopsided Republican victories in most congressional and presidential elections until the election of 1932. Regional dominance by one party also made it less important for individual politicians to claim unyielding loyalty to party principles in order to get ahead. Where one party ruled, a variety of agendas proliferated within it. A more individualistic candidate style began to appear during this period, a change the reformers cheered.

Another impetus for reform included the shocking revelations of business influence over party-run state and local governments in 1905 and 1906. Corruption turned public opinion against the parties. Press disclosures of governmental malfeasance from New York to San Francisco fueled a variety of reform measures aimed at cleaning up the electoral system and the processes of state and local government (Link and McCormick 1983, 30). Progressives seized on the public distaste, dominated the national agenda, and reformed the partisan era out of existence.

Progressives successfully altered many state and local electoral systems in order to tame party power. During the first decade of the twentieth century, the Australian "secret ballot" gained wide adoption and local governments replaced the parties as providers of ballots. Many other electoral reform proposals also gained prominence. Benjamin Parke De Witt, writing in 1915, summarized the progressive agenda for transforming elections: "a group of measures to give the people greater control over the nomination and election of candidates; as, for example, direct primaries, corrupt practices acts . . . and an adequate system of registration; and, secondly, a group of measures designed to give to the people control over candidates and policies after election as, for example, the initiative, referendum and recall" (De Witt 1915, 197). Stricter voter registration laws, adopted in many jurisdictions, required clear proof of residence and registration well in advance of the election. Corrupt practices acts, passed in the 1890s and early 1900s, outlawed cash payments to voters and corporate donations to parties and candidates (Link and McCormick 1983, 52). Spearheaded by reformist Governor Robert M. La Follette of Wisconsin, the direct primary received widespread adoption in states from 1900 to 1910. Many states also adopted initiative, referendum, and recall, allowing the public to directly propose and pass laws and constitutional amendments, vote on measures approved by state legislatures, and remove suspect elected officials in the middle of their terms. In the first two decades of the twentieth century, progressives also stimulated the adoption of nonpartisan elections in more than 60 percent of cities with populations of more than 5,000, and in elections for two state legislatures (Minnesota and Nebraska) (Ware 1987, 60).[3] A major goal of these reforms was to "improve" the electorate by limiting corruption and party power.

Class bias also appeared in electoral reforms. Twenty nonsouthern states also adopted literacy tests for voting between 1900 and 1920 (Kleppner 1982, 53–54). Although progressives argued for electoral reforms that, they claimed, would benefit all, progressive innovations served to reduce turnout among immigrants and voters with less income and education (Kleppner 1982, 63). Cumulatively, these electoral reforms shrank the electorate considerably. Presidential election turnout dropped from 75 percent in 1892 to 49 percent by 1920.[4] Historian Paul Kleppner estimates that personal registration require-

3. Minnesota reverted to partisan legislative elections in 1970.

4. Turnout fell in the elections of the 1920s in part because of female suffrage. Yet, according to historian Paul Kleppner, the "party of nonvoters" during the 1920s was only about half female and "also enlisted higher proportions of male voters than earlier." The nonvoters during the 1920s were concentrated especially among "com-

ments alone decreased turnout by 30 to 40 percent in the counties where they were in force (Kleppner 1982, 61).

In addition to making popular mobilization by the parties more difficult, progressive electoral reforms also weakened the internal discipline of the parties. The direct primary allowed individual candidates to spurn the preferences of party leaders and seek nomination from party voters. Herman Finer, assessing the consequences of progressive reforms in 1932, found three negative effects of the direct primary upon party hierarchy and discipline:

> Firstly, it becomes less easy to distribute nominations among the orthodox and heterodox groups in the party. . . . Secondly, differences which were formerly settled in private can now be ventilated and settled in public. . . . Nothing is so bitter as civil war, especially among professional warriors: nothing is so difficult to quiet as its aftermath. . . . Finally, party officials and workers are chosen at the primaries also, [producing] a weakening of cohesion and responsiveness throughout the body of the party. (Finer 1932, 435–36)

Progressive governmental reforms further weakened the hold of parties over government. The goal was to move from a "party state to a bureaucratic state" (Skowronek 1982, 291). Patronage employment proved an obvious target. Beginning with the national Pendleton Act of 1883, patronage employment was slowly reformed out of existence in Washington and many states (Skowronek 1982, 69). In its place came a "merit system" of public employment, in which jobs were filled on the basis of substantive knowledge demonstrated through competitive examination, not party loyalty.

Additional reforms sought to weaken the legislature, the seat of

---

ing-of-age voters, citizens of immigrant parentage, and those toward the lower ends of the education and income scales" (Kleppner 1982, 152).

party power in government, by strengthening and more efficiently organizing the executive branch. Both nationally and in many states, progressives secured establishment of independent boards and commissions to regulate policy areas where the corrupt legislature had been remiss (Link and McCormick 1983, 59). Political executives appointed these boards, and their members usually served fixed terms. Some required bipartisan membership. In 1913, for example, Congress established the Federal Trade Commission to regulate unfair business practices and the Federal Reserve Board to regulate the national banking system.

This transferred power from parties to "professionals" who could practice efficient regulation in the public interest. In truth, the progressives' interests were also well served by these changes:

The progressive reformers were often members of professions, and one of their prime objectives was to take responsibility for various policy areas away from government and into the hands of independent boards and agencies on which the professionals would have much greater influence. (Ware 1987, 131)

The popularity of regulatory agencies during this era grew from widespread acknowledgement of party corruption and the growth and increasing conflict among interest groups. Rising industrialism produced growing controversy in several policy areas. The policy environment proved less consensual and more conflictual. Labor-management relations, food and product safety, trade practices, child labor, and the regulation of transportation and utilities all became hot arenas of political contention. The early twentieth century witnessed a large growth in interest groups to address these concerns. The American Federation of Labor became the largest of several labor organizations. The National Association of Manufacturers spoke for small business, while the National Civic Federation represented larger industrial and financial concerns. Reform groups appeared to combat alcohol, child labor, and political corruption (Link and McCormick 1983, 56).

The groups arose because new public problems produced new conflicts that consensus-oriented parties did not wish to address. By wading into areas of hot dispute, parties risked internal splits and electoral defeat. This left an opening for aspiring interest group entrepreneurs, and they filled it with innovative advocacy techniques that became standard over the course of the twentieth century: "they organized their members, raised money, hired lobbyists, pressured governmental officials, and inundated the public with their propaganda" (Link and McCormick 1983, 57). John Aldrich calls these entrepreneurs "a new brand of benefit seekers" pursuing policy agendas in ways that circumvented parties (Aldrich 1995, 296).

Given the increasing ill repute of party politics during this period, the progressive response gained much support from "reform" interest groups. That response was to "professionalize" the disputes through nonpartisan regulation. This mode of policy-making shrank the importance of elections and enhanced the importance of interest groups: "Citizen influence through electoral participation was only tangentially and tenuously linked to policymaking by administrative bodies. Interest-group participation became a more appropriate means to shape such decisions, but that route was not practically available to most citizens, and especially not to lower-class citizens" (Kleppner 1982, 151).

The rise of an independent press also spurred party decline in the early twentieth century. By the late nineteenth century, large urban newspapers had become profitable, independent businesses, free from dependence on party organization. Journalistic entrepreneurs created

"chains" of newspapers—Hearst, Munsey, and Scripps-Howard—
from coast to coast. Journalism slowly became a profession, with
reporters interested in the facts rather than in promoting a partisan
message. Publishers Joseph Pulitzer and William Randolph Hearst
found that their newspapers sold well if they indulged in sensational
coverage of sports, gossip, murder, and scandal. The partisan press
survived only in less populated rural areas (McGerr 1986, 130).

The change in the press helped to lower popular interest in elections. Instead of a consistent and fervent partisan message, the public
received more sporadic and complicated coverage of politics. "The
independent press made politics complicated and unexciting; sensa-
tionalism made it unimportant" (McGerr 1986, 135). The new owners
of newspapers were wealthy businesspeople often sympathetic to progressive reform and sharply aware that revelations of political scandal
would sell papers. The "respectable" independent press catered
increasingly to the tastes of the "educated middle and upper classes"
while the sensational press sold well among the less well-off (McGerr
1986, 136). The changes in the press helped to stratify political knowledge by shrinking political interest among the disadvantaged, in
whose favorite papers politics became one small part of a parade of
sensational disclosures. As a result, "the well-to-do had the opportunity, unavailable to any other social group, to disseminate their con-
ception of politics and partisanship and set the agenda of public life"
(McGerr 1986, 136). That agenda called for less partisan and more
efficient government, goals close to the hearts of progressives.

By the 1920s, parties proved far less useful as tools for ambitious
politicians to achieve their goals. Electoral reforms had reduced popular participation and party dominance over voting procedures.
Governmental reforms lessened party power over government employ-

ment and legislative control over policy making. The press no longer conveyed a heavily partisan message, and campaigns stopped featuring sensational rallies that commanded public attention. The "educational" campaigns urged by reformers had deteriorated into "advertising" campaigns involving simplified messages about the qualities of particular candidates. In presidential elections, candidate personality became more important in campaigns, party labels less so (McGerr 1986, 183). A major transformation of American politics had occurred. For many Americans of lower education and income, politics became a complex, frustrating, and limited part of their lives. The politics of the 1920s resembles that of the late twentieth century more than that of the late nineteenth century. Although several urban machines continued to function, parties played a much-reduced role in elections and governance during the decade. Only a major jolt to the political system would resurrect the importance of party in the public's mind. That jolt came in the form of the Great Depression and the New Deal.

PARTIES AND THE NEW DEAL

The shocking decline in the nation's economy from 1929 through 1933 destroyed the livelihoods of millions of Americans and created a new importance for politics in their lives. Voter turnout rose during the 1930s as a charismatic president, Franklin Delano Roosevelt, cemented together a new partisan coalition through his innovative response to the economic crisis. Turnout in the 1936 presidential election was 5.1 percent above that of 1928 (Kleppner 1982, 85). The new Democratic coalition included many new voters (Petrocik 1981, 38) and also new converts to the party, particularly among African American, Jewish, and working class voters (Petrocik 1981, 38; Ladd 1978, 57–69). The arrival of organized labor as a major political force within the Democratic coalition made partisan politics more of a class divide than it has been before or since (Ladd 1978, 71–72). Among the public, party identification achieved a renewed importance in the 1930s as political energies coalesced around the issue differences dividing Democrats and Republicans. To support Roosevelt's New Deal involved endorsing unprecedented government efforts to aid the economy and assist the victims of the economic downturn. Political rhetoric between the parties during the decade was harsh and strongly focused on the economic issues dividing the parties. Parties became more important in the electoral system in that they came to matter more to voters. The Democrats reaped the benefits as they created a national majority coalition—of white southerners, African Americans, Jews, Catholics, and working class voters—that would last for a generation.

While parties enjoyed a new preeminence in elections, the Roosevelt administration spurred several governmental reforms that furthered party decline over the long term. Roosevelt set the tone during his first term by seldom conferring with party leaders in Congress over the substance of his reform legislation. Roosevelt's advisors sought to address the economic crisis not by strengthening party power, but by strengthening the bureaucratic hand of the president: "New Dealers shared the progressive's antipathy to party politics and their understanding that a strong and responsible executive required the demise of partisan responsibility" (Milkis 1993, 13). Although the Democratic party enjoyed some patronage opportunities from the large public employment programs of the thirties, formal control of the programs remained in bureaucratic hands. This hostility to parties also appeared in the administrative reforms of the executive branch proposed during Roosevelt's second term. Roosevelt secured passage in 1939 of an executive branch reorganization bill that enhanced the bureaucratic authority of the presidency while reducing the power of Congress and its party leaders. The bill created an Executive Office of the President, increased presidential staff, and gave the president the power to reorganize the executive branch, subject to congressional veto (Milkis 1993, 113–22). The plan gave the president more initiative in administering government at the expense of the partisan legislators in Congress.

The policy environment of the 1930s shifted strongly against the parties as Congress ceded power to the president and the executive bureaucracy. Congress surrendered authority to the president over several important areas of economic policy. The tariff, that useful partisan issue of the late nineteenth century, produced more complex and unstable coalitions during the 1930s. Congress found that by ceding authority over the tariff to the executive branch, they could guarantee adequate protection for local industries without receiving blame should protection fall short (Coleman and Yoffe 1990). Roosevelt's personal emphasis on fiscal policy—control over taxes and spending—also placed it under increasing executive control. Presidential spending and taxation proposals began to guide the national budget (Peterson 1985). Approval of federal welfare legislation shifted the allocation of benefits to citizens from urban party organizations to federal bureaucrats (Coleman 1996a, 39). Creation of automatic spending programs, such as unemployment compensation and Social Security, provided benefits bureaucratically without any explicit legislative or partisan intervention.

All these changes would gradually lower the importance of parties to voters. Economic policy, crucial to all citizens, became more the personal responsibility of the president and less the collective charge of the parties. Presidential preeminence in economic policy and the creation of automatic spending programs "contributed to declining party allegiance and declining focus on parties in the public, placed the systemic locus of policy initiation and control away from party hands [and] encouraged declining party differences at periods of peak public interest" (Coleman 1996a, 45). Further, the larger federal bureaucracy caused interest groups to work directly with federal administrators and ignore parties: "a politics of administration tends not to nationalize and reform parties, but to link interests directly to national governmental institutions, thus making intermediary organizations such as parties less important in the scheme of things" (Milkis 1993, 12).

POSTWAR PARTISAN DECAY

Executive power grew in Washington and the states after World War II. With greater executive and bureaucratic control over policy, it is little wonder that parties became less important to citizens. The reformed electoral system hardly placed parties at the center of elections, anyway. Ambitious politicians found political parties increasingly less useful in satisfying their goals of reelection, good public policy, and political influence. In John Aldrich's formulation, changes in the historical setting had created a set of formal institutional rules for conducting elections and making and executing policy that placed parties at a profound disadvantage. The second half of the twentieth century produced additional changes to entrench party weakness further.

The arrival of the new technology of television additionally curtailed the electoral importance of parties. Prior to TV, elections depended more on personal contact between campaigns and voters. Local party workers were key conduits in providing that contact (Herrnson 1988, 12–20). The ability of local parties to provide volunteer or patronage workers in elections remained a key organizational strength of parties before television. Now candidates for statewide office, the U.S. House, and even the state legislature use television to contact voters. The shift to TV began in the 1960s and is now complete. Candidates for major office need money for television ads and have to raise it themselves. Since primaries decide party nominations, candidates must set up their own organizations early in the election cycle in order to raise money and recruit their own volunteers. Parties play no role before the primary and only a limited fundraising and advertising role between the primary and general election. "Politicians can appeal over the heads of political parties directly to the public. . . . Parties are less effective in connecting politicians with the public, and the negative ads on television and the costs of broadcast time create a greater sense of distance between politicians and the public" (Nye 1997, 17).

Along with the rise of television came an increasing geographic mobility of Americans. Many ethnic urban neighborhoods disappeared with suburbanization. As more Americans moved from region to region, traditional community loyalties and partisan commitments weakened. The community homogeneity that supported Stephen E. Schier's partisanship in 1884 has vanished from most of America. Partisan mobilization encountered new obstacles as a result: "People who do not plan a long stay in a community are unlikely to invest much of their time or interest in its politics or problems. Local organizations are in constant flux as their membership regularly turns over.

And since census data show that the propensity to move is highest among the best educated and most affluent Americans . . . leadership recruitment is confounded as well" (Mackenzie 1996, 21).

The historical setting of the sixties and early seventies produced additional problems for parties. During that time, confidence in government plummeted, partisan identification among the public weakened, and the number of self-described independents rose (Nie, Verba, and Petrocik 1974; Nye, Zelikow, and King 1997). Why? "The issues that loosened party ties were racial conflict and Vietnam, capped off with Watergate. These issues caused substantial discontent. They led the public to turn against the political parties and the political process more generally" (Nie, Verba, and Petrocik 1974, 350). The war in Vietnam also split the Democratic party in 1968 and produced further changes in the electoral system that weakened parties.

The contentious 1968 Democratic presidential nomination process spawned calls for reform of the nomination system. Prior to 1968, presidential nominations remained one of the few bastions of party organization control in American politics. Although some delegates to the nomination convention were chosen through primaries, in most states, party leaders or caucuses picked the delegates. In some states, such as Georgia, the party chair handpicked the delegation; in others, such as Iowa, they were chosen through a system of participatory caucuses and conventions. Vice President Hubert Humphrey gained the 1968 Democratic nomination without entering a single primary. Opponents of Humphrey at the national convention, fueled by their strong opposition to the Johnson administration's conduct of the Vietnam war, demanded changes in the nomination process rules to "open up" the system. The 1968 convention approved creation of a commission on delegate selection, headed by Senator George McGovern (South Dakota) and Representative Don Fraser (Minnesota) to propose rules changes for the 1972 nomination contest (Polsby 1983, 9–53; Shafer 1983; Kirkpatrick 1976).

Opponents of the old system were infused with a righteous indignation about the party organization and its "regulars" and manifested a moral zealousness reminiscent of the most militant progressives. They successfully proposed new national party rules mandating proportional representation of candidate preferences at all stages of delegate selection in the states. Party leaders and elected officials could no longer pick submissive delegates; rather, candidate factions would "fight it out" in public delegate selection contests. The complex rules adopted by the national Democratic party caused many states to abolish their suddenly unwieldy caucus and convention systems and move directly to primaries for selecting delegates. The absence of party leader control in choosing delegates made the process into an unpredictable marathon that accentuated party divisions (Polsby 1983, 64–71).

Political scientist and Democratic member of Congress David Price argues that "displacing party and elected officials for the sake of candidate and issue activists is not likely to produce a more representative and responsive convention" (Price 1984, 204). So it proved. The immediate result of the reforms was a very divided Democratic convention in 1972 that nominated an insurgent candidate, George McGovern. He went on to suffer one of the great electoral defeats in American history. In 1976, the party nominated the little-known former governor of Georgia, Jimmy Carter, who in 1976 narrowly defeated incumbent President Gerald Ford, the candidate of the scandal-plagued Republican party. Carter was not rewarded with reelection in 1980. In the 1980s, the party softened its strictly proportional selection rules and allowed more party and elected officials to attend conventions as ex-officio delegates.

The short-term consequences for the Democrats were negative because the party's insurgents valued participation over consensus when choosing a nominee. Over the longer term, the reforms created the current presidential nomination process, involving open, competitive delegate selection in both parties over six exhausting months. The process rewards candidates who can campaign full-time for years before the contest formally begins and have great personal wealth to fund their advertising in so many states. It also rewards the early states of Iowa and New Hampshire, the first two states in the process, which can give candidates vital momentum for the marathon. The current process involves no party organization control; it is simply an open competition among candidates to get supporters to vote in primaries or attend caucuses on their behalf.

Now, presidential candidates have at each other in the search for delegate support. Proportional representation allows many candidates to compete and gain some delegates: "instead of pressing politicians toward coalitions that would assemble a majority in each state, factionalism [is] encouraged" (Polsby 1983, 67). As the candidate-based factions fight it out, many candidates run short of money and support and drop out of the contest. Only the battered "front runner" and a few rivals make it to the convention. The candidate with the largest number of delegates entering the national convention then is anointed the nominee on the first ballot. National conventions no longer seriously deliberate over the identity of nominees, as they did for multiple ballots during the partisan era. Instead, they are "designed as entertainment" to showcase the obvious nominee (Polsby 1983, 77). As a result, presidential elections become more candidate-centered and less party-centered. National conventions, one of the last citadels of party organization strength, thus fell.

Reforms of the national system of campaign finance also spurred the rise of candidate-centered campaigns at the expense of parties. Alarmed by the rising costs of campaigns (due in large part to increased dependence on televised advertising) and the invitation for corruption in the money chase, Congress passed a Federal Election Campaign Finance Act in 1971, restructuring the financing of presidential elections. Although altered somewhat by subsequent Supreme Court opinions, beginning in 1976, presidential nomination and general election contests became publicly financed according to the provisions of the 1971 law. Candidates, not parties, stand at the center of the new set of finance laws. Candidates for a major party's presidential nomination can choose to fund their campaigns with their personal money in unlimited amounts or can elect to accept public funds. To receive public funds, candidates had to qualify by raising $5,000 in each of twenty states. After that, candidates receive matching federal funds up to $250 for individual contributions to the campaign. Individuals are limited to $1,000 contributions to each candidate. In return for public money, candidates face limits on how much they can spend in contesting the nomination overall ($31 million in 1996 dollars, indexed for inflation by law) and in each state. In the general election, candidates can either accept total public funding ($62.2 million in 1996 dollars, indexed for inflation by law) or fund the race through personal cash (Sorauf 1992, 7–12; Wayne 1996, 45). Political parties can spend up to two cents per voter to aid their presidential candidates, a limit also indexed for inflation. This amounts to a small fraction of what candidates can spend. Presidential elections became increasing candidate-centered during the twentieth century, and so did presidential campaign finance. The 1971 law limited the role of parties in presidential elections in several ways. The campaign subsidies go to candidates, not parties. Prenomination financing of candidates encourages party fragmentation as the candidates fight for the nomination (Price 1984, 242–44).

The revelations of Watergate prompted another round of campaign finance reforms in 1974 that are still largely in effect today. These amendments to the 1971 act restructured congressional elections in a way that initially disadvantaged parties. As with the new presidential rules, the individual candidates, not the parties, stand at the center of the regulated system. All candidates for Congress have to disclose all contributions received and expenditures made by their campaigns to the bipartisan Federal Elections Commission (FEC). Congressional candidates can receive a maximum of $1,000 per election from individuals (meaning, in effect, $2,000 from wealthy contributors, for individuals could contribute $1,000 in both the primary and general election). Interest groups have to form federally regulated Political Action Committees (PACs) for purposes of making contributions. PACs, like candidates, have to file complete records of receipts and expenditures with the FEC. PACs can contribute $5,000 per candidate per election, meaning a maximum of $10,000 per candidate in an election year, since candidates run in primary and general elections. Political parties initially were subject to an identical limit. This law placed the political party on an equal financing footing with any individual interest group. As a result, the party percentage of campaign contributions to congressional candidates plummeted while the number of PACs soared, as did the PAC proportion of the total campaign contributions to candidates (Sabato 1984, 277). The new laws also increased greatly the importance of campaign fund-raising consultants. Additionally, individual contributions to national party committees, previously unlimited, could now not exceed $20,000 per calendar year. The laws caused parties to raise and spend less than interest groups to influence congressional elections.

Overall, a remarkable combination of forces combined to weaken the importance of the parties by the 1970s. The electoral structure put in place during the progressive era remained hostile to parties. Voter loyalty had waned; party organization control of nominations was weakened further by reforms of the presidential nomination process. Television made parties less important in campaigns. Fund-raising laws moved parties to the margins of electoral politics. David Broder, one of America's leading political journalists, spoke for many observers when he claimed in his 1972 book, *The Party's Over,* that "parties have been weakened by their failure to adapt to some of the social and technological changes taking place in America. But, even more, they are suffering from simple neglect: neglect by presidents and public officials, but, particularly, neglect by the voters" (Broder 1972, xxiii).

A PARTY RESURGENCE?

Some political scientists claim that American parties have rebounded from their nadir of the 1970s. Paul Herrnson argues that national party organizations—the party's national committees and their House and Senate campaign committees—today "have adapted to the candidate-centered, money-driven, high-tech style of modern campaign politics" and "are now stronger, more stable, and more influential in their relations with state and local party committees and candidates than ever" (Herrnson 1998a, 50, 79). Herrnson bases much of his case on the new fund-raising prowess of the national parties and their ability to hire and work collaboratively with political consultants to get their congressional candidates elected (Herrnson 1998a, 60–64). Much evidence supports Herrnson's conclusions about national party fund-raising. To explain how it has grown, we must examine changes in campaign finance law that made it so.

Campaign finance law allows two sorts of political contributions: those with "hard money" and those with "soft money." Hard money contributions are those subject to legal limits and full accounting, described in the previous section. In 1978, the Federal Election Commission responded to complaints from state and local party officials that the hard money limits prevented parties from raising adequate funds to function well in presidential and congressional elections. In response, the FEC allowed the national party committees to spend unlimited amounts for "election related activities" such as bumper stickers and get-out-the-vote efforts at the state and local level (Corrado 1997, 171–72). In the parlance of campaign finance, this is soft money in that such contributions have no legal limits, although they must be reported to the FEC. The soft money rule prompted the national parties to raise millions of dollars from corporations, labor unions, and individuals that had given the maximum amount of hard money allowed under federal law.

In 1996, soft money fund-raising and spending reached a new high due to aggressive solicitation and a shower of six-figure contributions to the parties. The National Republican party raised $138.2 billion, a 178 percent increase over 1992, while the national Democratic party raised $123.9 million, an increase of 242 percent over four years earlier (Corrado 1997, 175). The national parties spent funds in innovative ways, most notably on "issue advocacy" spending for campaign commercials that celebrated the traits and accomplishments of the party and its presidential and congressional candidates. These were legal because they did not "expressly advocate" election of a particular candidate (Potter 1997, 227). The Supreme Court in 1996 also opened up another loophole for party spending, allowing them to make "independent expenditures" of their hard money—that raised under contribution limits—for ads for party candidates. The court previously had banned such spending as not independent but collusive with the candidates. A majority of justices changed their mind, allowing another spigot of party spending to open in 1996 (Sorauf 1998, 223).

Simply judging by money spent in 1996, Herrnson's generalization about national party power seems correct. However, an enhanced ability to raise more money for elections is the only major evidence for party resurgence (Frendreis 1996, 386). Truly strong parties are more than cash cows for candidate-centered politics. Parties remain remarkably weak in the affections of the public (Coleman 1996b, 370; Wattenberg 1996). Party mobilization of the public remains in deep decline. Split ticket voting remains high and voter participation in national elections remains at a seventy-year low. Beyond their ability to raise money to subcontract with political consultants, parties remain quite weak in the electoral system. The lion's share of all funds spent in elections is still raised and spent by candidates (Coleman 1996b, 371).

The policy environment nationally remains inhospitable to parties. Recent studies found at best a slight influence of party organization activities on elected officials' policy decisions (Cotter et al. 1984; Leyden and Borrelli 1990; Dwyre 1992, 1993; Wright 1994). A merit-based bureaucracy still implements policy, and presidential authority in the political system continues to encourage more personalistic and less partisan politics. Important benefit programs remain automatically distributed to voters, free from party control. Party responsibility for the economic and social quality of voters' lives remains, in the electorate's eyes, quite low. Hence they pay little attention to parties (Coleman 1996b, 381).

The current strength of American political parties can best be judged by recourse to Alan Ware's definition of strong parties offered at the beginning of this chapter. A strong party controls the identity of its candidates, decides on the campaign issues for candidates, provides the lion's share of resources for election campaigns, and influences governmental appointments (Ware 1988, x). By this definition, the current resurgence in national party organization entails a greater (although still a minority) share in campaign resources. In all other aspects of party power, American parties remain much weaker than during their golden age. Then, parties commanded every one of Ware's criteria of power. We remain far from seeing those days again.

CONCLUSION

Ambitious politicians at the end of the twentieth century find political parties far less useful for achieving their goals of reelection, good public policy, and political influence than they did one hundred years ago. Parties remain useful to politicians for organizing the legislature and providing election services, but their other powers and functions have vanished. Progressive reformers created an electoral regime poisonous for party power. The changing historical setting took its toll, as the policy environment of government grew less congenial for parties. New, conflictual issues stimulated the rise of executive-dominated, regulatory government. Welfare programs removed the material incentive for voting from the control of political machines. Automatic benefits such as Social Security, unemployment compensation, and Medicare made many voters less dependent on party control of government to receive much-needed assistance.

Twentieth-century history has been unkind to parties in other ways. Increasing mobility destroyed many homogeneous neighborhoods where partisan attachments were strong. Television created a capital-intensive form of campaigning that parties adapted to slowly, only getting into advertising in a big way during the last decade. Parties contact fewer people during campaigns and make little difference to most Americans. Partisan mobilization as practiced in New Haven in 1876 seems inconceivable today. Parties, candidates, and interests have created new means of drumming up support that are far more effective in today's environment. Activation is far more efficient than old-style mobilization.

Parties once served as the fulcrums of American politics, drawing citizens quite effectively into their competition over power and conflict over issues. Widespread corruption, an unfortunate accompaniment of party power, prompted reforms that weakened parties and reduced electoral participation. Over the last one hundred years, according to John Aldrich, parties have changed from having "control" over their office-seekers and holders to now working "in service" to them (1995, 7). A major party now is "designed by and meant to serve its office seekers and its new brand of benefit seekers"-policy-oriented party activists, many of whom are active interest-group members (1995, 296). Today's parties play at best a supporting role in a politics dominated by an intense mosaic of political elites engaged in carefully targeted strategic activation. Parties collude with interests and wealthy individuals to raise money so candidates can target well limited segments of the adult population in elections. Meanwhile, government remains a complex, bureaucratic web of policies, each policy the concern of a particular set of candidates, bureaucrats, and elected officials. Activation strategies by interest groups drive much policy change, not mass mobilization by parties in elections. Popular control of government is less sure as a result.

CHAPTER 3

Candidates, Parties, and Electoral Activation

The evolving politics is a candidate-centered, technocratic

exercise in impersonal manipulation. It is also a politics of

extraordinary expense.

William Crotty, *American Political Parties in Decline*

odern campaigns differ from the mobilization efforts of the partisan era in three fundamental ways. First, candidates operate more individually, less as part of a partisan organizational effort. Second, the tools for success are much more expensive than those employed one hundred years ago. Third, because of the first two factors, candidates have very strong incentives to target the electorate carefully, given their limited resources. GOP political consultant Frank Luntz explains contemporary campaign strategy: "As campaign costs continue to spiral upwards, the necessity to target voters accurately and send them the right message at the lowest possible cost has become crucial. As a result, there is a trend in political campaigning toward dividing and subdividing the electorate into smaller, more narrowly defined subsections" (Luntz 1988, 200). Candidates for office operate as independent entrepreneurs with limited resources marketing themselves to prospective primary and general election voters. At their disposal are many tools for gathering all-important financial resources, researching the preferences of voters, and persuading voters to cast their lot with the right candidate. The candidate and his or her campaign have a strong incentive to deploy these tools as efficiently as possible in a harshly competitive environment.

These incentives explain much of the difference between activation and mobilization. During the partisan era, more primitive election tools, combined with party organization strength, produced a much more inclusive style of campaigning. The art of targeting remained primitive, resulting in partisan campaigning that produced a greater public involvement in parties and elections. Daniel M. Shea calls this approach a "shotgun" strategy aimed at reaching as many people as possible with partisan appeals involving the concerns of most voters (Shea 1996, 8). By contemporary standards this was hopelessly inefficient: "it did little to link the right message with the right person" (Shea 1996, 9). Today, candidate-centered campaigns employ rifles, not shotguns, aimed at finding and pushing the right message for the right voter: "no word better captures the tactics of modern campaigning than 'targeting'" (Shea 1996, 9). The arrival of better voter targeting techniques and new incentives for campaigns to independently pursue voter targets caused activation to supplant mobilization.

This chapter explains how candidates and parties use the new targeting arts to activate limited sections of the adult population to participate in elections. The key group in electoral politics today is the group of "likely voters." Each candidate must first solidify his or her base of support among them. An even more crucial subset includes those likely to vote but undecided between candidates in a given election. Candidates and parties spend extraordinary resources identifying and attempting to persuade this sliver of the public to vote in a desired fashion. New technology permits this efficient deployment of resources. Unlike partisan mobilization of the past, millions of Americans are ignored in this process. "The new campaign technology ignores communities with a history or pattern of nonvoting. Earlier mass mobilization techniques, such as rallies and door-to-door campaigning, were addressed to all citizens" (Baer 1995, 53). The electoral environment today involves fewer voters but more complex strategic choices by candidates. To understand the arts of activation in campaigns, we must begin with the choices candidates confront.

WHOM TO ACTIVATE?

Recall that John Aldrich identified two problems that candidates must solve in winning votes for election. First, voters must be supplied with reasons to turn out on Election Day. Second, voters need reasons to support one candidate over another (Aldrich 1995, 48). As a candidate with limited resources, how should one supply information to overcome voters' information deficiencies? Clearly, by activating those with the greatest marginal propensity to participate. Thus the first task of any campaign is separating the good targets from the less promising targets by focusing appeals "on those they believe already are, or are most likely to become, their supporters" (Aldrich 1995, 48).

Candidates for state and national office confront two groups of citizens who determine their electoral fate: primary electorates and the general electorates. Partisan activists who vote in primaries are far different from the party organization "regulars" of one hundred years ago. The regulars "tended simply to carry out what the office seekers and holders desired," but they have been replaced by "policy-type benefit seekers" who seek to bind candidates to their ideological agendas (Aldrich 1995, 183). The activist elites within each party have "grown, on average, more ideologically extreme over the last three decades" (D. King 1997, 172). Thus candidates must balance the agenda of an ideologically extreme primary electorate with that of a much larger, more centrist electorate in November.

This divergence produces three impacts on candidates. First, partisan activists will recruit candidates who reflect their agendas. Second, the need for the nomination and for the support of the activists in the general election will pull candidates toward the agenda of the party elites. Third, this partisan "pull" will continue throughout an elective career for politicians who hope to move up to higher elective office. The way to office always leads through primaries, and activist elites dominate them (Aldrich 1995, 191–92).

The tendency of candidates to deviate from the political center and to maintain this deviation during their careers complicates the task of winning elections. Campaign strategy involves convincing swing voters in primaries and general elections that a particular candidate who may well differ from them on many issues should nevertheless get their vote. This is not an easy task. It is so formidable that an entire profession has sprung up in recent decades to assist candidates with it by employing new campaign technologies.

The situation of candidates is more complex yet, because the electoral environment includes other elites of great strategic importance to them. Since capital-intensive campaigns are expensive, fund-raising in recent decades has become an ever-larger task for candidates for major office. National campaign finance law limits the amounts individuals and PACs can contribute, so candidates must constantly scrape up new funds from new people, rather than relying on a few "fat cat" supporters or party coffers as they did in the old days. This need for contributors further empowers the more ideologically extreme partisan elites and can compound the difficulty of reaching swing voters in the fall. Fortunately for candidates, direct mail communication technology (discussed later in this chapter) permits a candidate to present private, segmented appeals to each group, allowing candidates greater flexibility in their message.

Contributions are just one of several ways that interest groups can influence elections. Groups usually enter elections through PAC contributions, in-kind assistance of resources or volunteers, and independent expenditure or issue advocacy advertising campaigns. They, like many party activists, "become involved in the electoral arena only to forward their policy preferences" (Maisel 1993, 130). Occasionally active in primaries, groups more commonly deploy resources in general elections. Given their limited resources and the contemporary campaign techniques at hand, they pursue activation strategies in elections that satisfy their policy goals. The growth and variety of group activities in elections receives attention in the next chapter.

By Aldrich's formulation, institutional rules and the historical environment have changed, thus altering how candidates approach the public. The rise of primaries, the decline of party identification, and the advent of television and new campaign technologies produced a situation in which rational candidates employ activation strategies and disdain more traditional styles of partisan mobilization. Political parties are now secondary to the relationship between candidate and voter in politics (Price 1992, 133; Bibby 1994, 25–29). Important campaign functions controlled by parties one hundred years ago—such as campaign themes and voter contact—now fall under the control of the new profession of campaign consultants. Their loyalties and efforts center on individual candidates.

THE ROLE OF CONSULTANTS

Changes in campaign technology provided candidates "new means of winning" beyond reliance on party organization and the party label (Salmore and Salmore 1989, 255). Television, radio, and direct mail supplanted rallies and personal campaigning. Polling and focus groups provided new intelligence for voter targeting. Campaign finance laws of the 1970s formally limited the ability of individuals, interests, and parties to provide great sums to any particular candidate. Candidates had to raise funds on their own and to do that, they needed professional help. Direct mail consulting mushroomed as a result of the campaign finance reform laws (Friedenberg 1997, 24). A new profession of "promoters" arose in the sixties and seventies to meet the demand from candidates for professional help (Johnson-Cartee and Copeland 1997, 12).

Today, over three hundred firms provide campaign-consulting services nationally. They include many firms specializing in particular aspects of campaigning: campaign management, campaign finance development, survey and audience research, get-out-the-vote, grass-roots activation, media buying, television production, direct mail, and scheduling (Sabato 1984; Thurber 1995, 5). They commonly tout their ability to provide campaigns, in the words of one consultant, "a cost-effective strategy to maximize the votes it will receive" (Schoenfield 1998, 1). The field has professionalized rapidly. George Washington University and American University, both located in Washington, D.C., now provide degree programs in campaign management.

The professionalization of campaigns represents perhaps the final triumph of progressive reform over political parties. To Sidney Blumenthal, professional consultants

embody many of the virtues espoused by turn-of-the-century progressives. They are usually dispassionate critics of politics, wary of control by party bosses. In the consulting trade, these attitudes are institutionalized. Consultants are professionals without binding ties. In an important sense their politics are made possible by entrepreneurship, their ability to sell themselves to clients. This is the progressive ideal of individualist middle-class citizens in a transmuted form. The consultants are the answer to the progressive's problems. William Allen White, a progressive, . . . argued for a "permanent cure" for the political machine system, which progressives regarded as the bane of democracy. The permanent cure is the permanent campaign. (Blumenthal 1980, 7)

By "permanent campaign," Blumenthal means the professionalization of campaigns in which governing becomes an exercise in campaign "positioning" (1980, 7). When parties lost power over government policy to governmental executives, individualistic permanent campaigns became a sound strategy for executives seeking reelection. The Clinton presidency of 1995 and 1996, discussed later in this chapter, provides a prime example of such a permanent campaign. Proper positioning requires image-making and strategic calculation, clearly the stock-in-trade of consultants. The rise of the consultants provides for a dominance of politics by professionals that displaces the parties. Instead of corrupt parties, is it not better to be governed by professionals? Such is the current conventional wisdom. Professional politics focuses on goal-oriented efficiency. Activation is professional goal-oriented efficiency applied to campaign politics. These professional techniques, detailed below, are legion.

THE TOOLS OF THE TRADE

The consulting business includes many firms of varying size that assist candidates in performing three campaign functions. First, an effective campaign runs on accurate knowledge of the citizens most likely to determine its fate. The "knowledge firms" include those that provide database management for turnout and fund-raising and a variety of voter research services: polling, focus groups, and audience research. Second, adequate funding is the sine qua non of a successful campaign, and the campaign finance laws of the 1970s make securing adequate funding a very time-consuming activity. The "money firms" specialize in fund-raising by direct mail and other techniques. Third, a successful candidate must market him or herself well through a variety of media. The "media firms" include those specializing in television spots, radio commercials, direct mail to voters, and media buying. Twenty years ago, a candidate for statewide office might hire a general consulting firm to handle all of these tasks. Given the growing specialization of the profession, major candidates now usually hire separate knowledge, money, and media specialists. What follows is a description of each of these specialties.

Few Americans have heard of database management firms, and little do unsuspecting citizens realize how much information about them these companies collect for campaign use. Database management firms work year in and year out to create good "lists" for use by campaigns. The quality of the lists improves the quality of the targeting, thus making campaign activation more effective. A good list is one that will "yield" a highly positive response for a campaign. This helps direct mail, telephone canvassing, and get-out-the-vote (GOTV) efforts (Friedenberg 1997, 95). A leading database firm is Aristotle

Industries, which can provide detailed subsets of voters requested by campaigns. As Shawn Harmon of Aristotle observes: "as a result, searching for all female Democrat voters who are over 65 years old is not a problem" (Friedenberg 1997, 96). The firms are gaining steadily more information about voters, recently developing the ability to identify homeowners and whether a child is present in the home (Friedenberg 1997, 99).

The largest number of "knowledge" firms include those involved in voter research. The most common form of this is survey research or polling, provided by dozens of firms nationally. Any serious candidate for major office first needs a "benchmark" poll, costing about $25,000 and involving sixty-five to seventy detailed questions about the candidate and his or her likely opponents. This first, comprehensive poll gives a campaign strategic information about the effort's strengths and weaknesses. Adverse findings in a benchmark poll have ended many a budding campaign. As the campaign progresses, the candidate may commission a series of "brushfire" polls done every week or two to determine if the campaign's themes are affecting targeted voters in the desired way. A better-funded campaign may do nightly "tracking polls" that give more thorough results concerning the campaign's persuasive efforts. A "quick-response" poll may also be commissioned in response to a dramatic event that might affect the campaign and its message or in response to a new advertisement by the campaign or a rival (Shea 1996, 124–25). To supplement polls, firms also commission focus groups, aggregations of selected (often swing) voters who discuss the candidates and issues in depth with a moderator over a two-hour period. Many pollsters believe such in-depth discussions, videotaped by the campaign, add further depth to the public opinion results found in surveys (Shea 1996, 124).

Well-funded campaigns frequently employ instant audience response systems, or "dial groups," to assess campaign commercials, debates, and speeches. A group of from fifteen to one hundred carefully selected voters receives a dial, which they employ to register approval (100 on the dial), neutrality (50), or disapproval (0) with the ads, comments, or behavior of a candidate they watch on videotape or on live television. Consultants Richard Maullin and Christine Quirk, who specialize in audience response systems, provide the following example: "We recruited undecided swing voters during the Los Angeles mayoral campaign in 1993 and showed them ads from the leading candidates. The quantitative results of the session showed one candidate's ads were much more effective with this key group than any of the others. With this up-to-the-minute information in hand, the session moderator was able to interact with the participants and probe the reasons behind their reactions" (Maullin and Quirk 1995, 28). A related technology, the "mall group" involves showing mock ads to targeted swing voters recruited in shopping malls. This technique, perfected by President Clinton's pollsters Mark Penn and Doug Schoen, provided essential strategic information for his 1996 reelection campaign, noted later in this chapter.

An ethically more suspect sort of research is the "push poll." This term actually applies to two distinct campaign practices. The less controversial method of push polling involves early polling about positive and negative characteristics of the candidates in order to determine which bits of information seem to change voters' candidate preferences. A sample question: "If you learned that [candidate A] opposes a woman's right to choose an abortion, would this make you more or less likely to support him?" (Sabato and Simpson 1996, 246). This allows candidates to assess their own and their opponent's vulnerabilities and discover promising bits of negative information for future advertising. A more suspect form of push polling is actually a media or persuasion strategy. Phone banks on the eve of an election call voters and disclose sensational and often misleading information about a particular candidate in order to push people to vote for his or her opponent. Here is an example from the 1994 Florida governor's race, targeted at the Republican candidate, Jeb Bush: "Bush's running mate has advocated the abolition of Social Security and called Medicare a welfare program that should be cut. We just can't trust Jeb Bush and [lieutenant governor nominee] Tom Feeney" (Sabato and Simpson 1996, 257). Many tightly contested races feature this nasty variant of push polling.

A large part of running for office involves raising money to pay the campaign professionals to target the electorate well in order to activate more pliable voters to cast their ballots for you. Federal campaign finance law requires that candidates for national office must raise limited contributions from many people. This produced a boom in firms that help candidates raise political money. Campaigns raise funds in two ways: through direct mail and personal solicitation by the candidate. Consultants provide services that assist either task. They include direct mail firms, telephone and direct (personal) contact firms, and computer services firms that help manage contributor lists, fund-raising events, and compliance with state and federal campaign finance laws. Also assisting are list management firms that help with targeting and media firms that produce videos for possible contributors to watch (Friedenberg 1997, 24).

Candidates frequently despise campaign fund-raising, but consultants have found that "no one can raise money more effectively than the candidate" and "no campaign ever lost because the candidate spent too much time raising money" (Himes 1995, 62). Direct solicitation targets include individual contributors inside and outside of the district or state in which one is running, political action committees, and state and national party committees. All this effort focuses candidate time and attention on political elites with particular issue agendas, not the mass of citizens mobilized by partisan efforts in days of old.

Direct mail fund-raising firms either purchase potential contributor lists from database firms or develop their own lists. They then prepare highly charged, negative letters designed to excite readers and cause them to contribute. A successful direct mail fund-raising letter combines "pure emotion along with the inflammatory issues and controversial personalities of the day into a financially successful package that has only limited risk for the client" (Luntz 1988, 159). The risk is limited because direct mail operates as a "silent killer," spreading a very negative message that is unlikely to receive much public scrutiny. Direct mail fund raisers find that negative and ideologically extreme messages work best. According to Democratic direct mail guru Roger Craver, "you work the polar positions of an issue. The issues we mail on are so polar that they bring out the passion" (Luntz 1988, 159).

Financial resources gathered through direct mail and personal solicitation pay for the primary expense of any campaign, the marketing of the candidate through various media. Many campaign consultants work in "media" firms, advertising candidates through television, radio, print, and direct mail. Most Americans claim to get their news primarily from television, making it the central medium of persuasion for major campaigns. TV allows for activation through commercials in a manner far more efficient than the person-to-person party mobilization of the late nineteenth century: "one television spot can reach more voters than a team of volunteers in a year of canvassing" (Shea 1996, 171). The impact of television is primarily visual. GOP consultant Robert Teeter found in studies he conducted that "80 to 90 percent of what people retain from a TV ad is visual. . . . If you have the visual right, you have the commercial right. If you don't it almost doesn't matter what you're saying" (Luntz 1988, 77). The method of effective advertising is known widely among consultants. Effective ads (1) develop only one idea, (2) capitalize on visual elements, (3) are repeated frequently, so each targeted viewer sees the ad three to five times, (4) are created based on polling and audience research, (5) tell a dramatic and compelling story, (6) often feature negative information about rival candidates, and (7) cut through the "clutter" of ads close to election day (Friedenberg 1997, 160–68). The majority of campaign spending by candidates for major state and federal office goes for television ads.

Another often-used form of advertising involves radio spots. Certain firms specialize in radio commercials, and the consulting profession widely appreciates radio's utility. Radio is a useful campaign tool for several reasons. Far less expensive than television, the radio listening market is quite fragmented, with listeners evidencing much stronger station loyalty than do television viewers. This allows campaigns to target particular types of listeners precisely. Radio can convey vivid mental images to listeners. Radio is almost as ubiquitous as television, with 80 percent of the public claiming to listen to it every day. It is easier to run longer ads on radio than television. Radio is also an excellent medium for negative advertising. The negative message can arrive at its intended destination in a less flamboyant fashion than TV provides, and usually below the level of media scrutiny given to televised ads (Friedenberg 1997, 140–43).

Direct mail and telephone persuasion operate in a fashion similar to radio advertising. Mailings reach voters as well as potential contributors. Direct mail efforts allow the campaign to send inexpensive, repetitive messages to key audiences, permit negative advertising that is hard for opponents to detect, and can be targeted very precisely (Robinson 1995, 142). Push polling and other forms of telephonic contact with voters possess similar utility for campaigns.

The precise targeting of candidate messages—in ways similar to telephoning, direct mail, and radio ads—also flourishes through newer technologies. Since the mid-1980s, presidential and statewide campaigns have used satellite technology to permit live candidate interviews, usually with local television anchorpersons. This allows a customized candidate message and a less critical reportorial reception than a candidate might receive from full-time campaign reporters. Cable television has begun to fragment the television audience, allowing for more precise targeting of voters by advertising on cable stations. The Internet allows candidates access to an elite audience with high voting norms. Internet users are disproportionately white, well educated, high income, and 81 percent are registered voters (Martinez 1998, 3). Candidates for major office create their own web pages and take out banner ads on other strategically important pages. All of the new technologies promote a more efficiently targeted activation message that promises to yield the most support per dollar spent. Indeed, campaigns operate on this premise in using any of the persuasive media described above. The logic of this efficiency insures that broader, inclusive messages for the general public, common during the party era, appear less frequently today.

TO WHAT END? CAMPAIGN STRATEGIES

Campaign consultants thrive because they provide candidates with strategies for successfully employing the many possible campaign tools available. Tools are useful only if they help a candidate win. Linking the tools available to the end of victory is the task of campaign strategy. That strategy must operate on a realistic comprehension of the strengths and weaknesses of the candidates and the limitations of that candidate's financial resources. The financial threshold for funding a campaign for national office continues to rise, driven by the increasing costs of the campaign tools listed above. As of the year 2000, a competitive House candidate needs to spend at least $400,000; a U.S. Senate candidate from $2,000,000 to $30,000,000, depending on the size of the state. Candidates for major state offices also must spend amounts in the hundreds of thousands of dollars at minimum.

Once adequate funds arrive, the campaign must spend strategically. Longtime Democratic pollster William Hamilton states the key question a winning strategy must answer: "In order to win, what must be communicated directly to which group of voters (most of whom are not seeking the information) with a limited budget?" (Hamilton 1995, 169). To answer this question, a winning strategy involves three subsidiary tasks. First, careful research must divide the electorate accurately into supporters, opponents, and the uninterested or undecided. Polling and analyzing the voting history of the electorate helps to identify these three groups. Second, a campaign must allocate campaign resources efficiently toward getting the necessary number of votes to win. Third, a campaign must identify how to win by directing campaign resources—money, time, effort, and message—to those key voters who will decide the outcome (Bradshaw 1995, 31–36). A successful strategy accurately answers the following questions: "Who is the target audience? What is the message? What resources are needed to reach the target audience? When will the target audience be reached? How will the audience be reached?" (Shea 1996, 172). At each step of the way, consultants are hard at work.

Identifying the electorate involves studying the voting history of the district and buying lists from database consultants. Without this information, no campaign can expend its resources efficiently. "Testing the message" involves a cycle of polling, perhaps accompanied by focus groups and dial groups. Major campaigns usually have two or three consultants working collaboratively as a brain trust: a pollster, a media specialist, and perhaps a generalist campaign manager. In the early phases, a benchmark poll helps to identify candidate image and issue strengths and weaknesses, and the supporters, opponents, and undecideds in the electorate. During midcampaign, a series of polls with fewer questions than the benchmark poll permits a test of how well the campaign is meeting its targeted goals. These polls also allow a campaign to fish for issues to employ in the campaign, often by using push-poll questions. As the election nears, polling aims at defining the "persuadables" to target with appropriate media. Better-funded campaigns will do tracking polls during the final weeks to assess daily how well they are hitting their targets in the electorate (Hamilton 1995, 170–77).

Who are the "persuadables" who get so much attention? "These late-deciders tend to be the least-interested, least knowledgeable, least partisan of the voters who ultimately cast their ballots" (Johnson-Cartee and Copeland 1997, 62). How do they tend to make up their minds? According to consultant Joel Bradshaw, their final selection "is made more on the traits and characteristics of the candidates, and issues serve as a backdrop" (Bradshaw 1995, 38). Important traits for these swing voters include incumbency, party ideology, and candidate style or image. Careful voter research can yield the best possible appeal the campaign can make to this target audience.

Then, the message must arrive as intended by the campaign. Direct mail is one method that has proven effective in close elections, particularly those for lower office not featuring heavy television advertising due to its expense. Although somewhat expensive, direct mail can be finely targeted and, as noted earlier, can provide a more private message to swing voters. In a crucial 1996 state senate race in North Carolina, database analysis for the Democratic candidate identified a key swing group of middle-class suburban mothers—"soccer moms." The campaign then began a series of mailings and phone calls to this target group, mailing ten different pieces during the last two weeks of the campaign. The underdog candidate won by 2,500 votes (Crone 1997, 50).

Bigger campaigns depend more on television and radio advertising, much of it negative. Consultants argue that negative advertising works because a more jaundiced public is ready to believe the worst about candidates (Sabato 1984). A deeper historical change explains the rise of negative advertising. Weaker parties have made negativity a strategic imperative:

In periods of strong party identification, challengers are swept into office as a result of national tides favoring a given party. Today such tides are weaker, and attachments to particular incumbents for reasons other than party are stronger. The result is that challengers who hope to win must give voters compelling reasons to vote for them and must also explain why they should replace apparently satisfactory incumbents. Conversely, incumbents no longer protected by a majority party label can become vulnerable if challengers have enough resources to disseminate telling attacks widely. They must then answer such attacks and offer equally compelling reasons that voters should not choose the challenger. This process we have just described by definition requires negative and comparative messages. (Salmore and Salmore 1989, 160)

It is strategically necessary, and it works. Individuals weigh negative information more than positive information in individual impression formation, assessments of likability, and judgmental decision making (Fiske 1980; Hamilton and Zanna 1971). Negative information is weighed more heavily than positive information in political perception and behavior and when forming evaluations of presidential candidates (Lau 1982, 1985). Given this, imparting negative information about your opponent to undecided, low-information voters on the eve of an election can produce victory.

Examples of successful negative advertising are legion. Bill Clinton's ad attacks on George Bush's broken "read my lips" tax promise helped propel him to the presidency in 1992. Also that year, New York Senator Alfonse D'Amato, a Republican, buried his opponent, State Attorney General Robert Abrams, under an array of ads vilifying his "liberalism." Often, negative messages prove most memorable and acceptable to their target audience when delivered with a splash of humor. In 1984, Republican challenger Mitch McConnell defeated Democratic incumbent Walter Huddleston in the Kentucky Senate race on the strength of humorous negative ads employing bloodhounds to track the junketing senator overseas. Every competitive race for major office in America now includes negative advertising.

Television advertising, particularly negative advertising, however, damages our political system in several ways. First, it occurs in a "low information environment" for many swing voters, whose candidate preferences often rest on scant knowledge. Success often results from televised manipulation of the ignorant. Second, extensive television advertising, whether negative or positive, actually increases the disparity of information between the better-informed and less-informed segments of the electorate. "The more the candidates advertise, the more their message reaches only the better-informed segments of the electorate" (Ansolabehere and Iyengar 1995, 55). Third, negative ads depress the voting intentions among those who watch them. In a controlled experiment, political scientists Stephen Ansolabehere and Shanto Iyengar displayed negative and positive versions of campaign commercials from California senatorial and gubernatorial campaigns in 1992 and 1994. "People exposed to the negative versions of the advertisements registered lower intentions to vote, expressed less confidence in the political process, and placed less value in their own participation" (1995, 104). These results held up even when controlling for age, income, partisanship, and past participation.

Ansolbehere and Iyengar argue that the "collective good" of civic involvement shrinks as a result of individual campaigns pursuing their strategic interests. But who is to restrain them? Rational candidate behavior becomes irrational for the community: a "tragedy of the commons." As economist Thomas Schelling puts it: "people so impinge on each other in pursuing their own interests that collectively they might be better off if they could be restrained, but no one gains individually by the restraint" (Schelling 1978, 111). Candidate-centered politics have an internal rationality that requires narrow activation of selected parts of the public through techniques that may actually shrink the electorate. We have come a long way from the election of 1876.

THE PARTY ROLE

The current role of parties in electoral politics reveals just how far we have come from the era of partisan mobilization. The parties' basic task involves facilitating the success of individual candidates, who occupy the center of electoral politics. Parties do this by providing money and services. The candidates get the party label through a primary, a process beyond party organization control. Although party organizations have increased their ability to deliver money and services to candidates, their influence on elections remains sharply limited: "Although parties provide the largest single source of funds to candidates, this amount is just a fraction of the overall expenditures. Moreover, few candidates overtly link themselves to a party ticket to appeal to voters. It is indeed rare to find a candidate even mentioning his or her party in campaign advertisements" (Shea 1996, 12).

The party entities most helpful to candidates include the national and state party committees and the campaign committees of party incumbents in the national and state houses and senates. Nationally, the campaign committees include the Democratic Congressional Campaign Committee, Democratic Senatorial Committee, Republican Senatorial Committee, and Republican Congressional Campaign Committee. National campaign finance law contributed to the fundraising abilities of these organizations. Since "hard money" contributions are limited to federal candidates under current law, the various party committees have raised large amounts of "soft money," which they use for providing services and advertising for their candidates. The services include video and audio production facilities, polling, phone canvassing, and campaign consulting.

In 1996, the various committees of both national parties undertook extensive issue advocacy spending for television advertising. This is "political speech that may mention specific candidates or political parties but does not 'expressly advocate' the election or defeat of a clearly identified federal candidate through the use of words such as 'vote for,' 'oppose,' 'support,' and the like" (Potter 1997, 227). Heavy party fund-raising fueled the effort. The Democratic National Committee raised $101.9 million and other Democratic committees raised an additional $20.9 million, while the GOP counterparts raised $111 million and $27.2 million respectively (Herrnson 1998b, 45). Presidential candidates were particular beneficiaries of the ads. State parties paid for much of the issue advocacy advertising with money sent them by the national party committees. The national committees sent the money to avoid spending hard money. By federal law, 40 percent of national party spending had to be with hard money, but the national parties also could spend only a legal maximum of $12 million in hard money during the 1996 election cycle. They raised more soft money than they could legally spend. The solution? Send it to state parties, who operated under no such hard money limit (Wayne 1998, 75). National parties also spent funds on voter identification and registration efforts aimed at activating targeted subgroups of the electorate. As the section below reveals, those efforts followed the logic of activation by disproportionately contacting those most likely to vote—individuals with high incomes and education.

Although parties have become useful advertisers for candidates, their broader importance in the electoral process has not increased. Candidates run their own operations and view party organizations as useful supporting players but in no way central to the vital relationship between candidate and voter. Campaign consultants reflected this conventional wisdom in a 1994 survey by *Campaigns and Elections* magazine, a trade journal of the profession. Sixty-two percent of the 202 consultants responding to the survey believed that parties were "getting weaker in terms of organizational strength and their ability to influence elections" (C&E Survey 1994, 58). In the task of activation, parties play a subsidiary role. Party organizations may provide some resources and assist candidates where they can, but most important resources flow to candidates, who exercise autonomous authority over them. Hence the growth of the consulting profession, operating independent of parties and employed largely by candidates.

THE TARGETS: BIASES OF ACTIVATION

The preceding sections reveal a vast assemblage of talented individuals in campaign organizations seeking the attention and votes of the public. From the public, campaigns need money and votes. Campaign strategy bifurcates over the differing means of producing these goods. Each effort—for money or for votes—can only be effective if limited resources receive efficient deployment. The logic of campaign work requires segmenting the public and commanding the attention of only particular citizens. Those lucky citizens include the "policy-type benefit seeking" elites strongly motivated by certain issues who bestow primary nominations and campaign contributions (Aldrich 1995, 183). Successful campaigns activate a base of supporters who vote and a group of swing voters in whose hands the outcome of an election rests. When the campaign rifles aim at these people, they miss many, if not most, citizens.

Those likely to be targeted must have substantial political knowledge in order to know their own political interests and how to pursue them. They must possess a considerable sense of political efficacy—the belief that if they act, they will be politically effective. They also must have ample political interest in order to be worth contacting at all. That means that the likely targets of campaigns have relatively high education and income. Figures 3.1 and 3.2 display the 1996 distribution of political interest, knowledge, efficacy, and party contact among the American public by education and income.[1] The citizens listed at the right end of the figures are those most efficiently garnered by campaigns. They know more and have greater interest in politics than most citizens, making activation messages more effective. Because they believe they can make a difference in politics, they may welcome activation contacts as opportunities to achieve their own political goals. Accordingly, the major parties in 1996 contacted higher-income and more educated citizens most frequently. Even when awash in soft money, the parties pursued selective activation, not inclusive mobilization.

1. The results in figures 3.1 and 3.2 and tables 3.1 and 3.2 derive from a series of questions from the 1996 National Election Study conducted by the Institute for Social Research at the University of Michigan. Political interest is the percentage stating they were "very much interested" in the 1996 election campaign. The external political efficacy index is a summative score of agree/disagree responses to two statements: "People like me don't have any say about what the government does" and "I don't think public officials care much what people like me think." A score of 100 means the respondent disagreed with both statements, a score of 50 indicated disagreement with one statement, and a score of zero indicated agreement with both statements. Political knowledge is measured by a factual question about which party controlled Congress before the election, an item that correlates strongly with other information measures (Delli Carpini and Keeter 1995, 189–90, 215). Party contact involves yes/no responses to the item: "Did anyone from either of the political parties call you up or come around to talk to you about the 1996 campaign this year?" The data is archived at the University of Michigan by the Interuniversity Consortium for Social and Political Research.

Michael Delli Carpini and Scott Keeter, in their study of what Americans know about politics, find that education is the key variable promoting more political knowledge (Delli Carpini and Keeter 1996, 190). Education serves to make individuals more aware of the possible benefits of political participation and also lowers the costs of such activity. It also plays a major role in sorting individuals into social networks in which participatory norms are stronger (Nie, Junn, and Stehlik-Berry 1996, 74, 172, 190). Stephen Rosenstone and John Mark Hansen explain how such people become the natural targets for activation. First, campaigns seeking to activate individuals, "target people who are both convenient and predictable, people with whom they share social connections." Second, they target "people who are identifiable and accessible, who are members of voluntary associations." Finally, they "target people who are likely to respond and to be effective. They target the educated, the wealthy and the powerful" (Rosenstone and Hansen 1993, 239–41).

In the nineteenth century, political parties contacted the large majority of eligible voters, regardless of their education and income. Contemporary party contact, now more likely by telephone than in person, involves an efficient allocation of limited resources. Tables 3.1 and 3.2, reporting the results of National Election Study surveys during presidential elections of the last twenty years, reveal that parties no longer contact most voters. The pattern of contact in 1996, charted in figures 3.1 and 3.2, is part of a long-term bias in party activation. Not only did parties contact a minor fraction of the public, but those of higher education and income were most likely to receive that contact. This pattern is consistent with the logical framework of Rosenstone and Hansen, producing targeted activation, not mass mobilization.

Figure 3.1 Political Interest, Efficacy, Knowledge, and Party Contact by Education in 1996

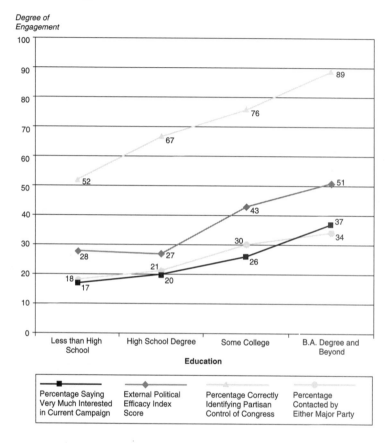

Table 3.3 further illustrates the results of activation strategies. Its data come from a landmark 1989 survey concerning the participatory behavior of Americans.[2] Those who volunteer to work in campaigns,

2. The Citizen Participation Survey, conducted in 1989, questioned a random sample of 2,517 people in depth about their participatory behavior. The questions and

Figure 3.2 Political Interest, Efficacy, Knowledge, and Party Contact by Family Income in 1996

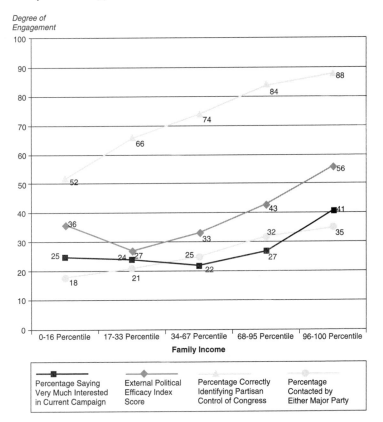

Degree of Engagement

0-16 Percentile | 17-33 Percentile | 34-67 Percentile | 68-95 Percentile | 96-100 Percentile

Family Income

Percentage Saying Very Much Interested in Current Campaign

External Political Efficacy Index Score

Percentage Correctly Identifying Partisan Control of Congress

Percentage Contacted by Either Major Party

contribute money to campaigns, or receive requests to do so possess significantly more of education and higher amounts of annual fam-

results detailed in table 3.3 come from this survey, now archived at the University of Michigan by the Interuniversity Consortium for Social and Political Research. The results are weighted to achieve a representative sample.

Table 3.1 Party Activation by Education, 1976–1996

	Percentage contacted by either major party during the election year					
	1976	1980	1984	1988	1992	1996
Grade School/ Some High School	18	18	16	18	13	18
High School Diploma	28	23	22	20	17	21
Some College, No Degree	35	27	27	26	21	30
College Degree/ Post-Grad	39	31	31	32	28	34

SOURCE: National Election Studies, University of Michigan.

Table 3.2 Party Activation by Income, 1976–1996

	Percentage contacted by either major party during the election year					
	1976	1980	1984	1988	1992	1996
Income 0–16 Percentile	15	15	17	16	10	18
Income 17–33 Percentile	22	25	22	19	16	21
Income 34–67 Percentile	29	23	24	25	20	25
Income 68–95 Percentile	35	25	29	27	28	32
Income 96–100 Percentile	44	39	27	40	23	35

SOURCE: National Election Studies, University of Michigan.

-

Table 3.3 Differences in Participation and Activation by Education, Income, Partisan Identification, and Ideological Strength

	Volunteer for a candidate in 1988?			Contribute to a candidate, party, PAC or other political organization that supported candidates in 1988?			Asked to contribute to a candidate, party, PAC or other organization that supports candidates in 1988?		
	Y	N	Sig.[1]	Y	N	Sig.	Y	N	Sig.
Average years of education	14.3	13.0	.000	14.7	12.6	.000	14.5	12.5	.000
Average family income	$35,000–39,999	$25,000–29,999	.000	$35,000–39,999	$25,000–29,999	000	$35,000–39,999	$25,000–29,999	.000
Average strength of ideology[2]	1.25	.97	.000	1.18	.94	.000	1.14	.92	.000

SOURCE: Citizen Participation Survey, 1989.

1. Probability that differences are nonexistent in the population from which the survey was drawn.

2. Variable coded with moderates at zero, slightly conservative or liberal = 1, conservative or liberal = 2, strongly conservative or liberal = 3.

ily income that those who are less active. Also, those who contribute, volunteer, or are asked to do so possess significantly stronger self-described ideology than those who aren't asked or aren't active. David King's finding of ideological extremism among activists (1997) finds support in table 3.3.

Beyond the activist ranks lie the all-important swing voters. Each campaign works hard to identify them and aim television messages toward them as the election nears. The Clinton campaign's early and accurate targeting of this group, detailed in the following section, is testament to their importance in determining election outcomes. Swing voters in the 1996 presidential election tended to be suburban, middle-income, married, and with children (Morris 1997, 236–37; Stengel and Pooley 1996, 19). Although less elite than the activists, such swing voters hardly resemble the low income and less educated Americans who have withdrawn from the electorate. The rifle of activation is very seldom aimed at that half of the population even during presidential campaigns, as the example of the 1996 Clinton reelection effort reveals.

THE STATE OF THE ART: THE 1996 CLINTON CAMPAIGN

No recent campaign better illustrates the successful art of electoral activation than President Bill Clinton's 1996 reelection effort. Sidney Blumenthal claimed in 1980 that presidents "must campaign early and often. And the easiest way to do that is to turn governing into a campaign; there is no line of separation. Consultants, then, are brought into the sanctums of government to use the prerogatives of office to further the politician's cause" (Blumenthal 1980, 9–10). The Clinton presidency followed this advice thoroughly in 1995 and 1996. Democrats suffered a historic midterm electoral defeat in 1994, when they lost control of Congress for the first time in forty years. The president had low approval ratings during the early, triumphant days of the new Republican Congress in 1995. Clinton assembled a team of political consultants to help steer him from this unpromising situation to victory in 1996.

The consultants, including presidential advisor Dick Morris, media specialists Bob Squier and Bill Knapp, and pollsters Mark Penn and Doug Schoen, met frequently in early 1995 to devise a strategy for governing and campaigning that would lead to reelection. Penn and Schoen argued that the president should announce a "contract with the middle class" to counter the GOP's "contract with America" then making its way through Congress. The pollsters argued that Clinton had to reassure middle-class voters that he understood their need for safe streets and good education for their kids (Penn and Schoen 1997a, 221). Clinton then proposed such a contract, including crime and education measures.

To drive the message home, the consultants arranged for television advertising beginning in June 1995 that would tout the "I care about the middle class" theme. Clinton had urged this. Doug Schoen recalled the president telling him that "If we don't spend $10 million on television in 1995, I could lose this thing" (Stengel and Pooley 1996, 8). The first ad buy, totaling $2.4 million, emphasized the president's support for capital punishment and stiff sentencing laws. These ads ran in smaller, strategically important media markets, far beyond the notice of the Washington press. In August, the consultants ran ads attacking Republican proposals to trim Medicare growth.

The national Democratic Party ran these issue advocacy ads with soft money they had raised. This method of advertising would continue throughout 1995 and well into the 1996 election campaign.

Campaign finance law made it illegal for such spending to be coordinated with a candidate, but in 1995, Bill Clinton was not formally a candidate (Potter 1997, 237). Hence he helped write the scripts of many ads that appeared during the coming months. For twelve months, the Democratic ads ran without an effective Republican countereffort. Dick Morris claimed that "by the time the Republicans ran their first ad, we had spent about thirty million dollars on issue advocacy ads without any opposition. Thirty million dollars is about three quarters of the total amount of money either Bush or Clinton spent on media in all of 1992, primary and general elections combined" (Morris 1997, 277).

All ads were pre-tested with mall groups, a methodological innovation by Penn. Proposed spots were shown to voters in kiosks located in shopping malls in sixteen swing states. At the kiosk, an employee "would ask a voter questions about his or her political affiliations and views of the president and then enter them on a computer. After viewing the spot, the viewer would then answer another series of questions. The whole thing took ten minutes" (Stengel and Pooley 1996, 10). This technique yielded overnight samples of some two hundred persons and replicated the way people encountered the ads—by themselves, on television.

The ads helped the president "frame" public perceptions of the major Washington event of 1995, the two government shutdowns brought on by budget disagreements between the Republican Congress and the Clinton White House. "Clinton's ads had convinced millions of swing voters that the Republicans had shut down the government, while the president had bravely defended the elderly" (Thomas et al. 1997, 40–41). After the shutdowns, Clinton shot ahead of his Republican opponents in the polls. The task then became to hold the lead with swing voters. Morris and his fellow consultants had the White House staff develop a steady stream of small-bore domestic policies concerning smoking, childcare, crime, and education that the president touted throughout 1996 in order to win the approval of swing voters. By early 1996, the White House was efficiently executing this campaign strategy through policy and advertisements, while potential GOP opponents carved each other up in the early primaries and caucuses.

Penn and Schoen's polling research guided the strategy. In October 1995, they had completed an in-depth "neuro-personality profile" of the American electorate. They identified two "swing groups" in the electorate. "Swing I" comprised 29 percent of the electorate and leaned toward Clinton. They were "less concerned with partisan politics and more interested in family-oriented middle-class programs." Although "supportive of many progressive causes, their first priority is programs that will help them feel safe physically and financially" (Penn and Schoen 1997b, 231). Many of these were what Penn called the "swing-rich" middle—young, upscale, suburban parents (Thomas et al. 1997, 16). "Swing II" totaled 25 percent of the electorate who support some "common sense" domestic programs like raising the minimum wage or helping their aging parents but remained "moderate-conservative" concerning many social values (Penn and Schoen 1997b, 232). Clinton would have trouble appealing to this group. The pollsters then listed a variety of policies that Swing I voters indicated they wanted from government. These issues became the centerpiece of the administration's domestic initiatives in 1995 and 1996.

To prepare for the all-important State of the Union Address scheduled for January 1996, Penn and Schoen in December polled the public with twenty different one-paragraph summaries of the "vision" of the Clinton presidency. The survey results figured into Penn's daily meetings with the speechwriters. The resulting speech received high public approval. As the national convention neared in August, the consultants recommended a whistle-stop train tour to Chicago. Why? Because, Penn claimed "every vote we need to win the election is within five hundred miles of the convention center in Chicago" (Morris 1997, 320). Once the trip was arranged, the pollster sought out a campaign theme. Their polls revealed that 61 percent of American liked "building a bridge to the 21st century," easily the most popular of the options polled. This became the thematic centerpiece of the president's acceptance speech and campaign (Stengel and Pooley 1996, 21).

Clinton's major opponent, Bob Dole, had a much tougher time getting to his party's national convention. He narrowly survived early, bruising primary battles, featuring some $22 million in advertising by his opponent Steve Forbes, most of which involved negative messages about Dole (Thomas et al. 1997, 64). By May, Dole had spent the maximum amount legally allowed him during the primary season fending off the attacks of his challengers. He then was left without funds for the general election until August, after the national convention ended. He also had a full-time job as majority leader of the Senate that proved so cumbersome that he resigned from it in June. The Clinton campaign ran attack ads aimed at Dole throughout this time, pairing him with the unpopular House speaker Newt Gingrich and chiding him for "quitting" his job as majority leader.

The Dole campaign did not complete an in-depth survey of the public until May 1996, less than six months before the election. Its findings resembled those of Penn and Schoen, certainly not good news for Dole. Further, Dole's one possible policy departure that might "shake up" the race, a large tax cut, was not a winner with the electorate (Stengel and Pooley 1996, 16). A Dole pollster, Doug Ward, knew their campaign was in trouble when he examined the new Clinton-Gore website in June 1996. "The Clinton/Gore themes were almost identical to theirs . . . both sides were finding the same results in their polling and research. The difference was that Clinton used his polling and research. The Dole people ignored theirs" (Thomas et al. 1997, 104). Dole himself followed no consistent strategy, and neither did his advertisements. Eventually, the Republican National Committee decoupled their message from the Dole candidacy, arranging its entire get-out-the-vote effort, from TV ads to direct mail, around the message: "Don't Give Bill Clinton a Blank Check" (Thomas et al. 1997 194).

The Clinton campaign, following a well-researched strategy, proceeded smoothly through the autumn. As Republicans ran attack ads, mall testing allowed the Clinton consultants to determine which response ad was most effective before putting it on the air (Morris 1997, 289). "Clinton's response ads were tested, refined and retested until they actually left voters feeling better about the president than they had before seeing the original Dole attack" (Stengel and Pooley 1996, 15). After each of the debates, instant polls by Penn revealed the president had done well. Only in the final weeks of the campaign, when reports surfaced about illegal soft money contributions to the Democratic National Committee for issue advocacy ads, did the race tighten a bit. The president won 49 percent of the popular vote and cruised to a large win in the Electoral College—379 to 159 for Dole. The adroitness of Clinton and his campaign did have some public opinion costs, however. A survey in January 1998 revealed that only

33 percent of voters believed Clinton "governs with a consistent core of beliefs" while 58 percent believed he was "driven by polls and the politics of the moment" (Brownstein 1998, 23).

The 1996 case provides several unsettling lessons about the contemporary politics of activation. Although the potential for popular mobilization is greatest during a presidential campaign, neither the Clinton nor the Dole campaign had any serious interest in achieving it. Both developed strategies for activating their bases and swing voters within an electorate limited to half of all adults. The costs of this narrower project were more manageable, the benefits more probable. A small group of swing voters became the central audience for three months of a national campaign. It was as if America had been transformed into a nation solely inhabited by prosperous, suburban, middle-class, married couples. The state and national parties might have used the large amounts of soft money spent on TV ads for a partisan "shotgun" mobilization, but instead "rifled" messages at swing voters. The party organizations were subordinate players in a candidate-centered politics of activation.

Presidential domestic governance also came to focus on a narrow band of issues of concern to the suburban swing voters. The alluring efficiency of activation, abetted by campaign technology, helped to shrink the national agenda to the issues most serviceable to the president as presidential candidate. National governance is thus transformed by the rationality of activation. Other players also help to shape the agenda through campaign activation, however. They are the ubiquitous interest groups, motivated by issues of moment to them, deploying money and volunteers during the election months. Their goal is public policy, and campaign activation strategies can work for them, too. Chapter 4 explains their abundant campaign work.

CONCLUSION

The perennial challenges for any campaign remain convincing citizens to vote and to support that campaign's candidate (Aldrich 1995, 48). Aided by professional consultants with their polling and advertising technologies, individualistic candidates dictate that campaigns meet these challenges with tactics less inclusive than those of the partisan era. For candidates, resources are limited, competition is often severe, and time passes quickly during a campaign. Efficient execution of a well-researched and carefully targeted strategy is essential to victory. Parties merely seek to enhance the ability of candidates to execute campaign strategy well by providing ads, phone canvasses, and get-out-the-vote activities, all aimed at carefully selected segments of the electorate. These central players in today's electoral arena, however, pay little attention to the effect of their collective behavior on the quality and quantity of electoral participation in America.

Candidates and parties no longer pursue popular mobilization or evidence any serious interest in it. Time and technology have consigned such inclusive strategies to a past era when parties stood at the center of our politics and reached throughout the public with their messages. Now, success in elections need not require such an inefficient and exhausting approach. Professionals can engineer victory with a smaller proportion of the eligible electorate than thought possible one hundred years ago. Organized interests have learned this lesson as well, as the next chapter demonstrates. One big problem, however, results from the dazzling expertise deployed in contemporary campaigns. This marvel of efficiency comes at the expense of the healthy electoral participation essential to constitutional democracy.

CHAPTER 4

Interest Organizations and Electoral Activation

As political parties have lost much of their relevance over
the last several decades and hence their ability to mobilize
the public, interest groups have acquired resources that have
made them more powerful than ever before.

Marvin Wattenberg, *The Decline of American Political Parties 1952–1994*

I nterests are the great beneficiaries of the politics of activation. In
governmental lobbying and political campaigning, more interests are active and use a greater variety of effective tactics than
ever before. In the 1970s, business groups, long evident on the
Washington scene, increased their number and resources (Edsall
1984). Social and political movements of recent decades, led by
aggrieved groups of citizens—African Americans, feminists, gays and
lesbians, and Christian conservatives—eventually created stable interest organizations that seek to influence elections and government.
Sociologist Paul Burstein labels both movements and traditional

interest groups as "interest organizations" that differ fundamentally from political parties (Burstein 1998, 45).[1] Most notably, interest organizations, unlike parties, do not run candidates for office. This gives them additional room for maneuver. If the controlling logic of activation is efficiency, interest organizations face fewer constraints than parties in achieving that efficiency. Interest organizations are not held accountable on issues of public concern during elections and can employ a wide range of activation strategies without concern for majority opinion or majority rule (Aldrich 1995). Activation by interests in elections and lobbying may at times resemble popular rule but in no way guarantees it.

This chapter explains how interest organizations became some of the most effective practitioners of electoral activation (the following chapter explains their dominance of governmental lobbying). Interests have many goals, and producing helpful electoral outcomes is just one of them. Most groups also must devote considerable time to membership maintenance and to influencing the actions of government between elections. Consequently, the resources any particular group can devote to electoral activation are limited and must be deployed carefully to insure the maximum positive effect. The configuration of resources varies greatly across groups. Economic interests often deploy money, their most plentiful resource. Large membership organizations, like those of Christian conservatives described in this chapter, can deploy thousands of activists to help spur sympathetic voters to head to the polls. At times interests hitch up with parties or candidates, or propose policies for a popular vote in state-

1. For compositional ease, I use the terms *interests, groups,* and *organizations* when referring to interest organizations in this chapter.

wide initiatives. In all cases, carefully crafted activation is the recipe for success.

INTEREST GROUP CAMPAIGN STRATEGIES

What are the primary electoral strategies that groups pursue? Jack Walker refers to electoral efforts as an "inside" strategy of organized interests that involves "working the system" as do the kindred strategies of lobbying and litigating (Walker 1991, 110–11). Groups adopt two subordinate objectives in pursuing their policy goals through elections. One is to "influence the outcome of electoral contests" by promoting the election of favored candidates. The second is to "influence the activity of eventual office holders and, thereby, government policy" by demonstrating their electoral clout to incumbents (Schlozman and Tierney 1986, 206–07). Toward those ends, groups provide resources for party or candidate activation efforts or directly activate voters themselves. They also tap their own members for time, money, and votes to assist with group electioneering.

Any individual interest group faces large obstacles in fathoming how to influence elections efficiently. Targeting is potentially a very complex task. Given the thousands of national and state candidates every year and the thousands of groups seeking to influence election results, large uncertainties confront any group entering the electoral arena. The immediate need of any group is information that will assist in allocating resources to influence campaigns. Any closely contested election in which the group strongly prefers one candidate to another becomes a priority race. Given this information, a group must then raise resources and deploy them effectively. In doing so, they follow an old strategic maxim: "one must apply maximum force to the point of decision" (Hazelwood 1995, 33).

Groups gather information about election contests in a variety of ways. The national party committees provide several information services for sympathetic PACs: handicapping races, arranging "meet and greet" sessions with candidates, and providing much election-related information, such as polls and district and state demographic analysis and news (Herrnson 1994, 55). Some PACs and groups rely upon particular experts in deciding which races to target. The Business-Industry Political Action Committee, headed by Bernadette Budde, provides in-depth analysis of national House and Senate races to a variety of organized business interests. A BIPAC endorsement and contribution usually triggers many more from corporate and business PACs (Gugliotta 1998, 12). Similarly, the AFL-CIO targeting effort in national House and Senate races also stimulates contributions from progressive organizations and individuals. Emily's List, a group supporting liberal female candidates, holds fund raisers for those it deems the "best bets" and thereby sends a signal to those sympathetic to its cause.

Another watchdog function performed by some organized interests involves rating the floor votes of incumbent members of the House and Senate. An estimated sixty-five to seventy organizations, including business, environmental, senior citizen, labor, farm, and ideological groups, report annual vote ratings (Hrebnar 1997, 187). The ratings usually range from 100 (a hero) to 0 (a zero) and serve as useful signals to kindred groups and individuals during election campaigns (Maisel 1993, 133). The purveyors of endorsements and ratings hope to maximize their own influence by spreading the word among their friends. This serves to simplify and make much more manageable the strategic choices that organized interests must make regarding elections. Without such efficient use of information, groups would be far less effective in influencing electoral outcomes.

However, information is of little use absent resources with which to act. Interests can either deliver votes through their own activation efforts or give money to campaigns that then deliver votes through activation (Herrnson 1998b, 38). Groups pursue money and votes in a variety of ways. PACs have proved to be a very convenient way to publicly and legally bring financial influence to bear on electoral outcomes. A 1994 survey of political consultants found that 59 percent of those polled believed that "the system of campaign contribution limits on individuals and PACs imposed during the last 20 years in federal and many state elections" has actually increased the influence of special interest money in politics (Campaigns and Elections 1994, 58). Political scientists tend to agree with this verdict (Wilson 1990, 50–53; Sorauf 1988, 286–89). PACs raise funds through several methods. Corporations may form their own PACs and solicit their employees for contributions. Unions can use member dues to fund PAC activities. Many ideological PACs gather money through direct mail letters often couched in negative and extreme terms (Godwin 1988, 59–65). Direct mail consultant Tom Walsh confides that "the more extreme the group's cause, the higher the response its list yields in a mail or telemarketing campaign" ("Early Returns" 1996, 5). The hunt for resources advantages more extreme opinions, as has the changing composition of partisan activism (D. King 1997).

Direct mail can also rally group members to their organization's cause by providing them with important electoral information. For example, the National Committee for an Effective Congress (NCEC) seeks to assist liberal Democrats running for the House and Senate with electoral analysis and other in-kind campaign services. They raise money and disseminate information about their targets through a direct mail campaign that vilifies conservative Republicans. In the 1980s, the National Conservative Political Action Committee (NCPAC) used direct mail in a similar fashion but spent its money on harshly negative advertising against liberal Democratic incumbents. Through direct mail, NCEC and NCPAC activated supporters to give money and vote.

Interests face a complex choice concerning the deployment of their funds. One option is simply to contribute PAC money to candidates. Those funds are limited to $10,000 ($5,000 each in the primary and general election), an increasingly small sum as campaigns have grown more expensive in recent years. Then there is the question about how to allocate it. Business PACs for decades gave heavily to Democrats, many of whom were cool to business agendas, because Democrats held control of Congress. This "incumbent" strategy disappeared in the mid-1990s when Republicans took over Congress. Now, most business PAC money goes to Republicans (Hrebnar 1997, 202–03). Business now invests in incumbents who are more sympathetic on policy, a seemingly more efficient allocation of resources in that it fulfills both "incumbent" and "policy" strategies. Still, some business PACs contribute to both candidates in close races in order to maintain access to the winner regardless of the outcome (Hrebnar 1997 196–200).

Labor and ideological PACs tend to follow a "policy" strategy consistently, regardless of which party controls Congress. This satisfies the expressive goals of many of their members (and, in labor's case, the material goals of many members as well) but leads to uneven success in policy. When the "good guys" win, the policy rewards can be great, but the loss when they are defeated can be equally severe.

The pattern of PAC giving in 1996 reveals the strategic choices made by interests with campaign money. Three thousand PACs gave $204 million to federal candidates, but fewer than 450 PACs contributed 76 percent of the total. Corporate PACs contributed $76.8 million; trade association PACs $60.2 million; labor PACs $48 million; and ideological PACs, $24 million. Seventy-five percent of all contributions went to incumbents, reflecting a PAC perception that this is an effective way to maintain access to decision makers. Open seat candidates received 12 percent of the contributions and challengers (the riskiest investment) a mere 13 percent of the total. Overall, PAC contributions accounted for 30 percent of all spending on House races and 15 percent of all spending in Senate races. PACs are a significant, but not a majority voice among those who contribute (Herrnson 1998b, 41–43). Their electoral influence is greater than these totals suggest. Many individual contributors follow PAC guidance when allocating their funds during campaigns. Also, organized interests expend funds in other ways to affect electoral outcomes.

Large soft-money contributions from private interests to political parties in the 1990s were one of those ways. The national Democratic and Republican Party committees received $263 million in soft money contributions in 1996. Corporations and unions are the largest soft-money contributors (Herrnson 1998b, 45). Substantial PAC funds also went for independent expenditures in which a PAC spends money to affect an election directly, without coordinating with a favored candidate. This usually takes the form of television advertising. It is a risky undertaking, because it may offend and actually impede the chances of the candidate it seeks to help because of the often extreme, single-issue nature of the ads. This tactic is less frequently pursued than it was during the 1980s (Hrebnar 1997, 209).

One growing mode of spending, however, is issue advocacy spending. Such ads must not "expressly advocate" election or defeat of a particular candidate (Potter 1997, 227). Unlike independent expenditures, issue advocacy spending need not be reported to the Federal Election Commission, giving groups who so spend the advantage of camouflage. The AFL-CIO announced a plan to spend $35 million on such ads in the 1996 House races, and they were eventually joined by business, environmental, and other groups in a grand total of an estimated $135 million in spending for issue advocacy ads in 1996 (Marcus 1998, 13). A national survey found that 57.6 percent of Americans recalled seeing an issue ad in 1996, and these ads were more negative in content than any other sort of political ad or coverage on television (Beck, Taylor, Stanger, and Rivlin 1997, 7, 10). Here is an example of language from an AFL-CIO ad: "Working families are struggling. But Congressman [X] voted with Newt Gingrich to cut college loans, while giving tax breaks to the wealthy. He even wants to eliminate the Department of Education. Congress will vote again on the budget. Tell Congressman [X], don't write off our children's future" (Beck, Taylor, Stanger, and Rivlin 1997, 11). Such ads may prove effective in pursuing group goals (although the AFL-CIO fell short of gaining a Democratic House in 1996), but more negative messages on the air may reduce voting (Ansolabehere and Iyengar 1995, 99). Thus targeted messages, aimed at activating key voters, may further weaken the frayed participatory norms that so robustly prevailed during the era of partisan mobilization.

In addition to activation through advertising, groups also attempt to activate their own memberships during an election. They often set up phone banks to contact members and remind them to vote on Election Day. Which members are most likely to be targets for activation? Given the limited time and resources of group leaders, probably those who are the most likely to respond positively to the call (Rosenstone and Hansen 1993, 239–41). A recent study of activation by Ohio unions found exactly that. Union members with higher education, political interest, and a history of union participation were most likely to heed the call (Heberlig 1996). Thus "biases towards those with greater resources exist even in organized labor, in spite of its traditional emphasis on the working class" (Heberlig 1996, 22). This bias is intrinsic to activation and is the core characteristic that differentiates it from older-style partisan mobilization. Old-style mobilization lacked the tools to precisely identify likely supporters; contemporary activation does not. Interests thus contribute to the bias in political participation through the efficient use of activation strategies.

GRASSROOTS ACTIVATION:
CHRISTIAN CONSERVATIVES IN 1994

The ability of unions to activate members is overshadowed by the powerful role that churches play in this process. Churches have a greater political impact in activating their members than do unions for two reasons: more Americans are church members than union members, and church members attend services more frequently than union members attend meetings of their locals (Verba, Schlozman, and Brady 1995, 386–87). Churches transmit important civic skills, such as speaking, discussing, and writing, to their active members. No institutions in American society impart these skills to more persons of lower socioeconomic status than do churches (Verba, Schlozman, and Brady 1995, 387). The center of gravity for the more politically active churches, however, concerns socially conservative issues. The rise of Christian conservatives rests heavily on the construction of social networks in churches that promote the political participation of their members. The ability of group entrepreneurs to activate church members proved vital to the Republican electoral victory in the 1994 congressional elections.

Religiously inspired discontent about abortion, gay rights, promiscuity, and the absence of prayer in public schools, among other issues, stimulated creation of a large Christian conservative movement in recent decades. The election of Bill Clinton proved a catalyst for action. Clinton, a politician dogged by charges of marital infidelity, pot smoking, and avoidance of the draft, espoused positions on many social issues contrary to those urged by Christian conservatives. By the mid-1990s, the movement included an estimated four million members nationally, among them 200,000 activists consistently engaged in electoral politics (Wilcox 1996, 71). The activists tend to be middle class, well educated, and with good incomes and are distinguished from the larger population of political activists by their high degrees of religious commitment and church attendance (Green 1995, 4). Church activity imparted citizenship skills that made activation an inviting strategy for a number of groups espousing a socially conservative agenda.

The largest such organization, the Christian Coalition (profiled in chapter 5), was founded by televangelist and former Republican presidential candidate Pat Robertson in 1989 and headed for most of the 1990s by Ralph Reed, an able political entrepreneur. Reed adopted a pragmatic, low-key leadership style aimed at maximizing the influence of the group within the Republican party and minimizing intra-party divisions. By 1994, the group claimed 1.5 million members and 1,100 chapters in fifty states. Another substantial organization is Concerned Women of America, founded in 1979 by Beverly Lahaye. It voices a culturally conservative message and builds membership through local women's prayer and Bible study groups. CWA actively lobbied during the Supreme Court confirmation hearings of Robert Bork and Clarence Thomas. By 1994, it had 1,200 affiliates and sev-eral thousand members. The Family Research Council, another such organization, is the political arm of Reverend James Dobson, who also heads a conservative religious movement called Focus on the Family. His Focus on the Family radio program broadcasts on 1,500 stations daily. Gary Bauer, head of the Family Research Council dur-ing most of the 1990s, was a former domestic policy advisor to President Reagan and evidenced a more combative style than Ralph Reed. Befitting his aggressive style, Bauer sought the Republican presidential nomination in 2000. FRC had twenty-six state affiliates and claimed more than 100,000 local activists by 1994 (Wilcox 1996, 62–64).

Conservative Christian ministers proved an important segment of the activist ranks of these organizations. A 1992 study of Baptist ministers by James Guth found that membership in the Christian Coalition or Focus on the Family spurred the ministers' political activism. Clergy who were members of these organizations were par-ticularly likely to participate in voter registration drives, the sort of activation activity emphasized by these conservative Christian groups (Guth 1996, 165). Organizational affiliation with the groups seemed at least to facilitate, if not cause, activism by sympathetic clergy. Further, ministers involved in the Christian Coalition and Focus on the Family were significantly more involved in political activities than ministers who were active in liberal organizations (Guth 1996, 168). As authoritative figures at the center of the social networks of their churches, such ministers could be powerful activators of church members.

The target of the activators—the above organizations, their members, ministers—is the white evangelical Protestant segment of the American public. Evangelicals believe in a personal conversion experience, a doctrine not shared by the Catholic and the more established, "mainline" Protestant denominations. They differ from other Americans in several ways. Evangelicals are less likely to have finished high school and to have a college degree but are more likely to be active in their churches. They are more likely to be in single-earner families and more prone to believe religion has a major influence on their lives. Many of them find their primary social networks in their churches, and most of their friends attend the same church (Ammerman 1987). White evangelicals are socially conservative on abortion and gay rights and are less tolerant than other Americans of fellow citizens who live by different values (Wilcox 1996, 49).

This constellation of attributes made evangelicals an appealing target for entrepreneurial activation in elections. Active church participation increased their citizenship skills, church-based social networks helped to reinforce their issue attitudes, and the salience of certain social issues increased their motivation for political participation. For group entrepreneurs, the costs of activation are low. Church affiliation makes evangelicals easily targeted; relatively homogeneous views on social issues makes them susceptible to the right message from national organizations. In the right situation, activated Christian conservatives could prove a dominant voice in electoral politics.

That situation occurred in the congressional elections of 1994. President Clinton faced growing public unpopularity that year, given earlier controversies about gays in the military and the failure of his ambitious national health plan. Clinton's strong support from Hollywood and its "countercultural" values epitomized to many Christian conservatives all that was evil in American life. Thus group entrepreneurs had their bogey that could help activate millions of followers. Their work was aided by an important strategic error by the opposition during the 1994 campaign. Representative Vic Fazio, chair of the House Democratic campaign committee, sought to demonize Christian conservatives by charging that Republicans were willing to turn over their party to the "intolerant religious right." Unfortunately for Fazio, this attack backfired. It received little notice by the broader public but did intensify the motivation of evangelical groups and activists. Fazio's charge failed to turn the election into a referendum on the Christian right (Soper 1996, 119).

During the campaign, the activation efforts by conservative Christian organizations came to fruition on several fronts. First, national organization leaders such as Ralph Reed worked pragmatically to hone a unified Republican message that downplayed "hot" social issues. Reed financed research and polling that led to the creation of the "Contract with America," a ten-point plan for reducing the power of the national government that strategically omitted those social issues threatening to divide the Republican coalition. Also, from 1989 to 1994 the Christian Coalition had trained thousands of local activists at leadership conferences in many states and deployed these leaders to spread the pro-Republican message throughout their social networks. Both the Family Research Council and Concerned Women of America similarly instructed their activist memberships. During this time, all of the organizations likewise facilitated the election of their members and other sympathetic activists as party officials and state convention delegates in many states. By 1995, a survey estimated that thirty-one state Republican parties were substantially or predominantly under the influence of conservative Christians (Persinos 1994).

The Christian Coalition also took a hand in recruiting candidates for Congress and other offices, at times preferring sympathetic outsiders who seemed more electable over some of their most committed members who wanted to run. Reed's pragmatic concern with electability was evident. Volunteer recruits easily totaled in the thousands nationwide. Many conservative Christian organizations dispatched activists to particular congressional campaigns. One House candidate, Republican Steve Largent of Oklahoma, had so many volunteers that he dispatched many of them to help the kindred Senate campaign of Jim Inhofe. Both ultimately won (Bednar and Hertzke 1995, 100).

The central activation strategy of conservative Christian groups, however, concerned potential voters. The common means involved voter guides distributed at conservative Christian churches, usually on the weekend before the election. The Christian Coalition distributed most of them, claiming a national distribution of 33 million guides, involving a workforce of 75,000 volunteers (Green 1995, 16). Distribution was particularly heavy in the states where white evangelicals were most numerous: 500,000 in Oklahoma, 3 million in Texas, 1.5 to 2.5 million in Georgia, and 1.7 million in Virginia. The guides typically contrasted the positions of candidates for governor, senator, or congressman on a few carefully selected issues. The Christian Coalition proved pragmatic in its portrayal of favored candidates in the guides, even leafleting in favor of Republican Governor Pete Wilson and Senate candidate Michael Huffington in California, although both supported abortion rights. The California Senate guide, for example, avoided the issues of abortion and gays in the military (both of which Huffington supported) and focused instead on term limits, health care, and taxes (Soper 1996, 221).

Extensive and careful activation, an unpopular president, and a demoralized opposition allowed Christian conservative groups to score a big victory on Election Day. Republicans gained fifty-two House seats, allowing them to take control of the chamber for the first time in forty years; they also gained ten Senate seats to take control there as well. The University of Michigan's 1994 National Election Study revealed the effectiveness of Christian conservative activation. Forty-three percent of evangelicals who claimed to regularly attend church were activated in one (or more) of three ways: by receiving a contact from a religious group, seeing information in the place of worship, or being urged by a pastor or church leader to vote. White evangelicals made up an unprecedented 51 percent of the Republican electorate and 27 percent of the overall electorate, according to Mitovsky International exit polls. Among these evangelicals, Republican House candidates received 76 percent of the vote. Evangelicals mentioned abortion and family values as important issues in their votes far more than did other exit poll respondents (Soper 1996, 118–24).

This win gave Christian conservatives an esteemed place in Republican governing councils. The leaders of the major Christian right organizations have kept in regular contact with the new Republican congressional leadership. The Christian Coalition spent one million dollars lobbying for passage of the Contract with

America and proposed a "Contract with the American Family" in 1995 that focused more on social issues such as school prayer, restrictions on abortion, and limiting Internet pornography. The divisiveness of these issues, however, did not yield legislative progress for Christian conservatives. Tactical missteps by congressional Republican leaders culminating in two government shutdowns, the renewed popularity of President Clinton, and internal squabbling over the agenda status of conservative social issues prevented much progress in 1995 or 1996. Successful electoral activation wins elections but doesn't always settle policy. In policy competition, interests need the additional activation strategies detailed in the next chapter.

This case reveals the unique resources of Christian conservatives in the politics of activation. Their target public is easily identifiable, enmeshed in social networks sharing a common social agenda, and provided with citizenship skills by church activity. This permits a broad and effective form of electoral activation, one that was particularly well executed in 1994. Such advantages will sustain the place of Christian conservatives in national, state, and local politics. Their 1994 success also grew from the simplicity of urging support for a simple partisan ballot. This common national theme made the message to sympathetic voters simpler, further lowering the costs of activation. Rarely in our politics can interest entrepreneurs present such a simple message to such a large, strongly inclined, readily identifiable, well-organized audience of voters.

Christian conservatives, however, remain a mixed blessing to the Republican Party. The movement's controversial social views at times proved an impediment to the party. During the 1996 GOP convention, Christian conservative activists sparred with the GOP nominee,

Bob Dole, over the abortion language in the national platform. In 1997, James Dobson of Focus on the Family threatened to bolt from the Republican Party because he believed it was downplaying important social issues. Strong convictions can yield both impressive electoral activation and frustration with the piecemeal operations of government.

INTEREST GROUPS AND DIRECT DEMOCRACY

Christian conservatives also have tried to make policy through direct democracy via initiatives voted upon by state electorates. Their record at this is decidedly mixed in the 1990s, winning anti–gay rights initiatives in Colorado and Maine but not in Oregon and failing with anti-abortion initiatives in several states. The politics of initiatives prove more difficult for interest entrepreneurs than partisan elections did for Christian conservative activators in 1994. An initiative is a policy proposal requiring explanation to the public, a much more ambitious and costly persuasion process than boosting a particular partisan label. Since persuasion regarding initiatives is expensive, groups with large financial resources come to the fore in initiative politics. Without a shower of costly advertising, initiatives usually go down to defeat.

Heeding the call of progressive reformers, twenty-four states now provide an alternative means of lawmaking that involves direct votes by the people. These initiatives come in four forms: constitutional, direct, indirect, and advisory. Constitutional initiatives allow the public to amend their state constitution directly. Direct initiatives allow an interest group to draft a proposed law and submit it for a popular vote. In indirect initiatives, the proposal is first placed before the legislature, and if that body does not act on it in a given period, it goes before the voters. Advisory initiatives merely vent the public will but change no laws.

The arguments in support of initiatives all strongly endorse participatory democracy as a highly desirable lawmaking mechanism. Reformers argue that initiatives bind state law to the will of the people when the legislature ignores it, thus promoting governmental responsiveness and accountability. Direct popular lawmaking can serve to break "special interest" domination of state government, retarding the incidence of corruption. Referendum campaigns can produce public education about important current issues, furthering each citizen's right to petition the government for redress of grievances. Placing initiatives on the ballot increases voter interest and election turnout and allows citizens to make laws on "tough issues" frequently avoided by timid, reelection-minded lawmakers (Cronin 1989, 10–11).

Although these arguments held sway earlier in the century when most states adopted initiative procedures, do they prevail in light of recent evidence? The rise of activation technologies presents a powerful challenge to participatory lawmaking. These technologies are increasingly capital-intensive, making money steadily more important in initiative politics. The Supreme Court sustained the importance of money in initiative politics in *First National Bank of Boston v. Bellotti* 435 U.S. 765 (1978). The case concerned a Massachusetts law prohibiting corporate expenditures on ballot proposals about "taxation of income." The court ruled that limitations on spending by corporations in initiative campaigns constituted "an impermissible legislative prohibition of speech based on the identity of the interests that spokesman represents." This effectively protected, on First

Amendment grounds, unlimited spending by interests in initiative campaigns. With unlimited rights to unleash activation technologies on statewide electorates, well-heeled interests now frequently find the direct initiative a promising means of achieving their policy goals (Hrebnar 1997, 175).

A group can pick its issue and in doing so, define and limit its potential opposition. By clarifying its issue target, it can raise and deploy resources for a project with great immediate benefits for the group's policy goals. No elected middlemen are needed to achieve policy, just one conclusive popular vote. Further, no state or federal laws limit what a group can spend on an initiative campaign. It's no surprise, then, that well-financed interests often command the politics of state initiatives. In 1994, the seventy-four initiatives up for vote in various states set an all-time record (Hrebnar 1997, 178). This was topped in 1996, when 106 made the ballot (Broder 1998, 11).

Professional political consultants hired by organized interests dominate initiative politics (Magleby and Patterson 1998, 167). Although groups can phrase the proposition as they wish, voters have little information and are subject to volatile changes of opinion. As one initiative consultant puts it: "they filter conflicting interpretations of the issue and its ramifications. The result can be a wild roller-coaster ride. Major shifts in voter preferences, which might take weeks to develop in a candidate campaign, can occur virtually overnight in a ballot measure campaign" (Mandabach 1995, 19). Groups that can contain this volatility and direct voter preferences effectively have a large advantage. Money is the essential resource for framing the issue well and pressing the message home to an inattentive electorate. Ability to spend promotes success at each step of the initiative process.

First, what should the wording of the proposition be? Consultants can pretest ballot questions to determine which versions are most acceptable to the public. Wording the question well allows pollsters to employ its language in poll questions, making their surveys a more reliable indicator of the initiative result. The 1994 Save Our Sealife campaign in Florida is a case in point. Before gathering signatures for the initiative, consultants "did extensive testing in polls and focus groups designed to produce ballot language that was brief enough to avoid troubling voters, but just detailed enough to elicit voter interest and sympathy" (Hill 1995, 30). This wording also allowed for accurate polling and helped to ensure a large majority in support of the initiative. Once persuasive wording is created, ballot access is the next hurdle. This aspect has been professionalized as well. Over 60 percent of signature-gathering efforts in initiatives are professional, usually by firms charging up to $5 per signature (Campaigns and Elections "Citizen Initiatives," 1994, 36). During the actual campaign, ads are carefully crafted via polling and focus groups in order to get across a "winning message to people who have limited attention spans" (Sonis 1994, 63). Mobilizing the entire voting-age population is not the task here; rather, it involves activating a majority of likely voters to support your side of an initiative campaign.

Once the ballot is set, states usually send voters a thick pamphlet detailing the contents of the initiatives, written in very technical prose. One survey found that "most voters do not read the pamphlet or use it as a source of information for decisions on propositions" (Magleby 1984, 146). That makes television advertising the key to the fate of particular propositions, particularly in larger states, and television advertising, as we have seen, is quite expensive. Given the propensity of voters to vote "no" to unfamiliar proposals, the cost of getting a proposition approved is quite high. One study of initiatives in several states found that "campaign spending is the single most powerful predictor of who wins and who loses" (Zisk 1987).

INITIATIVES IN CALIFORNIA

The state of California provides a useful case for examining the impact of activation strategies upon the initiative form of direct democracy. As the nation's largest state, much scholarly evidence exists about its initiative politics. Its great size and diversity also provide insights about how initiatives might function if implemented nationally. A state with a strong progressive reform tradition, the initiative is heavily used and enjoys strong public support. In California, has the initiative in practice fulfilled the hopes of the participatory democrats who embrace it?

Certain features of the initiative process are particularly important when evaluating the California case. Procedures for placing initiatives on the ballot should not favor particular interests or factions of the public over others, if the popular will is to receive undistorted expression. Also, campaigns for the initiative should be educational and balanced, with both sides' arguments thoroughly presented to the public. Third, voters should base their choices on adequate and accurate information about the contents of the initiative. Failure of the process in any of the above respects would severely diminish the democratic utility of initiatives. Activation strategies present a strong challenge to all three of the above-mentioned aspects of the California initiative process.

The rules for ballot access in California are restrictive, advantaging interests and causes with the funds to purchase professional assistance in gathering the requisite number of signatures. For an initiative that would amend state law, more than 400,000 signatures—5 percent of registered voters—must sign petitions. For the less frequently used petitions to amend the state constitution, 8 percent of registered voters or over 600,000 signatures are necessary. As the voter registration rolls have increased in recent decades, so have the required signature totals and the costs of gathering signatures. An increasing number of moneyed interests have employed professional techniques to gather signatures and run initiative campaigns.

The breakthrough year for the modern initiative business in California was 1978. State residents passed Proposition 13, a stiff constitutional limitation on state property taxes, advocated by Howard Jarvis, an anti-tax advocate. One initiative campaign professional called Proposition 13 "the last amateur campaign" (McCuan, Bowler, Donovan, and Fernandez 1998, 73) in that it was not heavily funded by particular interests and did not deploy the activation tactics of professional initiative consultants. Proposition 13, prompting drastic changes in state finances, signaled interest groups that the initiative process might be a useful way to pursue their own goals. The number of ballot initiatives doubled in the 1980s, and the "initiative business" of professional petition, campaign, and advertising consultants grew in both size and importance.

Firms involved in the promotion of initiatives have existed since the founding of the Whitaker and Baxter consulting firm in 1930. Today, between fifty and seventy consultant firms are active in initiative campaigns (McCuan, Bowler, Donovan, and Fernandez 1998, 63). Why the proliferation? Veteran signature solicitor Kelly Kimball states one reason: "they are the biggest paydays in politics" (Magleby and Patterson 1998, 161). Signature solicitors make millions on petitions and ad consultants can make millions on statewide media buys. Consequently, consultants often approach interest groups to pitch possible initiative campaigns. Joe Cerrell, a Los Angeles consultant, claims that "people go out and propose these initiatives so they can make money. It's become a straight business" (Schrag 1998, 211).

Interests, for their part, can realize several advantages though initiatives. Groups can win, and in doing so change state law. Rarely, however, do groups representing narrow interests actually prevail with initiatives. A recent study found that "narrow based, well organized groups who seek to protect clearly identifiable interests and seek exclusive, divisible benefits for members" (such as corporations and unions) won passage of only 14 percent of the initiatives they proposed from 1986 to 1996 (Donovan, Bowler, McCuan, and Fernandez 1998, 82). A narrow interest can win, however, if it cloaks the initiative in broad, appealing goals and language, as an example from 1984 illustrates. That year, Scientific Games of Atlanta funded an initiative to create a California lottery, which passed in large part because some of the funds were to be diverted to public education. The lottery in fact gives public schools less than 3 percent of their total revenue, but the public widely believes it to be a big revenue source for education. This has impeded public support for subsequent school funding proposals. Scientific Games, meanwhile, has reaped vast profits from the initiative that they subsidized (Schrag 1998, 198).

Even when a narrow interest loses, its proposal can move up the state political agenda. For example, unions placed initiatives 214 and 216 on the ballot in 1996. Similar in content, the two initiatives sought to regulate state health maintenance organizations (HMOs). Although both failed, in the three months after the election the legislature passed 27 HMO regulation bills that included many of the provisions in the initiatives (Gerber 1998, 203). This example reveals one of the several virtues of a losing initiative campaign. Even in defeat, an interest can raise the agenda status of an issue, signaling the state legislature that action is needed. Likewise, major initiative campaigns in California often attract national media attention, thereby encouraging kindred interests nationally and in other states to take up the cause. A losing campaign can also spawn new, effective, interest group coalitions, as is illustrated by the coalitions formed among labor unions on account of their common work on issues 214 and 216. Lessons from defeat can also teach interests how to reframe issues in order to broaden their appeal in future advocacy.

Although narrow interests seldom win the initiatives they propose, they do tend to be successful in defeating hostile initiatives. From 1986 to 1996 in California, narrow interests defeated measures sponsored by other narrow interests 86 percent of the time. Narrow groups also stop many initiatives sponsored by broader interests (Donovan, Bowler, McCuan, and Fernandez 1998, 96). Broad or diffuse groups, representing the poor, environmentalists, homeowners, or consumers, usually seek to deliver nonrival and nonexcludable benefits, reducing the incentives for individuals in the broader target public to join and advance the group cause. Narrow groups, offering rival and exclusive benefits for members, don't have this problem. Given their stronger member incentives, we would expect narrow groups to block many initiatives sponsored by more diffuse interests. Indeed, narrow interests have prevented passage of initiatives sponsored by less well-organized "groups associated with diffuse constituencies" 65 percent of the time (Donovan, Bowler, McCuan, and Fernandez 1998, 90). A particularly successful defensive strategy for more narrow groups involves the sponsorship of counterinitiatives. In this situation, an interest sponsors an initiative on the same subject as a hostile initiative, but with content that is more favorable. The two initiatives may confuse voters, causing both to lose. From 1968 to 1990, for example, thirty-seven initiatives on the ballot in California were counterinitiatives to another initiative already on the ballot (Banducci 1998, 112). During this period, counterinitiatives received much heavier funding than did the rival initiatives on the same topic. Counterinitiatives averaged over $5 million in campaign spending, while the original initiatives themselves averaged only $1.4 million (Banducci 1998, 121).

Despite these frequently effective strategies employed by narrow groups, groups supporting broad and diffuse interests have a fair record of success in California initiatives. When confronting narrow interests, the diffuse interest prevailed on initiatives 35 percent of the time from 1986 to 1996. When broad interests competed against each other over initiatives, the broad interest sponsoring the initiative won 58 percent of the time (Donovan, Bowler, McCuan, and Fernandez 1998, 95). Many successful campaigns involving duels by diffuse interests involved relatively low spending but particularly charged issues, such as Proposition 187 in 1994 (concerning illegal immigrants) and Proposition 209 in 1996 (banning affirmative action in the state university system). Narrow interests did not enter the battles over either of these issues. Although the problem of narrow interest dominance is absent in these two cases, both give critics of initiatives additional ammunition. The successful "broad interests" have been labeled anti-immigrant (187) and racially prejudiced (187 and 209), suggesting that majority policy-making may not be properly solicitous of minority rights in a racially diverse state.

Interests dominate public campaigns over initiatives with a variety of activation techniques. Consultants identify groups of likely voters for direct mail campaigns. Mailings "can now be targeted with something approaching the precision of a global positioning satellite . . . the endorsements in the mailing reflect the targeted voter's politics and with which the voter will likely identify" (Schrag 1998, 213–14). The lion's share of funding, however, goes for radio and television advertising. Explaining a proposition in a minute or less requires oversimplification, and intentional distortions frequently appear as well. A classic example of ad deception involved the campaign against a 1982 "bottle initiative," pushed by environmental groups, requiring a deposit on bottles that would fund recycling. A coalition of out-of-state beverage and container companies formed a counter-campaign under the title of "Californians for Sensible Laws." Their ads failed to mention that the bottle "tax" was a refundable deposit, falsely depicted Oregon residents as opposing their (actually very popular) bottle law, and dubiously claimed that the proposition would shut down the voluntary recycling industry in California. One ad even featured a Boy Scout asking why "the grown-ups" behind Proposition 11 were shutting down "Mr. Erickson's recycling center and putting us scouts out of business" (Cronin 1989, 218). Not surprisingly, Proposition 11 lost.

Such an environment is unlikely to encourage knowledgeable and rational voting. Studies of voting behavior in California initiatives reveal that the progressive ideal is not matched by experience. One study of voting on Proposition 10, a 1980 rent-control initiative, found that "over three-fourths of the California voters did not match up their views on rent control with their votes on the measure" (Magleby 1984, 144). Admittedly, this was a particularly complex proposition. Simpler issues, such as Proposition 13 on property tax limitation in 1978 and Proposition 209 banning affirmative action in state university admissions in 1998, might have produced a less drastically misinformed result. Given such evidence, however, we cannot really know if or when the electorate knows what it is doing when voting on initiatives. Moreover, the electorate voting on initiatives is also an elite subsection of all those who go to the polls. An estimated 5 to 15 percent of voters "drop off" from initiative voting, and the remaining voters tend to be older and more highly educated than the electorate or population as a whole (Cronin 1989, 185). The information costs in initiative voting are high, and even a small and relatively elite electorate can find it difficult to vote rationally.

The rise of California's initiative business presents several disturbing lessons about the politics of activation. A particularly important weakness in the California initiative process is the cost of getting an initiative on the ballot in the first place. The high costs tilt the agenda toward narrow interests. Broader interests usually succeed with petitions only when dealing with hot issues like propositions 13, 187, and 209. Initiatives have become just another strategy for well-heeled narrow interests to make policy and influence the state agenda in California. A comprehensive study of recent initiative politics concluded that in California, "it is difficult to pass things, and even more difficult to pass something that threatens the well-established interests. . . . The contemporary process does not make it easy for advocates of large, diffuse, public benefits to take on 'the interests'" (Donovan, Bowler, McCuan, and Fernandez 1998, 100).

All this interest activity also demonstrates how the initiative process has weakened political parties in California. Professional initiative consultants provide a new way for interests to ignore parties in shaping public policy. Instead of dealing with the messy legislative process, they can go into business for themselves via an initiative and either win and make law or, in losing, perhaps place an issue at the top of the state legislature's agenda. This "weakens political parties because it allows groups to force public decision on issues framed by the groups themselves" (Magleby 1984, 189). Parties don't draft initiatives and very seldom play any role in interpreting them for voters during campaigns. The traditional party roles of compromising and moderating the demands of diverse interests are absent from initiative politics. Instead, groups deploy funds to take their agendas directly to a marginally attentive electorate.

Another loser in initiative politics is the state legislature. Initiatives in recent decades have circumscribed legislative power over criminal law, taxation, and environmental policy. A recent term-limit initiative requires frequent turnover of members, thus weakening institutional expertise. Direct rule of the people, thanks to the arts of activation, has actually empowered narrow interests at the expense of institutions—parties and the legislature—that have incentives to consider more consistently the broad, diffuse interests of Californians. Initiative politics signals not an advantage of the people over the interests, as its proponents argued, but an advantage of interests, particularly narrow, moneyed interests, in setting California's public agenda.

In each of its important aspects, the California initiative process comes up short. The popular will receives distorted expression because ballot access is driven by expensive, professionalized activation strategies for amassing signatures. Initiative campaigns are waged on television, with ads that frequently distort and oversimplify the matters at issue in an initiative. Balanced, educational discussion of the issues seldom occurs. Finally, voters often lack adequate information when choosing how to vote, making initiatives an often less than accurate and rational reflection of public opinion. The evidence from other initiative states, such as Oregon, Michigan, and Massachusetts, reveals that these shortcomings extend far beyond California (Magleby 1984; Cronin 1989; Zisk 1987; Bowler, Donovan, and Tolbert 1998). The realities of initiative politics have dimmed the great hopes of progressive reformers.

Participatory theorist Benjamin Barber argues that "referendum and initiative processes divorced from innovative programs for public talk and deliberation fall easy victim to plebiscitary abuses and the manipulation by money and elites of popular prejudice" (1984, 156). The evidence above confirms his generalization and suggests that his prescription for public deliberation knows few practical and successful applications in contemporary politics. The logic of activation does not require deliberation by citizens. That is a costly and inefficient enterprise for candidates and interests who seek to win popular support in elections. Barber's "innovative programs" of public dialogue will fail to take root without strong incentives forcing them into our politics. When it serves the interests of parties, candidates, and interests to bring these techniques into the arena, they will arrive there. No amount of reformist preaching can substitute for the proper incentives among electoral players. The California initiative case illustrates this point. Designed to prompt popular deliberation over policy, it offers few incentives for citizens to master the arcane content of initiatives. It does, however, provide strong incentives for interests to use the initiative process to pursue their ends in government. This they have done. Workable reforms, as we see in our final chapter, must either comport with or adjust the incentives of parties, candidates, and interests, or they will fail to achieve their ends. That is the story of the initiative in California. A national initiative system, given our entrenched politics of activation, would surely suffer from similar pitfalls.

As the *New York Times* warned in 1911 when California first adopted the initiative: "While pretending to give greater right to the voters, the initiative deprives them of the opportunity effectively and intelligently to use their powers" ("Anti-Democracy in California" 1911, 12). By displacing partisan mobilization, proponents of direct democracy instead started in motion a process that now frequently features manipulative activation of marginally attentive voters with funds provided by wealthy private interests. The arts of activation in campaigns feature no more perverse result than this.

CONCLUSION

Interest groups use their resources in campaigns to affect the actions of government once the election is over. The efficient pursuit of their policy goals requires tightly targeted investments, whether in candidates (through contributions), campaign technology (through ads), or grassroots activation (through leafleting and phone calls). In today's electoral arena, however, the central players pay little attention to the effect of their collective behavior on the quality and quantity of electoral participation in America. Techniques that win often either confuse voters—in the case of initiatives—or repel them from politics altogether—in the case of negative advertising. Interests seek to prevail in elections, not to ensure a clear and representative public voice. They similarly seek victory, not representative results, when lobbying government, as the next chapter makes clear.

CHAPTER 5

Interest Organizations and Government
Lobbying by Activation

Lobby groups could no longer bank on some pricey
Washington superlawyer to make their pitch in private, they
had to generate grassroots movements to pressure scores of
legislators. That meant turning increasingly to the technologies of political campaigns and campaign organizers, pollsters and direct mail specialists to tap and manipulate public
opinion.

Hedrick Smith, *The Power Game: How Washington Works*

The flurry of activation efforts by interest organizations during
campaigns, examined in the previous chapter, has its counter-
part in their activities aimed at influencing the actions of government. Governmental politics, defined as "the decisions of national
and local governments," includes activation efforts as thorough and
intense as those during elections (Rosenstone and Hansen 1993, 71).
Just about every Washington interest group now finds activation a
vital tool in its struggle to prevail over policy. Interests employ activation widely toward state governments as well (Hrebnar 1997,
238–39; Hrebnar and Thomas 1993). The pervasive presence of activation in lobbying suggests that the distinction between electoral and

governmental politics is collapsing. Instead, we have government consumed by "image-making with strategic calculation [such that] government is turned into the perpetual campaign" (Blumenthal 1980, 7).

This chapter reveals how a burgeoning number of interests, utilizing new communication technologies, have perfected new activation strategies that enhance their influence over governmental officials. Groups use activation technologies frequently because they help them accomplish three goals: (1) getting and keeping members, (2) employing "grassroots" pressure upon officials, and (3) convincing the public of the worthiness of group causes. Nowhere are the arts of activation in government more advanced than in Washington, D.C., the primary focus of this chapter. The rise in lobbyists reflects national government's broad potential reach, a product of increasing social and economic complexity. With an estimated 91,000 lobbyists plying their trade in our nation's capital, the competition for effectiveness is intense among interests (Phillips 1994, 43). Innovative and effective activation strategies are the products of that competition.

The range of group strategies reveals the many possible means to the efficient exercise of influence. Their strategies divide into two types, "inside" and "outside." Inside strategies are "based primarily upon close consultation with political and administrative leaders, relying mainly on financial resources and substantive expertise" (Walker 1991, 9). Traditional lobbying long entailed largely inside strategies. Outside strategies involve "appeals to the public through the mass media and . . . citizens at the grassroots" (Walker 1991, 9). Activation is the core element of increasingly popular outside strategies. More and more interests use both inside and outside strategies when approaching government.

As the range of strategies employed by groups has expanded, so has the variety of groups actively pressuring Washington decision makers. Kay Lehman Schlozman and John Tierney catalog a wide array of interest organizations now active in our political life (1986, 38–51). Many groups are membership organizations, composed of individuals who elect to join. These include labor unions, farm groups, professional associations (such as the American Bar Association and American Medical Association), trade associations of kindred businesses (the American Bankers Association and Association of Dressings and Sauces), and broader scope "peak" business associations (the U.S. Chamber of Commerce and Business Roundtable). Also in this category are numerous "cause" groups composed of individuals sharing a common policy agenda (the National Taxpayer's Union and the Friends of the Earth), and "advocacy" groups that seek benefits on behalf of those unable to articulate their own needs (the Children's Defense Fund). Membership groups additionally include civil rights organizations (the National Association for the Advancement of Colored People and the National Urban League) and those concerned with social welfare (the National Rural Housing Coalition and Full Employment Action Council).

Alongside the many membership groups are numerous organizations that are not composed of voluntary members. Robert Salisbury terms these organizations "institutions" that have less need to "justify their political efforts by reference to membership approval or demand" (1984, 68). These include corporations, large hospitals and universities, radio and television stations, think tanks, and public interest law firms (Schlozman and Tierney 1986, 49). Foreign, state, and local governments also qualify as institutional lobbies, although they are more concerned with the opinions of the "membership" (that is, their constituents) than are other institutions. Large, complex institutions are affected by government actions in many ways and thus find it necessary to participate actively in governmental politics.

Given that each interest organization has limited resources, it behooves them to identify an advocacy niche in which they can maintain and deploy their resources with maximum effectiveness. The drive for effectiveness often leads kindred groups to form coalitions when influencing government. Without the right niche and interest allies, organizational effectiveness is in peril: "Since interests have to group, or network, in order to matter in making public policy, lobbyists need to behave and make choices economically, both for themselves and for those within their environment. Interests perform a lot of appropriately interrelated tasks and select good issues in order to gain an accepted policy niche. Their representatives desperately want that niche in order to be in the 'in crowd'" (Browne 1998, 227). The pursuit of effectiveness increasingly leads interest organizations to use new technology for the effective activation of their supporters. The newer activation strategies, detailed in this chapter, serve as an effective complement to the more traditional lobbying techniques still practiced before government.

TRADITIONAL LOBBYING TECHNIQUES

Traditional, "inside" lobbying techniques remain with us because they continue to create influence over the actions of government. *Influence* is the ability of a group to produce a desired outcome in government—whether that outcome involves stasis or change. All groups seek influence and at times use traditional lobbying to attain it. Most inside techniques usually do not involve activating a large public voice. Instead, professional lobbyists develop working relationships with governmental officials over time and present group arguments directly to them. The legislature is a central target of inside strategies. In addition to legislative lobbying, interests attempt a variety of inside techniques with the White House, bureaucracy, and courts.

In approaching the White House, direct contacts with staff can be helpful, particularly when a relationship with them is already established. Groups also seek representation on and audiences with presidential commissions and task forces and try to influence administration cabinet and subcabinet appointments. When approaching the bureaucracy, interests keep up regular contacts with agency personnel and actively participate in hearings and public comment opportunities concerning proposed administrative rules. They also serve on advisory committees in the bureaucracy. Interests approach the courts in a variety of ways. Interests also seek to affect judicial appointments, and to influence the "conventional wisdom" of the legal community through publications and law review articles. They also sponsor litigation and file amicus curiae (friend of the court) briefs in cases of importance (Schlozman and Tierney 1986, 325–73; Hrebnar 1997, 221–45).

Lobbyists incessantly seek out lawmakers and their staffs, targeting legislators of particular importance to their group's agenda. They include the chairs of standing committees and subcommittees considering legislation of importance to the group, and personal and committee staff concerned with topics of group interest. Legislative party leaders receive contact on high-profile matters. The number of interests seeking legislative attention has grown, however, while the number of lawmakers has not. That makes staff contact an important component of lobbying efforts.

Many interests employ in-house lobbyists, but some more well-heeled institutions and membership groups hire Washington talent to present their cases before governmental institutions. The hired guns can be found in lobbying firms, law firms, and public relations firms. Many lobbying firms include former lawmakers and Hill staffpersons who lobby for clients in policy areas where they previously worked as governmental officials and employees. The Duberstein Group, for example, was started by Kenneth Duberstein, a former legislative assistant and chief of staff to President Reagan. Corporations often hire Washington law firms to represent them, and the cost is not cheap. The most prestigious such firm is Patton, Boggs, and Blow, with 1,500 clients. Tommy Boggs, one of its partners, is the son of former House Majority Whip Hale Boggs. Public relations firms execute both inside and outside strategies. Hill and Knowlton, a leading firm with hundreds of clients, has divisions for lobbying, advertising, and other media work and hundreds of clients.

Although inside lobbying has an unseemly aura, the rules of the trade are not as ethically dubious as many suspect. The public views interest influence in Washington as involving illegal payoffs from unscrupulous money interests, as if "the halls of government are awash with bribes from lobbyists" (Hartwig 1995). Such tactics don't work and are very seldom employed. Lobbyist Bruce Wolpe summarizes the five commandments of successful lobbying. First, one must tell the truth. Truthful information that helps your cause is highly effective. Lies and misinformation can be found out and are highly destructive to one's lobbying effort. Second, never promise more than can be delivered. Pledging analytical and political support that does not come through is never forgotten. Third, know how to listen in order to understand accurately what is said. Lawmakers and administrators often are vague in their pronouncements in order politely to say "no." Fourth, staff are there to be worked with, not circumvented. They often know more than the administrators and lawmakers for whom they work. Discounting their expertise and influence can be fatal. Finally, spring no surprises. Lawmakers and administrators need to understand a lobbyist's proposal clearly, including its shortcomings. If they are later caught unawares by a weakness in a lobbyist's presentation, his or her credibility is impaired (Wolpe and Levine 1996, 13–19).

If inside lobbying is less than nefarious, that does not mean that its sum effect is representative of public opinion. Intensity rules in lobbying, as in electoral politics. Institutions and membership groups strongly involved in particular issues often gain disproportionate influence through the use of inside strategies. This has long been an important criticism of insider strategies. Inside lobbying, however, is now complemented frequently by outside techniques, spawned by new technologies that make activation strategies more useful in lobbying. The inside game is not as restricted in its scope of participants as it was. It is more complicated than in the past but, as we will see, not necessarily more representative of the public will.

One of Washington's leading lobbyists, David Rehr of the National Association of Beer Wholesalers, reveals how legislative lobbying in Washington no longer simply involves the traditional tactics. The old style of lobbying, according to Rehr, involved inside lobbying of a few important lawmakers, usually committee chairs. Before congressional reforms of the 1970s, committee chairs had great power over legislation within their jurisdictions. That made elite lobbying of legislative insiders a very efficient method. Now, power is more widely distributed in Congress, making it more difficult for interests to tightly target lawmakers. Successful lobbying must now involve grassroots tactics in which interests activate constituents to contact lawmakers. In the past, individual interests often went door-to-door contacting individual lawmakers. Now, kindred groups form coalitions and share the work of direct contact. Previously, most contacts were staff-centered, but now it is possible to cultivate "legislative champions" who will carry an interest's issues over time and even lobby their lawmaker colleagues for that interest. Some legislators now find principles and politics encourage them to consistently press particular group demands. The substance of group persuasion has also changed. While personal compatibility between elite lobbyists and lawmakers often proved influential in the past, now a group must have an abundance of defensible data and arguments in order to make headway on Capitol Hill (Rehr 1997). Many other observers echo Rehr's claim that "grassroots lobbying is everywhere" (Rubin 1997; Kollman 1998; Faucheux 1994). At the heart of the new style of lobbying lie activation strategies.

THE RISE OF ACTIVATION IN LOBBYING

In recent decades, the Washington political environment has become more complex, uncertain, and decentralized (Salisbury 1990, 227–28). Power is scattered throughout Congress and the executive branch. Given the uncertainty this complexity spawns, it is rational for interests to use a wide range of techniques, as Rehr suggests.

"Since no interest wins all of the time, rarely do lobbyists and knowledgable interests do only one thing or follow a single set of tasks. They target all directions if needed" (Browne 1998, 167). Activation becomes highly useful in this circumstance. Groups use activation strategies to further their three primary goals of getting and keeping members, rousing them to contact government officials through grassroots or "outside" lobbying, and convincing the public of the rightness of the group cause through advertising and public relations. Although institutions need not concern themselves with attracting members as must membership groups, they nevertheless can use their personnel and funds to pursue outside lobbying and to alter public opinion in their favor.

New technologies make activation by groups easier and more pervasive than ever before. Interests can identify their "targets" for activation through survey research and focus groups. Groups "narrowcast" advocacy messages to their employees, members, and targeted segments of the public through direct mail, the Internet, cable television, satellite technology, telephone, and fax. Employees and members then use many of these same technologies to contact members of Congress and administrators with the group message. The "warm transfer" is a technique popular among groups at this stage. Individuals dial an 800 number and their calls are routed automatically to the Washington office of their senator or representative. New communication technologies also make coordinated "coalition" advocacy by kindred groups more manageable and efficient, reducing drastically any duplication of effort.

As the previous chapter noted, the part of the public that serves as the primary target for group activation efforts includes those individuals who are, in effect, the cheapest to activate. The cost of activation decreases with the level of a citizen's political knowledge, resources, and involvement. Hence the primary targets are that minority of citizens who rank high in education, income, political efficacy, involvement in voluntary organizations, and membership in social networks with high participation norms (Rosenstone and Hansen 1993, 71–88; Nie, Junn, and Stehlik-Barry 1996, 74). The explosion of group participation in governmental politics is a manifestation of the popular participatory ethos of activation. Its methods encourage participatory democracy, but beneath this veneer is careful group strategizing to activate strategic minorities in order that particular group agendas may dominate the councils of government. Examining how groups recruit and keep members reveals this logic of activation at work.

GETTING AND KEEPING MEMBERS

Membership is a vital resource of interest organizations. Mancur Olson explored the problem of group membership in his impressive book, *The Logic of Collective Action* (1965, 5–66), by examining the conditions under which material incentives encourage group membership. Institutions solve the membership problem by employing people to work for them. The material incentive of the job makes activation efforts by their organizational superiors an easy task. But membership organizations face a more difficult challenge in maintaining their rank and file. Most interest organizations pursue what Olson terms a "collective good," that is, a good whose uses are nonrival (they are equally provided for all) and whose benefits are nonexcludable (no citizen can be deprived of them). Examples include governmental benefits that are universally available, such as police protection and national defense. However, groups may also seek collective goods whose reach of benefits is not universal but does stretch considerably beyond their membership. The National Education Association, for example, may improve the working conditions of all teachers, thus bettering the lot of many teachers who are not members.

The problem of collective benefits, then, is the "free rider" problem. Why should a teacher join the NEA if benefits come to her whether she is a member or not? Similarly, if the National

Association of Beer Wholesalers gets the beer tax lowered, all whole-salers benefit, regardless of whether they are members. Small "poten-tial" groups, like the dominant industries in a single sector of the economy—such as the steel producers—don't have this problem. Individual players in this situation can calculate that their own effort plays an important part in providing the collective good. Thus with-out their individual action, no collective good may result at all. This explains why so many narrow economic interests are well represented in Washington. Larger groups can solve this problem by providing "selective incentives" for individuals to join the group. These incen-tives are material benefits available only if one joins the group. Many effective economic groups have done exactly that. The National Farm Bureau, for example, remains a large organization by rewarding mem-bers with exclusive use of the bureau's system of cooperatives for marketing crops. Labor unions have secured passage of legislation in some states permitting closed shops, in which all employees must be union members. The benefit of the job comes only with union mem-bership.

Olson's theory is called a "byproduct" theory of group formation because individuals join groups not to pursue the political agenda of group leaders, but rather to gain selective material benefits. These groups' political agendas are thus byproducts of their actual reasons for existence. Although this may describe the membership of certain large economic groups, such as labor and farm organizations, indi-viduals who join for reasons beyond the merely material populate thousands of groups. James Q. Wilson identified two additional incentives for joining political organizations. One is the solidary incentive, "the intangible rewards arising out of the act of associat-ing that can be given to, or withheld from, specific individuals"

(Wilson 1995, 33–34). These include the pleasures of friendship and ego satisfaction resulting from interaction with fellow members and political notables. Another incentive is purposive, defined as "the intangible rewards that derive from the sense of satisfaction of having contributed to the attainment of a worthwhile cause" (1995, 34). The "joiners" of political membership organizations are more likely to be issue-conscious and issue-driven than their fellow citizens and will pursue great purposes through group membership. Environmentalists join Friends of the Earth to save the planet. Christian conservatives join the Christian Coalition to restore the moral fiber of the country.

Although solidary benefits can be selectively apportioned by interest organizations, purposive benefits cannot; they are collective. One can contribute to a great cause without necessarily joining any organization. Then why are issue-based membership organizations ubiquitous in Washington? Robert Salisbury (1969) provides an answer. He defined the benefits such individuals seek as expressive, not purposive. An expressive benefit is "selective, not collective in nature, providing value only to those who contribute to it" (Baumgartner and Leech 1998, 69). Thus joiners of Common Cause or the National Coalition to Ban Handguns do so to receive a particular feeling of accomplishment they cannot receive without joining. One can be active on an issue without joining such groups, but group membership can make one's activism more widely known and effective. Issue-based membership groups provide members with ample recognition of their expressive accomplishments, as the case studies later in this chapter reveal.

Interest organizations do not simply miraculously appear. Someone must market prospective benefits to potential members in order to form a group and keep it functioning. Salisbury calls such individuals "entrepreneurs" who are promising a mutually beneficial exchange to prospective members. The members receive selective material, solidary, or expressive benefits (sometimes a combination of the three), and in return the entrepreneur receives financial resources to operate the group. "In order to sustain a group organization, it is necessary to maintain an adequate flow of benefits both to members and to the organizers themselves. In short, there must be a mutually satisfactory exchange" (1969, 25).

Who are the entrepreneurs? They are, according to V. O. Key, the "influentials, the opinion-leaders, the political activists in the order" who, he argued, are essential to the health of America's democratic regime (1961, 558). They include Ralph Nader, founder of many public interest organizations, and Ralph Reed, the organizer of the Christian Coalition. Their role is highly important in that they "bridge the gap between the public and institutions usually filled by bureaucratic party organizations in other democracies" (Fowler 1994, 293). The proliferation of group entrepreneurs is thus another symptom of party decline. As more citizens find parties irrelevant for satisfying their material, solidary, and expressive needs, they turn to interest organizations led by entrepreneurs touting myriad agendas.

Entrepreneurs do not activate people to group membership in a vacuum. Several factors have shaped the context of entrepreneurial appeals in recent decades. The growth of national governmental power and responsibility in the 1960s created policy networks of interested individuals, many of whom became group entrepreneurs. Marian Wright Edelman, for example, founded the Children's Defense Fund after working in government on social welfare issues. Government policy thus reduced the information and transaction costs for entrepreneurial group activity. People involved in a given policy area know the policy as well as each other, making group organization easier. Further, some groups receive government grants to undertake federal program activities like job training and economic development (Barry 1997, 83). The national government thus helps to maintain some policy entrepreneurs. Entrepreneurs also frequently benefit from financial support of wealthy patrons—both individuals and charitable foundations. The Children's Defense Fund receives a large segment of its budget from charitable foundations, as do many other social welfare groups (Wade 1997). Televangelist Pat Robertson underwrote the extensive start-up costs for Ralph Reed's entrepreneurship with the Christian Coalition in the early nineties. Patrons lower the costs of group organizing and have helped to spawn group proliferation in recent decades (Walker 1991, 74–75).

Although patrons and government networks and funding are quite useful, most membership groups have to work constantly at raising memberships and money. Direct mail is the primary technology employed by national groups for this purpose. The technique can vary greatly in its cost. Generally, the better the targeting, the more useful the mailing in generating group memberships and contributions. The campaign involves three steps: (1) assembling a mailing list, (2) preparing the letter's "packaging," and (3) developing the right "pitch" in the text of the letter (Schlozman and Tierney 1986, 191).

Chapter 3 described the rise of mailing list firms that attempt to refine information about the public into efficient lists for mailing campaigns. Candidates use these firms, and interest groups do as well. The "package" involves the appearance of the letter and its contents, developed in order to attract recipients to open and read it. Direct mail specialists have found that an envelope with a licked stamp looks more personalized and is more likely to be opened than is metered mail; a high quality print on the exterior of the letter also gets it opened more frequently (Schlozman and Tierney 1986, 192).

The "pitch" of the letter couches the appeal in extreme language in order to spur an intense reaction from the reader. As one interest organization leader proclaimed: "getting members is about scaring the hell out of people" (Browne 1998, 23). Two 1994 examples from the conservative Christian Coalition and their liberal rival, the People for the American Way, illustrate the scare tactics. The Christian Coalition claimed that "many of the interest groups on the Left (including militant homosexuals, radical feminists and Big Government liberals) all have powerful organizations advancing their point of view in government." At the same time, their rival argued that "the unsettling truth is that, in nearly every state in the union, the grassroots power of mean-spirited and well-organized Right Wing political organizations is threatening people's rights and disrupting people's lives." In their letters, the two organizations agreed only that the state of the nation was perilous!

The result of such fervid appeals is that those who take the bait tend to "rarely have any real knowledge of the politics and policies made possible by their donations" (Godwin 1988, 147). Direct-mail members have trouble holding their groups accountable, since it is difficult for them to know exactly how their contributions are spent. Those who respond to direct mail appeals tend to be of two sorts. One group has lower levels of political interest than activists recruited by other means. They provide money for groups but little additional effort. A second group has high levels of political interest and activity, but they tend toward extreme political views and are more aggressive and supportive of aggressive political behavior

(Godwin 1988, 66–67). Thus groups usually activate individuals to membership in a way that advantages the most extreme opinions without providing clear accountability for the expenditure of the contributions received. Direct mail often increases membership efficiently, but not in a fashion that encourages temperate opinions or representative results. Unlike the process of partisan mobilization, when groups recruit members, the majority is not contacted, nor does it rule.

THE GROWTH OF OUTSIDE LOBBYING

One of the "hottest trends" in lobbying today is grassroots or "outside" lobbying (Faucheux 1994, 20). Outside lobbying involves attempts by interest group leaders to activate "citizens outside the policymaking community to contact or pressure policy officials inside the policymaking community" (Kollman 1998, 3). It is so common a practice now that "government relations people now realize that each issue brings with it three cost centers: lobbying fees, PAC costs and expenses for grassroots programs" (Faucheux 1994, 21). Most interest organizations spend long hours assessing how to employ outside lobbying to maximum effect. "The most sophisticated groups, such as the Sierra Club and the National Federation of Independent Business, today routinely combine inside and outside lobbying approaches in order to take full advantage of the respective strengths inherent in each technique" (West and Loomis 1998, 229).

Outside lobbying is elite-induced activation in the service of a particular group agenda. Most commonly it seeks to further a particular item of concern to an interest organization, at a time deemed ripe for maximum influence. The tactic works best, according to Jack Bonner, head of Bonner and Associates, a leading Washington grassroots lobbying firm, when an interest activates "politically important home district constituents who can demonstrate they understand both sides of an issue and can explain in their own words how this issue will impact their district" (Faucheux 1994, 26). Thus, even though the plea may be manufactured by an interest, it needs to look "real." The competition to produce "real" public messages on major issues can prove costly. In 1993–1994, during the height of a national debate over health care reform, interest spending on outside lobbying alone totaled an estimated $790 million (Faucheux 1994, 30). Although outside lobbying is particularly suited to membership organizations, corporations are also getting into the act. They are internally activating "company officers, shareholders, employees and vendors into a grassroots lobbying force" (Faucheux 1994, 26).

New communication technologies permit ever more effective outside lobbying. Dan Danner, vice president for federal relations of the influential National Federation of Independent Business, explains how changing technology facilitates outside lobbying:

The landscape had changed dramatically in Washington over the last twenty years. Lawmakers pay far more attention to the grassroots people at home. Not too many years ago, a smaller group of people controlled the national agenda—the party and committee leaders in Congress. That has fundamentally changed. New members are now willing to take on the traditional committee and party leaders with arguments about what the "people back home want me to do." The biggest single factor in this change is the new communication technology. What legislators do is reported that night on C-SPAN. Open, instantaneous reporting and the ability of people to immediately and cheaply respond to what they see. The key for groups is to effectively direct these grassroots possibilities. (Danner 1997)

Constituents can reach lawmakers quickly and groups can stimulate the contact. Lawmakers, used to "running scared" in an era when party loyalties are weak among the public, often find it prudent to be legislatively cautious (A. King 1997). The pursuit of reelection, good public policy, and influence in Washington (Fenno 1973) is always precarious in this era of unlimited exposure. A former House party leadership aide, now a Washington lobbyist, explains this legislative timidity:

Legislators are extremely cautious, and that's why grassroots lobbying works. We used to have terrible trouble getting a representative to go along with the leadership if they had encountered any contrary opinions when back home in the district. The representative was thinking, this might be a widespread opinion, so why buck it? Why get people mad at me? On a lot of issues that are low in importance for the representative, this is enough to keep them in line. Groups have figured this out and work the grassroots all the time now. (Plebani 1997)

A 1992 Gallup poll of 150 representatives and senators revealed the most effective outside lobbying techniques. Over 70 percent said they pay a great deal of attention to personally written letters from constituents, meetings with heads of groups, visits from CEOs of companies that have employees in the district, phone calls from constituents, and personally written letters from group leaders or officials from district companies (Faucheux 1994, 26). Capitol Hill is now awash with the results of these activation strategies.

How does outside lobbying work to persuade lawmakers? Ken Kollman argues that its effectiveness involves two dimensions. First, groups employ it to signal policymakers about the salience (importance) of a given issue to the public. Second, outside lobbying involves increasing the salience of the issue among the public, expanding the conflict around an issue (Kollman 1998, 62). By informing both decision makers and the public about the importance of an issue, groups hope to activate segments of the public to pressure governmental authorities on the group's behalf. The goal in this is "influential" lobbying, defined as advocacy that "changes policy-makers' decisions" (1998, 72). To succeed, groups must lower the information costs of those most likely to become active in outside lobbying. The targeted members of the public must understand the issue, how it affects them, and how they can exert influence with policy-makers (Rubin 1997, 189).

This sort of targeting need not be haphazard. Interests often employ focus groups and survey research to identify the types of citizens most likely to respond to activation appeals. For example, research may reveal that 55 percent of women favor health care reform, but more than 65 percent of women over 50 do. Within this group, Democratic women in the Northeast and Midwest may support it in even higher proportions. They become the "high yield" target segment that groups favoring health care reform seek to activate. Direct mail or telephone appeals to those most likely to become active ensue. This "targeted issue marketing," as it is called, operates on the premise that group advocates cannot reach everyone and that they do not have to do so (Rubin 1997, 197). Efficient activation need not require that most citizens have any knowledge of the issue in order for the interest to prevail.

Outside lobbying usually involves a fixed sequence of activities. First, research identifies those citizens available for activation. Next, targeting spots members of that group in critical legislative districts, whose activation will have the largest likely influence on the outcome. Then, "mass issue marketing" sensitizes lawmakers and the media to the issue, creating an environment in which targeted activation can get a better public response and be more influential with decision makers. After that, interests actively recruit from targeted segments of the public, most often through phone and mail contact. Next, the activation occurs. Targeted activists call, write, or visit public officials. Finally, interests conduct follow-up and maintenance with their activated citizens, thanking them for their efforts, asking them to report on their tasks, and keeping them informed about the issue in the future (Faucheux 1994, 30).

Lobbyist Bruce Wolpe lists five imperatives in the outside lobbying process. First, although the message delivered need not be spontaneous, it must reflect actual opinions of the citizens who are activated. The contact must ring true and not seem contrived by coming in the form of a single, common message or with highly technical argument. Second, the communication must involve some actual effort on behalf of the activated citizens. Their effort will demonstrate a genuine commitment and intensity that can move cautious legislators. Third, "astroturf" lobbying is a no-no. Counterfeit communications can be identified and destroy the credibility of the group that produced it. Many legislative offices now spot-check communications to make certain the person who apparently sent it did do so and shares the opinion voiced in the communication. Fourth, control is important. Groups should ensure that the tone of the messages is civil and that citizens do not demand too much time and attention from lawmakers concerning their communications. When activating citizens, they must be clearly informed about appropriate language and given realistic expectations about what response to expect. Finally, correct targeting is critical. Unless the right decision makers get the message, group resources are wasted. Some officials will never buy certain arguments. A poorly targeted campaign can produce inappropriate messages and even create a backlash (Wolpe and Levine 1996, 89–94).

In addition to targeted contact by large groups of citizens, two other outside lobbying strategies are also popular with organized interests. A high-end version of grassroots lobbying involves "grasstops" efforts. This entails personal contact with governmental officials by "powerful people who have a special relationship with, or power over, decisionmakers" (Rubin 1997, 194–95). These can be personal friends, campaign contributors, local business, community, or group leaders, local elected or appointed officials, and academic or other experts. These contacts trade on their familiarity with government officials and must be used rarely. They may not be willing to act on the basis of these relationships very often, and too frequent personal contact by them may presume too much of a personal relationship. Grasstops efforts are best reserved for truly critical situations in which their influence can be decisive for the group's agenda (Bergner 1997).

In recent decades many groups, particularly membership groups, have frequently used public protests to bring grassroots pressure to bear upon government. Protests can accomplish "mass issue marketing" by commanding the national agenda when thousands of people flood the Mall in D.C. They can also be targeted precisely to influence particular legislators and administrators. Smaller groups may send their activists to occupy legislative district offices and bureaucratic agencies, "sitting in" to obstruct business and gain media attention. Such confrontational tactics, however, seldom win a sympathetic response from decision makers, although they may command the local media agenda temporarily. Protest now is best viewed not as a spontaneous pouring forth of popular will, but as one of several activation techniques that is highly routinized. Citizen protest has become "a normal part of the political process" but "the recurring behavioral repertoires of both protestors and police, and their inter-actions with one another, have become institutionalized and therefore routinized, predictable and, perhaps as a result, of diminishing impact" (McCarthy and McPhail 1998, 84).

Outside lobbying is now so widespread that even governmental officials try to use it on their own behalf. Whereas lobbying often meant pressing demands on government officials, now some govern-ment officials work with groups to pressure other officials. Ronald Shaiko calls this "reverse lobbying," very evident in Washington dur-ing the 1990s. The Clinton administration formed coalitions with dozens of health care reform groups in 1993 and 1994, urging them to do outside lobbying of Congress on behalf of the administration's ambitious health care reform package. Similarly, House GOP leaders in 1995 organized "Project Relief," an effort of over one hundred trade associations to press regulatory reform legislation through the House and Senate via grassroots efforts (Shaiko 1998, 257, 267–77; Imig 1998, 167–69). Governors have employed similar tactics toward state legislatures in recent years (Schier 1998).

What effects does this flood of outside lobbying have upon America's political system? Ken Kollman examined the correspon-dence between outside lobbying efforts and both the salience and popularity among the public of the issue lobbied. The larger the out-side lobbying campaign, the more it corresponded with issue impor-tance (salience) and popularity in the general public. Thus "interest groups generally use more outside lobbying the more public opinion favors them"—surely a rational response (1998, 100). Outside lobby-ing, however, more consistently reflects the salience, not the popular-ity, of the issue among the public. Outside lobbying does not neces-sary boost popular policies. Instead, "there are some groups with intense supporters pursuing unpopular policies that use outside lobbying" (Kollman 1998, 100). Grassroots specialist Barry Rubin argues that if groups can shrewdly activate "a small minority of supporters, they can give the impression that support is deeper and broader than it actually is" (Rubin 1997, 200). This will reflect issue salience more than issue popularity. Activation of this sort is far less inclusive and representative than the partisan mobilization of the last century, which consistently identified and exploited popular issues.

PERSUADING THE PUBLIC

Mass issue marketing, mentioned above, is a central component of outside lobbying. Groups advertise broadly among the public to recruit members, raise the salience and popularity of their issues, and create the correct "environment" for more targeted activation of the public. Many institutions and membership groups regularly run "image" advertising in print and over the air in order to create a more positive public attitude about the organization. Some ads are general in intent and audience and are broadcast throughout society. Examples include the "I'm the NRA" series of magazine ads depicting the National Rifle Association in a warm and approachable fashion by profiling individual NRA members. Other image ads are targeted more narrowly. The agriculture conglomerate Archer-Daniels-Midland, for example, sponsors many image ads during Sunday morning network public affairs programs, reaching an elite, politically active audience with a beguiling message.

Many "advocacy" ads—arguing for a particular policy position— are also targeted narrowly. Mobil Oil has long run commentary pieces on the op-ed pages of major national papers, seeking to convince an elite, politically aware leadership. The famous "Harry and Louise" ads attacking the Clinton administration's 1993 health care reform plans were run by the Health Insurance Association of America, a trade association. The ads featured an 800 number that generated 350,000 phone calls from which 40,000 grassroots activists were recruited. These activists generated an estimated 200,000 contacts with members of Congress. The HIAA spent most of its $2 million outside lobbying budget for this issue just on fulfilling requests for information packets generated by the ads. Advertising for such efforts is usually targeted at reaching the 10 to 15 percent of the public most likely to contact legislators, according to Ben Goddard, the media consultant for HIAA's effort (Faucheux 1994, 25). Advocacy advertising seeks to increase the salience of issues and activate people to work for the group's agenda. They do not seek to change opinions so much as to reinforce them, and they serve to "channel and strengthen latent opinions and to provide information to support preexisting attitudes" (Schlozman and Tierney 1986, 176–77). They often involve sensational visual images, such as aborted fetuses or clubbed baby seals, in order to increase salience. Messages that "round up the usual suspects" for activation may well misinform or inflame the public about an issue through the distorted and often simplistic format of the advertising. Activation messages of this sort are often misleading for mass consumption.

CASES OF ACTIVATION IN ACTION

Through many techniques, activation has become a primary tool of influence over what government does. The following case studies reveal the centrality of activation to group effectiveness in Washington. Each of the following interest organizations is a major presence in national politics. All are membership organizations, highly skilled at the three arts of group activation. The following cases reveal how each of them uses activation strategies to keep and maintain members, execute effective outside lobbying, and persuade targeted segments of the public of the worthiness of the organization's agenda and activities.

The National Federation of Independent Business

A 1997 *Fortune* survey of 2,200 Washington political insiders named the National Federation of Independent Business as the fourth most influential lobbying group, and the most powerful business lobby, in national government (Birnbaum 1997, 23). This power is based squarely on activation. NFIB has fifty state offices, but the vital communication within the organization comes from its national headquarters to its 600,000 members, each the proprietor of a small business. The activation strategy is a simple one. Step one involves deciding "which senators and representatives will be the swing votes on the committees charged with [the relevant] issues." Then, NFIB activates "small-business owners who are influential in their states and districts and are willing to deliver a rock-hard message." The final step involves taking the members and aiming them at the legislators (Lewis 1994, A1).

NFIB's membership is organized by its tendency to become active. It is divided into the 400,000 "A" list (members who responded at least once to a direct mail activation), the 200,000 "AA" list (members who responded to more than one direct mail activation), the 40,000 "guardian" list (the most active members) and the 3,000 "key contact" list (members who have close relationships with public officials for grasstops efforts) (Faucheux 1994, 22). Each tier is activated as strategically necessary on particular legislation. Members are also encouraged to perfect their activist skills at federation-sponsored training seminars. NFIB sponsors little public advertising and no protests. These techniques are not efficient, according to Director of Federal Relations Dan Danner, because "our best work comes right from our membership. We are very member-oriented" (Danner 1997).

NFIB maintains a full-time staff of membership recruiters, who, in the manner of a corporate sales force, work particular geographic areas seeking additional members for the organization. NFIB has no chapter organization, so solidary benefits figure little in the decision to join. Although NFIB offers some useful information of selective material benefit for members (on their web page and via publications), the annual $100 dues primarily reward their expressive incentives. Members cast ballots several times a year that set NFIB's policy. Survey research by NFIB staff reveals that members are highly homogeneous in most attitudes concerning economic policy, strongly in favor of smaller government and less regulation. This configuration of uniform, intense attitudes permitted NFIB's recent successes.

The organization played a large role in defeating the Clinton health care reform in 1993–1994 through outside lobbying, targeting their membership with direct mail and phone banks. NFIB and its allies in the health insurance industry turned back an advocacy campaign led by the White House and a sympathetic coalition of trade unions, senior organizations, and consumer groups. Members of Congress in 1995 reported they considered NFIB the second most effective lobby on health care issues, ranking just behind the Health Insurance Association of America (Hansen et al. 1996, 143). NFIB also activated members and their PAC contributed substantial funds in support of Republican congressional candidates in 1994, when the GOP gained control of both the House and Senate (Danner 1997). In early 1995, NFIB lobbied hard for the Contract with America, coordinating their efforts with socially conservative groups like the Christian Coalition and developing strategy in regular meetings with the House Republican leadership. Congressional leaders, like the White House, now regularly encourage interest group activation in order to win major policy battles in Washington. NFIB has the activation savvy to persist as a major player in these fights.

The Sierra Club

The Sierra Club in recent decades has moved from a focus on wilderness trips and educational programs to operation as an important national force in environmental politics. Initially organized by local chapters, the group had only 7,000 members in 1950. Now, Sierra members number over 500,000 and the organization maintains a large Washington headquarters and sponsors lobbying activities in many states. The 1997 *Fortune* survey ranked Sierra as the most effective environmental lobby in Washington (Birnbaum 1997, 23).

In the early 1990s the Sierra Club commissioned a survey of their members to determine how to activate them more effectively. The more traditional inside lobbying practiced by the organization was not as successful as it once had been, and the "distance" between the national organization and its members drew criticism (Sease 1997). Members reported that the organization's staff used too many technical terms and needed to communicate more clearly. Sierra responded by enhancing communication with members and better explaining group policy-making procedures. The organization's web page and frequent mailings keep activist members well acquainted with group activities.

Like NFIB, Sierra stratifies its membership by their degree of political interest and activism. About 15,000 members receive Sierra's political newsletter, *The Planet*. Sierra staff count on this group to attend rallies and protests, contact public officials, and attend other political activities sponsored by the organization. A smaller set of 5,000 members, known as the "core group"—receiving the most activation appeals—include the officers of national, state, and local organizations and the most active volunteer members of the club. Sierra also maintains a "student coalition" of some 10,000 members that are "somewhat active" (Wilson 1997). Although the organization sponsors activism training for interested members, the great majority of members remains largely inactive concerning politics.

Sierra has a smaller proportion of active members than NFIB because individuals join Sierra for a wider variety of reasons. Although members get some merchandise discounts, material incentives seldom draw people to the club. Solidary incentives are quite strong, however. The organization sponsors nature trips for its members. One-fifth of the organization's membership is in California, where the socially oriented Sierra Singles attracts many members (Hamilton 1997). Many also join for expressive reasons, seeking to voice policy concerns about the environment. The governance committee of Sierra's national board of directors has formal authority over the organization's policy direction. Every two years, local chapters complete a questionnaire on issues, which goes to the governance committee to aid in its formulation of the national group agenda. This process, although not formally democratic, does allow local chapters to emphasize issues of great interest to them. Members can vent intense views through a ballot referendum procedure among the membership. If 2,000 members sign in favor of a referendum on an issue, a ballot goes out to all members.

In recent years, Sierra refined its outside lobbying activities. Members are activated through phone and mail on particular issues. Polling and focus groups allow the organization to test messages that might help broaden its base of supporters (Sease 1997). Sierra targets swing congressional races and has a PAC that contributes money to candidates. It also runs "issue advocacy" advertisements to influence congressional elections and the national agenda. One example of particularly efficient targeting involved the clean air regulations in mid-1997. The Environmental Protection Agency proposed stringent new rules that drew the strong opposition of business interests. As the Clinton administration discussed whether or not to back the EPA standards, Sierra spent $1 million in advertising on the issue in New Hampshire and did a "media tour" of the Northeast. Why? Because Vice President Al Gore, usually a friend of Sierra's agenda, would play a large role in the administration's decision. Gore, likely to seek the 2000 presidential nomination by contesting the New Hampshire primary, visited the state often. Thus, New Hampshire voters were a prime target for environmental persuasion. The Sierra effort was called the "Where's Al?" campaign, urging him not to waffle on the new regulations. Gore got the message while visiting New Hampshire. The administration eventually supported the EPA standards.

The American Association of Retired Persons

AARP is the largest membership group in America, with an estimated thirty million members. Why? The benefits it offers to its members are a major reason. In return for a mere five dollars per year, anyone fifty or older can join and receive many selective material benefits. These include group health insurance, specials rates on other forms of insurance, a motor club, a low-fee credit card, discount pharmaceuticals, and a discount card for hotel room and car rentals (Halpert 1997). Thus AARP resembles the "byproduct" group identified by Olson, whose members join for material reasons and not because of the organization's policy agenda (Olson 1965; Johnson 1998, 39–40).

AARP's vast membership is also stratified by level of political activism. National staff report that within the membership, approximately one million identify themselves as particularly interested in political issues. AARP direct-mails to as many as 400,000 activists involved in their various state and national lobbying programs. Its web page contains information on AARP's political agenda. The organization also sponsors activism training for interested members. Still, the proportion of members politically active for AARP is a small fragment of the total membership. AARP is probably able to keep its vast membership because it has no PAC, thus avoiding partisan controversies, and sponsors no protests, a controversial form of political activity among its senior citizen membership. Although members do not vote on policy, the national staff regularly conducts survey research on member preferences and reports those results to its national legislative council, which composes the organization's policy agenda.

Volunteer members make up the legislative council, which is subdivided into policy committees that meet throughout the year. The national staff aids the policy-making process at every stage. The committees spend several months every year redrafting organization policy, which the council as a whole and the organization's board of directors must then approve. Seldom is there great conflict over policy among these bodies. Although member opinions are represented in survey research, at times the organization takes positions contrary to the views of a majority of its members. During the health care reform debate in 1993, AARP endorsed a Canadian-style national health system. A majority of the organization's activists preferred this approach, but less than half of the overall membership did (Donnellan 1997). National staff claim, however, that on most issues, the national policy of the organization is consistent with the opinions of a majority of members.

The 1997 *Fortune* survey ranked AARP as the most effective lobby group in Washington (Birnbaum 1997, 23). AARP played a major role in lobbying for the White House health care reform in 1993–4, an ambitious and risky effort that failed largely because of the able activation tactics of rival groups (West and Loomis 1998, 75–108). Still, the wide geographical reach of AARP's vast membership makes it difficult for legislators to ignore. AARP also has combined outside lobbying and advertising with great strategic skill. Before the 1988 Iowa precinct caucuses, the AARP ran many televised issues ads about long-term health care for the elderly. Active AARP members in the state also received information from the national organization on the issue. One Democratic presidential candidate was so swamped with questions about the issue on the campaign trail that he called the AARP staffperson in charge of volunteer action and asked for AARP to "tell him what to say" about long-term care policy (Donnellan 1997).

The People for the American Way

PFAW, unlike the groups discussed above, is the offspring of a wealthy patron. Norman Lear, a Hollywood television producer, founded PFAW in 1980 and subsidized the organization in its early years as a response to the perceived threat of the religious right. The organization has no formal chapter organization and operates through direct mail with its approximately 250,000 members. It claims to be nonpartisan and has no PAC. Its major issues concern religious freedom, gay and lesbian rights, and freedom of artistic expression. Many of its largest contributors are Hollywood celebrities, including Barbra Streisand and Alec Baldwin.

PFAW offers its members no solidary benefits, because no chapters exist, and material benefits (hats and jackets) of only small value. Membership does provide information that may affect the material circumstances of a few members, but the primary incentive satisfied through membership is an expressive one. The direct mail appeals, couched in dire terms, seek to trigger such motivations among prospective members. PFAW has a carefully conceived direct mail program to maintain members and channel those interested into activist programs of the organization. Approximately 40,000 members belong to a PFAW "action network" that can be activated for outside lobbying. Three to four thousand clergy and some 300 lawyers also are affiliated with their own PFAW activist networks. The lawyers support litigation on behalf of PFAW's causes, and the clergy operate as media spokespersons and grasstops advocates for the group (Montgomery 1997). PFAW also sponsors regular seminars on the arts of activism for interested members, and its web page contains much useful information for the group's activists.

The organization's national board sets policy, assisted by its subcommittee on political advocacy. PFAW members do not vote on the organization's agenda. A 1997 survey of members found, according to national staff, that the group's agenda was very much "in synch" with that of its members. More active members indicated they did "not want to vote in the organization, but rather wanted us to tell them what to do in order to be more effective advocates" (Montgomery 1997). PFAW floods interested members with letters, e-mails, and phone calls to encourage and direct outside lobbying, and they undertake extensive grassroots training with their members. They also research and disseminate information concerning religious right organizations. PFAW's membership peak occurred when they effectively expanded the conflict over a Supreme Court appointment. PFAW ran television ads and stimulated outside lobbying about the proposed appointment of conservative Robert Bork to the Supreme Court in 1987. Bork was defeated, and PFAW was happy to claim responsibility for the victory.

The Christian Coalition

PFAW's much larger rival, the Christian Coalition, also grew from the activities of a wealthy patron. Televangelist Pat Robertson, a candidate for the Republican nomination in 1988, formed the coalition in 1990 with the expressed goal of promoting the conservative Christian agenda to a prominent place in national policy-making. He hired an able young group entrepreneur, Ralph Reed, to build a grassroots organization to pursue political advocacy. Using Robertson's mailing list from 1988 and a small contribution from the Republican Senatorial Committee, Reed began to build membership through direct mail and personal appearances. Using expressive appeals to religious convictions, the organization grew rapidly, from 25,000 in 1990 to 1.7 million by 1997 (Watson 1997, 50–52).

Since religious convictions are intense matters for many conservative Christians, credible expressive appeals well targeted to this segment of society garner impressive results. The coalition's web page and its activism training programs for interested members emphasize its expressive appeals. Direct mail also serves to reinforce the expressive appeal of the organization. During the coalition's first year, a new member received twenty-one direct mail solicitations emphasizing expressive reasons for supporting its efforts (PFAW files 1991). Solidary incentives attract membership as well. Conservative Christians inhabit social networks in which direct, personal recruitment into the coalition often occurs (McKigney 1997). The organization's state and local chapters and sponsorship of summer camps for members' children also satisfy solidary incentives. Local chapters are "groups of like-minded people who meet once a week and are very concerned," according to one former state director (McKigney 1997).

National and state boards direct the agenda and operations of the organization. Most of their decisions, however, involve "tactics, not real departures from any previous agenda. The coalition is very clear about its issues and both the board and membership seems to agree on them" (McKigney 1997). The group claims to not be a partisan organization and has no PAC. Still, it distributed millions of voter guides among conservative churches during the 1992, 1994, 1996, and 1998 elections that listed the issue positions of candidates in a fashion that usually favored Republican candidates. Its tax-exempt status as a nonpartisan organization underwent an ultimately unsuccessful challenge in federal court as a result (Miller and Glasser 1999). State and local chapters have actively contested school board elections, with some success, particularly in the Southeast (Wilcox 1996, 80–82). The organization also sponsors protests and demonstrations on particularly controversial matters, such as at concerts of the rocker Marilyn Manson.

Fortune magazine ranked the coalition as the seventh most effective lobbying organization in Washington (Birnbaum 1997, 3). One reason is its efficient, highly automated telephone system for activating its membership. It works as follows. Executive director Randy Tate first records a plea to his membership, usually about current legislation. The system then sends the recorded message, along with a call list, via modem to personal computers throughout America. Those computers then dial the selected coalition activists, deliver Tate's urgings, and "thus spawn a wave of letter writing and phone calling from thousands of people who have already been trained in political action." This system is "faster than the older and slower boiler-room style operations of the coalition's rivals" (Birnbaum 1997, 25).

The coalition has proven itself adept at outside lobbying. It opposed the 1994 lobby reform bill, fearing that it would restrict its outside lobbying efforts, and activated 250,000 people "to communicate their opposition to Congress using a combination of telephone trees, faxes, computer bulletin boards and talk radio. It did it all in twenty-four hours, and Congress shelved the bill" (Rubin 1997, 191). Similar tactics helped the coalition push many of the provisions of the Contract with America through the House in 1995. The organization also seeks to alter the public agenda through advertising on issues it deems of high priority. In 1998, the group sponsored ads criticizing gay and lesbian lifestyles and claiming that a homosexual orientation can be voluntarily abandoned. Representing controversial issues of high salience to its members, the coalition demonstrates the importance of expressive motivations in the politics of activation.

Large membership organizations, adept at the arts of membership activation, are an enduring part of national politics. Their power issues in large part from their activation capabilities. Corporations and other institutions now seek to emulate their success at outside lobbying. The power of expressive motivations in stimulating activism is evident in four of the five groups described above—only AARP garners members primarily through material incentives. All of the above groups are functionally oligarchic, but not in a way that seems to greatly violate member preferences. Otherwise their membership, fueled by satisfaction of expressive incentives, would decline.

The cases above do not fully capture the complex environment of group activation, however. All of the groups use traditional inside lobbying strategies as well as the outside approaches at which they are particularly adept. All also engage in coalition work with kindred interests on an ad-hoc and permanent basis. Elected politicians in Congress and the White House regularly assemble activation coalitions of sympathetic groups to win legislative and regulatory battles. Spurring targeted segments of the public into action helps to aggregate political resources for the fight. Such tactics can purchase influence efficiently for groups. Unlike political parties, interests need not rule nor aggregate preferences into a governing majority. They, more narrowly, seek to get what they want through inside and outside strategies. Increasingly, the way to do that is to master the arts of activation.

CONCLUSION

Interest activation in governmental politics continues to grow, a triumph of the participatory ethos. Jack Bonner, head of Bonner and Associates, a leading grassroots lobbying firm, argues that the reason for "the magnification of influence of interest groups is the explosion of participatory democracy that is now occurring. As a result of grassroots [activation], members of Congress are paying more attention than ever to what interest groups back home think about the world" (Bonner 1998, 197). The new technology of instantaneous communication makes activation less costly for groups, and activation promotes influence, the coin of the realm for interests. Those with higher education, income, and political knowledge are the grand beneficiaries of this advocacy revolution (Baumgartner and Leech 1998, 123). They are more likely to pursue the satisfaction of expressive goals by joining groups like the National Federation of Independent Business, Sierra Club, or People for the American Way, all of which have affluent and well-educated memberships. They dominate the professional associations so much in evidence in Washington. They direct think tanks, corporations, universities, and other institutions that increasingly use outside lobbying. And the field troops of any activation effort by an organized interest are very likely to have higher income and education than those who are less active.

All this activation creates a dizzying complexity in the national political system. Vast numbers of interests, working in shifting alliances, inhabit numerous and fluid "issue networks" also populated by administrators and legislators (Heclo 1978). On some issues, business groups fight against the agenda of professional associations. In the 1993–4 health care debate, for example, the Health Insurance Association of America (HIAA), representing insurance companies, and the American Medical Association (AMA), representing doctors, battled over many aspects of health care delivery. At times, business organizations form coalitions with citizens' groups to gang up on a rival business. Certain pharmaceutical companies joined with consumer groups to oppose a three-year extension on drug patents provided by implementing legislation for the General Agreement on

Tariffs and Trade (GATT) in order to curb the patent privileges of rival companies (Baumgartner and Leech 1998, 114). In each case, activation strategies proved central to the lobbying efforts.

What does the rise of high-tech activation by interests produce in our national politics? Terry Straub, vice president for public affairs of USX Corporation, identifies four troubling trends. First, policy debates become more extreme as interests activate citizens with dire rhetoric warning of the consequences of inaction. Second, all this activation produces a clogging of demands upon the national government, making it harder for individual groups to be heard and for government officials to make policy. Third, technology makes group demands and appeals immediate. Activation usually works speedily, increasing pressure on governmental decision makers. Finally, the flood of activation produces instability. Alliances shift from issue to issue. In campaigns and lobbying, group activation efforts increase the uncertainty surrounding lawmakers' reelection and policy-making tasks (Straub 1998).

All this trouble would be worth it if frenetic group activation mobilized a majority of citizens to direct the actions of government. Groups instead activate citizens to vote and lobby around narrow, particular agendas that have no necessary relation to majority rule. They do this, according to E. E. Schattschneider, because it is efficient: "there would be no such thing as pressure politics if a short cut to influence had not been invented. Lobbyists long ago discovered that it is possible to get results by procedures that simply ignore the sovereign majority" (Schattschneider 1977, 189). Interest organizations, regardless of their participatory trappings, face no public test of strength in elections and frequently seek to circumvent majority opinion through the use of inside and outside strategies. They advantage

intense opinions much more consistently than representative opinions.

The alternative, according to Schattschneider, is popular mobilization by political parties. Parties, when mobilizing as they did in the
last century, are responsible to the majority because their power
derives from them. They cannot avoid a periodic test of strength in
elections, as can interest organizations. Strong parties also can recon-
cile and aggregate antagonistic interests, lend coherence to government, and educate the public to common, broad political identities
(Ryden 1996, 9). Activation by groups, in contrast, rewards distinct
and intense interests, makes governance more complex and less coherent, and fragments political identities among the public. Interests,
given their narrow purposes, are only interested in activation. It is an
efficient means for pursuing influence. As America's parties weakened
by turning from mobilization to activation, they made both elections
and governance more vulnerable to the problems of rule by organized
interests.

CHAPTER 6

From Activation to Inclusion

Who cares what every adult thinks? It's totally not germane
to this election.

Anonymous campaign strategist, referring to the 1998 elections (Broder and
Edsall 1998)

T he statement above succinctly reveals the disturbing consequences of activation strategies in contemporary American pol
itics. Elections no longer engage or involve most of the public.
Their results determine the direction of national policy much less
than during the strongly partisan era of the last century (Ginsburg
and Shefter 1990). In the past, party elites had to encourage rule by
popular majorities in order to gain power. The dictates of majority
preferences, evident in the partisan verdict of the election, directed
elected officials' actions on policy. Campaign technology required
generic partisan messages, delivered "shotgun" style (Shea 1996, 8).
Conceptually simple and based on personal contact, the message
encouraged great participation from a public with strong and widespread partisan commitments and voting norms. In the partisan era,

despite its corruption, what the public of possible voters thought was totally germane to an election.[1]

In contemporary America, activation is not about majority rule. Parties, interests, and campaigns motivate strategic minorities, often those with unrepresentative and particularly intense attitudes, to vote, call, write, contribute, or demonstrate. Modern communication technology permits finely honed retail messages conveyed efficiently to targeted segments of the public—a "rifle" communication style (Shea 1996, 9). Rifles expend less lead and energy and hit targets more accurately than shotguns. That's why everyone in politics uses them today. Their careful aim targets the few and misses the majority of citizens.

CHANGING ELECTORAL RULES OR CHANGING POLICY?

How can we broaden political appeals to engage more citizens? This chapter identifies reforms more and less useful to this end. We must first sketch out the largest implications of the problems meriting reform. With the explosion of activation strategies has come party decay and a proliferation of interest organizations. Despite incessant and increasing activation efforts by interests, the "party of nonvoters" (Burnham 1982, 153) has grown enormously in recent decades. At the

1. Of course, the electorate during the partisan era of the late nineteenth century was restricted to white males at least twenty-one years of age. They constituted the public of all possible voters. The point here is that they figured much more prominently in the calculations of politicians then than the public of all possible voters does today. Why? Because partisan mobilization stimulated a much larger proportion of possible voters to visit the polls than are so stimulated by today's finely tuned activation strategies.

root of all these phenomena are two major forces: changes in the operation of domestic policy and in the rules of electoral competition. National government moved major economic concerns onto "automatic pilot" through entitlements and other automatic spending programs. As the delivery of economic benefits became more bureaucratized, the public looked less to parties for assistance with their material needs. Parties came to matter less on vital domestic policies as the twentieth century wore on. In tandem with a loss of policy control, parties also lost control of elections with the advent of the progressive reforms.

Walter Dean Burnham, a prominent scholar of elections, argues that renewing mass participation requires a transformation of both national policy and national election rules. A new, social democratic party rooted in the economic agenda of the working class can reintroduce the millions of lower-income citizens to the polling booths (Burnham 1982, 311). Such a claim is more ideological than empirical. One can question whether lower-income citizens will respond primarily to a class-based message. It is true that class-based partisan mobilization helped to democratize western European countries in the late nineteenth and early twentieth century and has contributed to the persistence of high voter turnouts in these nations. Although class proved a strong fulcrum for partisan mobilization in Europe's relatively homogeneous, industrializing countries, America's situation today is vastly different. Our economy and cultural makeup are much more diverse and complex than those of any European nation during the nineteenth century. Class consciousness is much less pronounced here, and the rise of racial and cultural issues in recent decades makes the credibility of a class-based appeal increasingly problematic. Such an appeal would have to convince millions of ill-educated, poorly informed citizens of the need to participate in order to achieve some abstract policy goals. The costs of the effort are huge; the likely benefits at best unclear.

Changing the national policy agenda might well enhance participation, but not in the way Burnham thinks. John Coleman (1996a) argues that the automatic economic policies of the "fiscal state" have made parties irrelevant to the material welfare of most citizens. Hence, party labels and party competition matter less to them. Parties might recover if Congress took more discretionary control over domestic economic programs—such as unemployment compensation, Social Security, Medicare, and other entitlements—and the parties voiced differing approaches on how to manage them. Then partisan conflict and mobilization might revive around the raised economic stakes of party competition.

This is unlikely to happen. Congressional politicians of both parties find it advisable to leave automatic benefits programs undisturbed, for fear of electoral retribution that might result from controversies surrounding a more active management of them. Social Security still deserves its reputation as the third rail of American politics. A more hands-on approach by Congress involves large uncertainties for legislators and great potential electoral risks, should accidents and bad management occur. Getting more citizens riled up and voting about such issues is an incumbent's nightmare in an age of activation.

Increasing Congress's discretionary role over economic policies that are currently automatic will also probably produce bad policy results. Many programs were made into entitlements for sound policy reasons. Unemployment compensation is immediately available during economic downturns; automatic Social Security and Medicare payments allow millions of citizens to plan their retirements intelligently. Without such automatic features, many Americans would have to depend on the forecasting skills of elected politicians from year to year to get their benefits. Potential recipients also would have to engage in an annual political tug-of-war to get those benefits. Should the legislature prove shortsighted, corrupt, or politically cowed by spending politics, the livelihoods of millions of Americans could be at stake. Government failure on this scale could stoke public alienation and lead to more empty polling booths, not fewer. If greater material security for vulnerable citizens weakens political parties, that is a price well worth paying.

The world of policy thus holds little hope as an antidote to the politics of activation. No working-class parties or sweeping increases in congressional discretion over domestic policy are likely soon. If we are to involve the public in elections and governance on a broader scale, the answer must lie in altering the laws regulating activation in elections and in governance. As Burnham argues, "electoral law makes a difference" (1982, 155). Legal reforms will fail, however, unless they are rooted in a careful understanding of the incentives that produced the politics of activation. Costs for popular participation must be lowered and parties, groups, and campaigns must perceive greater benefits in broader-scale activation. The potential benefit of such changes is great. Expanded incentives for inclusion can make elections more consequential to governing. Many of the "usual suspects" mentioned as constructive reforms, however, do little to expand incentives for inclusion. By reexamining the origins of activation strategies, we can identify reforms that might bring the public back into electoral politics.

ACTIVATION'S IMPLICATIONS

The roots of activation lie in the progressive assault on party rule at the end of the last century. Progressives effectively instituted laws that demobilized the public. Martin Shefter defines demobilizing measures as "reforms that effectively disenfranchise the voters who are likely to support their [progressives'] opponents, or ... bureaucratic reforms that deprive incumbents of the resources they use to link themselves to a mass base" (Shefter 1994, 96). Voluntary personal registration, civil service reform, and banning party-column ballots proved effective demobilizers. The creation of state and federal bureaucracies further curbed parties through a strategy of circumvention, defined by Shefter as "outflanking incumbent politicians by establishing executive agencies that stand outside the domain of electoral and party politics, and provide the reformers with privileged access" (Shefter 1994, 96). As bureaucrats delivered material benefits to citizens previously dispensed by parties, the importance of parties inevitably shrank.

Primary elections led to more individualistic campaigns, and postwar America witnessed a proliferation of interest groups and movements all seeking to use the public to press their agendas. American politics, in Alan Ware's terms, became less partisan and more "individualistic" (Ware 1988, 61–62). Candidates ran as individuals and voters increasingly preferred to choose candidates rather than parties when voting. Interest groups segmented the public through appeals to narrow agendas via advertising and direct mail. Functions long performed by parties—to aggregate antagonistic interests, lend collective coherence to government, and educate the public on their common identities—gradually decayed (Ryden 1996, 9).

Individualistic democracy places undue burdens on citizens and makes majority rule more difficult. Our electoral system is remarkably complex, requiring choices among many candidates and offices and verdicts about referenda issues. Knowledgeable voting, absent a strong party cue, becomes a heavy burden successfully accomplished by a relative few. Turnout declines as a result. Ware rightly argues that "one of the flaws in a view of democracy which values individual, rather than party, representation is that it assumes voters will have sufficient information on which to base their decisions" (Ware 1988, 61–62). This assumption doesn't suit contemporary America. Parties, interests, and candidates seek first to prevail in elections or over policy, not to inform. "Elites, enmeshed in a political battle of win or lose, have little incentive to encourage informed and systematic citizen evaluation of political phenomena" (Kuklinski et al. 1993, 244). Modern technology produces mountains of information, but no political institutions consistently attempt to make it widely understood by the public. Parties during the last century had a strong incentive to clarify and simplify the major issues at election time so that most of the public could grasp the party message. Today, such an approach is inefficient and needlessly expensive. Activation of targeted segments of the public through carefully tailored activation messages has replaced it.

The explosion of information and communications technology aggravates the knowledge gap within the public. Access to computers, cable television, and other information services stratifies by income and education (Delli Carpini and Keeter 1996, 273). Information is a fuel for activation. As access to information varies, so will the likelihood that one is subject to activation messages. Technology and activation in tandem need not result in the dispersion of necessary political knowledge among all citizens. Instead, America's increasing information stratification shrinks the number of productive targets for activation to an elite minority. E. E. Schattschneider, writing decades ago, argued that expanding the arena of conflict around an issue would make policy-making more responsive to the public (Schattschneider 1977, 20–43). Thanks to the growth of activation technologies, that is no longer the case. Interests can activate millions seeking to alter policy, but those millions are not necessarily representative of broader public opinion. Hence, today "conflict expansion does not necessarily redound to the benefit of the public" (West and Loomis 1998, 43–44).

Our current participatory ethos does nothing to ameliorate the problem of shrinking public involvement in elections. "An emphasis on participation faces the enduring problem that because of the multiple demands on citizens, many of which are more pressing than politics, participation is likely to be sporadic, at least partially informed, and unrepresentative in character" (Pomper 1992, 136). Since time is increasingly precious for citizens, nonparticipation in elections is increasingly rational.

Direct democracy as practiced "turns out to be a true paradise for active, usually very small, minorities" (Sartori 1987, 226). Our political system has become steadily less user-friendly for those without higher education, interest, and personal efficacy. In this context, the current participatory ethos furthers rule by an elite minority with particular and often unrepresentative issue agendas.

David Broder identified three problems resulting from low participation in elections. First, with low turnout, "it is the most motivated—and militant—elements at the edges of the ideological spectrum" who receive the most attention. Second, reduced turnout contributes to "shrinkage of the financial base" for candidates, enhancing the elite and extreme skew of that form of participation. Third, low turnout produces representative distortion: the young, the poor, and the nonwhite are less likely to vote and have their preferences influence the political system (Broder 1997, A19). Proponents of participatory democracy would solve these problems with a call to organize those at the margins of our political system. This is a futile approach, according to Sidney Verba, Kay Lehman Schlozman, and Henry Brady, authors of a major empirical study of political participation (1995). To them, "the cure contains the seeds of the malady . . . the participatory benefits of organizational activity are being reaped by those who are already politically involved" (Verba, Schlozman, and Brady 1997, 78). The political system is already quite crowded with groups pressing demands on government, and those groups usually include relatively elite individuals (see chapter 4). The costs of organizing the marginalized are quite high, and the benefit of their organization, given the organizational proliferation and crowding in our politics, is quite low.

The least costly form of participation is voting, but as turnout has declined, "individually motivated" forms of participation—those most evidencing an elite skew—have risen (Inglehart 1997a, 235). This contradicts the division of labor designed into the representative institutions of local, state, and national government. When voting ably aggregates popular preferences into a coherent, partisan electoral verdict, representative deliberation reflects majority preferences. But when the public increasingly abandons elections and parties for more "direct" forms of participation, the linkage between the majority's views and government policy frays. Increasingly, elections and governing reflect not a majority verdict, but a host of minority voices energized through activation. Popular government in America is on the wane. To restore it, we must identify the best features of the old partisan order and restore them to our politics.

THE BEST OF THE OLD ORDER

It's easy to identify those features of the partisan era that should never return: graft, a distorted partisan press, election fraud, abuses of patronage, coercive public voting. Other, less troubling aspects of the partisan era are gone, however, and probably will not return. Theda Skocpol notes that from the 1870s to the 1890s, intense party competition encouraged the formation of interest groups that learned from the model of partisan mobilization (Skocpol 1996, 24). Today, groups infest all locations on the political spectrum and often ignore partisan cleavages and conflict. During the partisan era, the parties resembled "two opposing armies arrayed against each other in more or less close formation; politics today is an altogether messier affair, with large numbers of small detachments engaged over a vast territory, and with individuals and groups frequently changing sides" (King 1978, 372). Then, parties were more powerful than groups and more central to the operation of the political system.

Several features of the partisan era are needed today. The American political system was more inclusive and election-centered during that time. Partisan messages reached all eligible voters in a fashion unfathomable in our current era of activation. The message was simple, based on a partisan label, and usually personally delivered, making it memorable. Partisan identification and voting norms were far stronger. Restoring partisanship and voting norms is a mighty project, one best achieved over decades. Still, we need to create incentives for parties, candidates, and groups to develop more inclusive messages. Only then will our electorate grow in size.

Elections stood more at the center of our politics during the partisan era because they required simple choices and were decisive in their results. Voters picked a party, one party won, and then ruled. Although the coercive public voting of the last century will not and should not return, we can certainly find ways to make our baroque electoral structure simpler and more comprehensible to more citizens. Government will better reflect the public will when we increase the number of voters and make elections simpler and more decisive. Verba, Schlozman, and Brady find that voting has the least representational distortion of any form of participation (1995, 468). By making it politically profitable for parties, interests, and candidates to maximize electoral participation, we encourage more representative elections and government. Some political scientists argue that strengthening the political parties is vital to this cause.

PARTY RENEWAL?

Advocates of party renewal admire the mobilization of the partisan era and seek to restore it through a variety of reforms. Before considering these proposals, recall what party renewal might entail. During the partisan era, political parties satisfied all of Alan Ware's criteria for party strength: the party organization chose candidates, decided the election agenda, had dominant control of electoral resources, and influenced governmental appointments after the election (Ware 1988, x). With these powers, parties produced inclusive appeals and elections determined much governmental policy. Restoring these powers is a tall order.

The many obstacles parties encounter in our present political system make this a huge task. Structurally, party organizations don't control nominations, and patronage has withered. The public is increasingly indifferent to parties (Wattenberg 1996, 167). The policy environment is complex and not sharply delineated by issues controlled by the congressional parties. Currently, national politicians are groping for an "organizing framework" for each party, and "the grounds for future party competition remain unclear" (Coleman 1996a, 206). Parties also confront many competitors that have taken over many of their traditional functions. Bureaucracies and individual legislators deliver constituent services earlier distributed by party bosses. Campaign consultants provide electoral services that were formerly the domain of the parties. Interest organizations, independent of the parties, provide money and campaign assistance to candidates. Between elections, interests incessantly activate segments of the public to influence policy, competing with (and often superceding) the wishes of party leaders and organizations. The media disseminates political information formerly spread by local party officials and a more partisan press (Goldman 1996, 32–34).

The Committee for Party Renewal of the American Political Science Association proposes several reforms to overcome the many impediments to party strength listed above. They advocate (1) substantially increasing the limit on hard money contributions by individuals to political parties from its current level of $20,000, (2) allowing individuals to give more money to parties than to candidates, (3) permitting parties to give unlimited campaign contributions to candidates through existing party committees, (4) providing full public disclosure of all party contributions and expenditures, (5) mandating substantial free television time for parties to speak on behalf of themselves and their candidates, and (6) giving parties sole sponsorship of party debates (White 1995, 12).

Each of these proposals will enhance the power of parties, but the cumulative transformation resulting from their adoption is likely to be, at most, incremental. Increasing individual contributions may encourage more hard money funding of parties, but the candidate-centered structure of our elections insures that most funds will continue to go to candidates. Raising the permissible level of hard money party contributions to candidates also does nothing to alter candidates' independence. They will continue to win nominations on their own, and voters show no signs of an increased disposition toward party voting. The explosion of soft money spending in 1996 made parties more important "subcontractors" of consultants and advertising, but candidates won or lost as individuals and voters prefer to view them that way. Free television time would drastically alter party power in elections only if the *only* time available was free time. Under this proposal, however, candidates will remain able to purchase their own ad time and parties will find it most efficient to use their free time allocations in the service of individual candidates. Why? Because the voters choose individual candidates, not parties, and successful advertising must address the world as the voters see it. Touting parties will not move voters. The party that does so will suffer a competitive disadvantage in elections. Still, free air time would increase party power in elections a bit by giving parties some additional control over a valuable technology. Party sponsorship of debates, however, makes little difference in electoral politics. With the exception of presidential debates, few voters pay attention to debates, preferring to get their information about candidates elsewhere, usually from advertising.

Many obstacles to party power are not addressed by these reforms. The individualistic nomination process remains. Parties receive no additional power of appointments in government. The reforms promise no change in a policy environment that is antithetical to party control over policy. The many competitors of parties—bureaucracies, interest groups, entrepreneurial consultants, and the media—are not challenged at all by these reforms. Still, one can hope that by increasing party power marginally, as these reforms would, voters might find parties more important and begin to choose between them more than they now do. True party renewal, however, becomes likely only when broader structural changes in elections, discussed later in this chapter, accompany these reforms.

RECENT REFORM MEASURES

Reforming campaign spending and interest group activities have been hot topics in Washington during the 1990s. There are constitutional limits, however, to what reformers can do to curb interest activation. Groups' rights to recruit members, persuade the public, and mobilize the grassroots to influence government all involve the expressive freedoms of the First Amendment. As Madison lamented, "liberty is to faction what air is to fire" (Madison 1961, 78). Given this situation, disclosure becomes the primary reform option. Congress pursued it in 1995 when it passed the Lobbying Disclosure Act. The first major lobbying reform in several decades, the act increased regulation of group advocacy in several ways. All lobbyists who expect to receive more than $5,000 or spend more than $20,000 over a six-month period must register and report on their activities. They must disclose the issues they lobbied on, the governmental offices contacted, the lobbyists involved, and the involvement of foreign entities (companies or governments) (Hrebnar 1997, 280). Conspicuously absent from reporting requirements, however, are the grassroots activities of interest groups and reporting requirements for religious groups. Efforts to include these provisions had doomed the bill in 1994, due to intense group lobbying. Reports filed during the first half of 1997 revealed that groups spent at an annual rate of $1.2 billion in their efforts to influence national government (McAllister 1998, A13). Such information can at least inform us of the scale of group activation efforts before government.

While groups flex their muscles, the current debate over campaign finance reform reveals the weakness of parties in our national politics. Much ink has been spilled and effort expended in recent years decrying the state of national campaign finance law and proposing reforms of it. Political scientist Gerald Pomper summarizes the reformist consensus: "The purpose of campaign finance reform should be to limit contributions from dubious sources and to promote a fair and relatively equal fight between major candidates" (Pomper 1997, 1). These are desirable goals, but they do not address the problems resulting from the rise of activation strategies. We can eliminate dubious financing and encourage competitive races, all the while relying on activation strategies that have developed in recent decades. Clean funding and competitive races do nothing to alter the narrow targeting of our candidate-centered politics, nor do they affect the activation imperatives of interest organizations.

The most popular campaign finance reform bills of 1998 exhibit these shortcomings. The House passed the Shays-Meehan campaign finance bill in the summer of 1998, and a majority of senators supported the McCain-Feingold reform bill, although a filibuster ended its consideration on the Senate floor. To their credit, both bills placed unregulated, interest group "issue advocacy" advertising under the contribution and disclosure provisions of federal election law. This would transform the ads into independent expenditures that interests must fund with hard money—contributions in amounts are limited by law and with publicly disclosed sources. Neither the sources nor the amounts of issue advocacy spending are now legally regulated.

The two bills, however, do nothing to alter our system's reliance on activation strategies. Instead, they actually weaken political parties. Both would totally ban soft money contributions to political parties, curtailing party power in elections by greatly reducing parties' financial resources. McCain-Feingold cushions the blow only slightly by raising the hard money limit for individual contributions to state parties from $5,000 to $10,000 and raising the total amount an individual can contribute in hard money to parties, PACs, and candidates from $25,000 to $30,000.

It is possible to curb the excesses of soft money contributions without crippling the parties' financial bases. Soft money contributions should be more thoroughly reported and speedily disclosed to the public. The currently unlimited soft money contributions from individuals could be capped at a level that does not greatly harm parties, perhaps at $25,000 to $50,000 per year. Still, one can overstate the harm done by these bills. Curtailing party money does marginally weaken them in our electoral system, but parties already face many structural limits and numerous competitors. As the "party renewal" proposals will not greatly strengthen parties, the campaign finance reform bills will not weaken them terrifically. If partisan mobilization is our goal, however, the bills do head in the wrong direction. Under Shays-Meehan and McCain-Feingold, activation will continue unimpeded, but parties will play an even smaller role in its execution.

A more ambitious proposal long advocated by reform groups such as Common Cause and Public Citizen involves public financing of congressional elections (Sabato 1989, 56–65). The specifics of such proposals vary, some providing total public funding to candidates in return for their agreeing to expenditure limits. Others propose implementing a variant of the partial public financing for candidates seeking presidential nominations. In such plans, candidates would get public matching of small contributions in return for an overall spending limit. Any public funding plans have to be voluntary, since the Supreme Court in *Buckley v. Valeo* 96 S.Ct. 612 (1976) allowed candidates to spend unlimited personal funds in campaigns. Public funding plans might produce elections that are more competitive and outlaw dubious contributions, but they do not discourage activation as it is currently practiced. Instead, the spending limits they place upon candidates might make the electoral activities of interests more important in election outcomes, thus further empowering intense and often unrepresentative minorities. Also, these reform plans, by giving money directly to candidates, bypass parties and further weaken party power in elections. One must look beyond recent reform proposals for solutions to the problems of activation.

THE EXPERIENCE OF OTHER NATIONS

Bypassing the conventional wisdom of reformers permits us to find ways to make American elections inclusive, as they were long ago. Fortunately, the experiences of other constitutional democracies provide a natural laboratory in which we can assess the effects of differing political arrangements upon popular mobilization. Most long-established democracies have far higher turnout rates in national elections and electoral rules and procedures that differ from America's.

Examining how elections operate elsewhere provides valuable instruction about useful reforms.

In stark contrast to the United States is the island of Malta, a small nation that consistently has the highest electoral turnout in the world. More than 95 percent of Maltese voters turn out for national elections (Hirczy 1995, 255). How does Malta do it? Unlike in America, the national government takes responsibility for registering all possible Maltese voters. Moreover, Maltese elections involve a simple and decisive choice. National elections choose a unicameral House of Representatives, with power over all subordinate jurisdictions—Malta has no federalism. A two-party tradition, based on long-standing class divisions, pits the Nationalists against Labor. Most Maltese choose between only the two major parties, not among a blizzard of individualistic candidates. Maltese do not vote for myriad offices and on multiple referenda, as normally occurs in the United States. Thus, the costs of choice are lower for voters in Malta than in America. The simplicity of the choices presented to the Maltese also produces the benefit of a decisive result.

Malta uses a single transferable vote (STV) balloting procedure for electing its representatives, another reason for the big turnouts. This procedure allows voters to rank candidates in order of preference. Candidates are then chosen in multimember districts. On election night, a "quota" for election in each district is established by totaling the number of votes and dividing it by the number of seats. The first-preference votes are then counted. Any candidates hitting the quota are then elected, and any surplus votes beyond the quota are allocated among the remaining candidates. This process continues until all seats in the multimember district are filled. If no candidate receives the necessary quota of votes, the lowest finisher is eliminated and his or her second preferences are then allocated. STV stimulates extensive mobilization of the electorate by parties and candidates. Why? Every vote counts toward filling the seats in the legislature. None are wasted, since anyone's list of preferences could determine which candidates win. This produces a strong incentive for parties and candidates to seek out every possible supporter, wherever they may be (Hirczy 1995, 261). Maltese elections involve partisan rallies of the sort found all over America in the 1870s and much straight ticket voting. The majority party rules the legislature and therefore, the government. Since every vote counts, candidates and parties get everyone out to the polls. In Malta, party voting and party loyalty produce clear, decisive, and representative electoral results.

The United States differs greatly from Malta, and these differences demonstrate many shortcomings of American politics. Almost one-third of Americans remains totally outside of the electoral system because they are not registered. Among those registered, interest in political parties has shrunk and levels of political interest and efficacy vary greatly. Voters must choose between a dizzying array of candidates, offices, and referenda. Elections are complex and seldom decisive concerning our national direction, given the prevalence of divided government, the separation of powers, and federalism. Our single-member districts produce many "wasted" votes in elections, particularly in landslides. Candidates and parties do not find that every vote counts. Low turnouts are common in districts strongly populated by partisans of one party. Those who are registered aren't consulted. The arts of activation make it possible to rule with far less than majority support among the adult citizenry.

Malta has limited utility as an example for the United States, a vastly larger nation with very different demographic characteristics, political institutions, and cultural traditions. Still, many other democracies share some of Malta's electoral traits, and just about all of them have higher turnouts than America. Although only Ireland has the STV, parliamentarism and universal registration are widespread. America's electoral system is as complex as any in the world. The United States is also the only major constitutional democracy in the world, besides France, in which registration is the responsibility of the individual (Katz 1997, 234–35). Australia also makes registration an individual responsibility but requires mandatory voting—as do Belgium, Greece, and eight other nations. Party-dominated elections, Maltese style, are found in many other democracies. The electoral role of parties in the United States is distinctively weak: "The rule in most democratic countries is that the great bulk of political money is party money, raised by the parties, administered by them and spent by them. But yet again, the exception is the United States, where individual officeholders and candidates are their own principal fundraisers" (King 1997, 71).

Our "user unfriendly" electoral system helps to explain why Americans "surpass Europeans in virtually every form of political perspective and activity that would seem to provide a motivational foundation for voting" but have turnouts far below the European norm of 65 to 80 percent (Wolfinger, Glass, and Squire 1990, 557). Since, however, "no nation can approach the United States in the frequency and variety of elections" (Crewe 1981, 232), the incessant demands placed upon voters serve to shrink turnout in any given election. Robert Jackman and Ross Miller, in a study of turnout in twenty democracies, found that the frequency of elections depressed turnouts across nations, controlling for other cultural, political, and electoral structure variables. The authors concluded "the distinctively high volume of elections" in America "depresses turnout by encouraging voter fatigue" (Jackman and Miller 1995, 483).

Another large impediment to participation is our registration requirements. The "motor voter" legislation passed by Congress in 1993 made voluntary registration easier by permitting it in a variety of government offices—including driver's license bureaus—heavily frequented by the public; but it expanded the registration rolls only modestly (an estimated 3 percent) and did nothing to stem declining turnout in 1994 and 1996 ("Low Voter Turnout Expected" 1996). Additional reforms might have more impact. Peverill Squire, Raymond Wolfinger, and David Glass estimate that merely eliminating the need to reregister once one moves would increase turnout in American elections by 9 percent (1987, 56). G. Bingham Powell projects that automatic registration would boost American turnout by 14 percent (1986, 35). Although automatic registration would raise turnout, and higher turnout would expand the scope of activation efforts, a substantial portion of adults—perhaps more than a third—would remain poor targets for activation under this reform. Its effect, although salutary, would prove incremental. Targeting would still pay, and activation would remain quite selective.

A more audacious change involves compulsory voting. Jackman and Miller find such laws causally significant in stimulating turnout in twenty democracies (1995, 481). Such laws also might change the rational calculations of citizens. Currently, political ignorance is viewed by many citizens as cost-free. They need not participate, so the incentive to gather political information, among those of low education and efficacy, is very small. A study by Stacy Gordon and Gary Segura revealed that compulsory voting laws had a causally significant influence in stimulating the political sophistication among a sample of 8,963 respondents in twelve democracies, even when controlling for individual and system structure variables (1997, 140). Why? "Nonvoters have little incentive to accumulate information. Driving those individuals to the ballot box certainly will not spur all of them to gather the requisite information. But, ceteris paribus, we should expect that at least a few of those who otherwise would gather no political information will choose to gather some. And this effect, of course, is absent in countries without compulsory voting laws" (Gordon and Segura 1997, 132). Compulsory voting in America could increase the electorate and its political sophistication. The following section assesses which incremental and more far-reaching reforms might best curb the shortcomings of the United States' ubiquitous activation.

LARGE AND SMALL CHANGES

Making popular politics in America more inclusive is a huge challenge. Successful reforms must overcome the many structural impediments to popular participation and party strength: primaries, voluntary personal registration, complex ballots, and frequent elections. Other challenges to inclusive politics are also well-entrenched: the many competitors to parties (bureaucracies, consultants, interests, and the media) and lack of public interest in parties. All this suggests that strengthening parties will prove difficult and probably won't do much more than alter popular politics incrementally for the better. Ultimately, we cannot revive the party mobilization of 1876–1892. Our electoral structure, political organizations, and popular attitudes have changed so much that we cannot realistically hope to resurrect electoral institutions of a century ago.

A more achievable and productive approach involves strengthening incentives for candidates, parties, and interests to maximize popular participation in elections. That will produce more elaborate, but ultimately more inclusive activation strategies. America should follow the example of almost all constitutional democracies and make accurate registration of voters a governmental responsibility. This reform would immediately enroll the almost one-third of the adult population not registered, lowering their costs of participation and making them more likely targets for activation strategies (Wolfinger, Glass, and Squire 1990, 966). The national government can take over the registration duties, or require it of states. In addition, each citizen should receive notice of the election and polling place via mail within a week prior to the actual voting, as is the practice in Sweden.

An even more effective, if controversial, method of expanding the scope of activation involves mandatory voting. Our individualistic culture may well reject this as too coercive, but its benefits are substantial. Mandatory voting promises to increase voter turnout and to stimulate political sophistication among the public. Admittedly, some additional uninformed voting will occur. The more frequently new voters go to the polls, however, the more useful they will find political information in discharging a mandatory duty. As Gordon and Segura (1997) discovered, the incentive for gaining knowledge increased under mandatory voting laws. If people want more information, they will get it, since parties, groups, and candidates will find benefits in searching widely to reach practically every adult. Parties, groups, and candidates also will find it efficient to simplify their activation messages and spread them broadly, because activation will become more expensive, advantaging economies of scale. Perhaps general messages of the sort dominant during the partisan era might return to our popular politics. Parties, properly strengthened, could serve as the best conveyors of broad, wholesale messages. They did it well in the past.

Reforms to strengthen parties are useful ancillaries to measures that expand the electorate. We might try to restore the partisan era by abolishing the direct primary and reinstituting the partisan ballot. Abolishing primaries will restore the nomination power to party conventions, which supposedly will help parties to mobilize voters as they did in days of old. Eliminating primaries, however, holds much less promise than restoring the partisan ballot. Direct primaries did accelerate the demise of strong party organizations, but it is far from clear that abolishing them will restore parties to their electoral preeminence. Nominations during the partisan era occurred in caucuses and conventions dominated by professional politicians who sought electoral victory in order to achieve their primary political goal, the pursuit of material gain. Today, elite activists motivated by ideological incentives dominate party caucuses and conventions. It is difficult to imagine them providing slates of nominees that would prove broadly appealing to the electorate. Rather, each party would tend more toward its activist extremes, furthering the downward spiral of popular alienation.

The party ballot, in contrast, could be a key to a more inclusive electoral politics. It would force voters to choose between party slates, not individual candidates, in the polling booth. This would encourage parties to consider the electability and issue coherence of their entire slate and discourage individualistic candidate campaigns. Parties might then return to the center of electoral competition. Would the party voting resulting from this reform encourage parties to move beyond activation strategies? That remains uncertain. At minimum, party appeals would return, creating fewer and simpler campaign messages in our electoral politics that might lower information costs for nonvoters and encourage them to return to the electoral arena. Should this happen, inclusive partisan mobilization might actually develop. Adoption of partisan ballots and mandatory voting, however, seems unlikely anytime soon. The candidates and interests dominating the individualistic electoral politics of activation will strongly oppose it.

Other, more incremental reforms might also strengthen parties and prepare the way for a return to mobilization. Parties must be better funded. The Shays-Meehan and McCain-Feingold approach of banning soft money would prove greatly counterproductive. Instead, we need to make it "easier for ordinary citizens [and interests] to give money to the parties" and "easier for the parties to give money to their candidates" (King 1997, 186). Restricting soft money contributions to $50,000 per person and quick disclosure of their origin and how they were spent will make party campaign finance more accountable without weakening parties. All limits on party committee contributions to individual candidates should be lifted. Parties could even be granted several hours of free television time to use in an election on every federally licensed station. This reform probably won't change candidate-centered activation messages during elections, but at least it would increase party power in the electoral process. By altering national laws on television licensing and state and national laws on campaign finance in these ways, parties may become the more likely conveyors of shotgun-style messages to a much expanded group of voters.

Another change in the electoral system would increase the partisan flavor of national elections, one requiring many states to amend their laws. Currently, every state but Maine and Nebraska apportions their

Electoral College votes in a winner-take-all fashion (Wayne 1996, 310). Maine and Nebraska, however, allocate votes by congressional district, granting one vote to the presidential candidate who wins the district and two bonus votes for the statewide winner. This district system, if adopted by every state, could enhance the role of parties in elections. House candidates and presidential candidates of the same party would find a common cause in securing victory in individual House districts. Sharing a more common electoral fate would make common partisan cause between House and presidential candidates more likely. A shared incentive for victory could also encourage a uniform partisan message in elections.

The above proposals have their shortcomings. They assume that the rest of the electoral status quo will continue unchanged. Elections would be more manageable for voters and produce more decisive results without primaries, referenda, and long, complex ballots. Unfortunately, all seem to be here to stay. It also seems unlikely that parties will erode the control bureaucracies and chief executives now have over public policy. Fewer elections with simpler and clearer choices—provided through shorter ballots and stronger parties with more control over policy—would strengthen popular control over government. Further, most elected officeholders will receive these reforms very coolly. Individualistic politicians may well find few incentives to expand the electorate. It makes campaign activation more difficult and encourages them to work more closely with their parties. By increasing turnout, however, we can both make elections more important and bolster party power.

Interests or, as Madison termed them, "factions" will always be with us. They have no incentive to expand the electorate or to develop inclusive messages in the present system. As Schattschneider argued, interests seek to get results efficiently, often in ways that "ignore the sovereign majority" (1977, 189). The reforms discussed above might alter interest behavior, perhaps encouraging them to devote some resources to more inclusive and partisan messages. We can, in any event, better regulate what interests do. The Lobbying Disclosure Act of 1995 helps in this regard. The provision in Shays-Meehan and McCain-Feingold requiring that interests fund "issue advocacy" spending through limited, hard money contributions and disclose these ad expenditures expeditiously is much needed. Interest organizations have the constitutional right to recruit members, persuade the public, and mobilize their grassroots for lobbying. Our best interest group reform is full and speedy disclosure.

Activation in our politics is likely to stay. Americans probably will never again march in partisan rallies, read a partisan press, and live in homogeneously partisan neighborhoods to the degree they did from 1876 to 1892. The partisan mobilization as practiced in that era will remain a historical phenomenon, one with important lessons for the failures of today's popular politics. Successful reform can grow only from a thorough understanding of the many structural, behavioral, and technological forces that created our current politics of activation. It remains possible to mobilize most citizens for participation in national elections that prove decisive for the course of government. We can do it by expanding the targets for activation to the entire adult population and by giving parties a stronger role in electoral activation. Only then can activation be transformed into a method of inclusion, not exclusion.

Some would argue that such sweeping change is impossible in the current political environment. However, the new institutionalism in political science, which holds that institutional operations derive from the rational choices of individuals involved in them, helps us understand the benefits of such change. According to this approach, institutional rules result from the rational choices of political actors and help to shape such choices. A major lesson of the new institutionalism is that changing formal procedures—such as election laws—produces lasting changes in political behavior. Without the direct primary and the demise of the partisan ballot, our individualistic politics would not have evolved as it did. The proper remedy to our politics must be structural. The right structural changes can create and maintain a much more inclusive popular politics. Mandatory voting laws hold great promise in creating this result. Short of this, the return of the party ballot, universal registration, and more modest party-strengthening measures can encourage electoral inclusiveness.

The ultimate barrier to such reforms lies not in current electoral laws but in the theory of participation that supports them. It is true that progressive reforms did create new participatory venues for the public—the direct primary, initiatives, referenda, and recalls. The abolition of the partisan ballot gave voters more choices among individual candidates. These participatory reforms, however, destroyed the inclusive electoral role of political parties and made possible the current politics of activation. The widespread contemporary belief that "the more participation, the better" is simply wrong. More participation is not always better for American democracy. Some forms of participation, particularly those fostered by the progressive reforms, served to advantage activist elites and interests while pushing millions of citizens to the margins of electoral politics. In contrast, appropriate participatory reforms will lower the costs of participation for all potential voters. This is the great virtue of the electoral procedures of the admittedly flawed partisan era of our past. We must learn this lesson again, by making voting simpler (lowering costs) and more conclusive for government through party rule (increasing the policy benefits of voting).

Activation ultimately remains a means, not an end. It currently operates to empower minorities but marginalize millions. A fresh form of partisan mobilization is possible, however, by employing many of the state-of-the-art techniques of activation. By changing laws to create the right incentives, we can resurrect a more inclusive politics. We can encourage parties, interests, and campaigns to take every citizen seriously. It happens in other constitutional democracies. Why can't it happen here?

Bibliography

Aldrich, John H. 1995. *Why Parties? The Origin and Transformation of Party Politics in America.* Chicago: University of Chicago Press.

Ammerman, Nancy Tatom. 1987. *Bible Believers: Fundamentalists in the Modern World.* New Brunswick, N.J.: Rutgers University Press.

"An Exclusive C&E Survey of America's Political Consultants and Party Leaders." *Campaigns and Elections* 15, no. 2 (March 1994): 58–59.

Ansolabehere, Stephen, and Shanto Iyengar. 1995. *Going Negative: How Attack Ads Shrink and Polarize the Electorate.* New York: Free Press.

"Anti-Democracy in California." 1911. *New York Times* (October 18): 12.

Argersinger, Peter H. 1985. "New Perspectives on Election Fraud in the Gilded Age." *Political Science Quarterly* 100 (winter 1985–1986): 669–88.

Arnold, R. Douglas. 1990. *The Logic of Congressional Action.* New Haven: Yale University Press.

Baer, Denise. 1995. "Contemporary Strategy and Agenda Setting." In *Campaigns and Elections American Style,* ed. James A. Thurber and Candice J. Nelson, 47–61. Boulder, Colorado: Westview Press.

Baer, Denise, and David Bositis. 1993. *Politics and Linkage in a Democratic Society.* Englewood Cliffs, New Jersey: Prentice-Hall.

Banducci, Susan A. 1998. "Direct Legislation: When Is It Used and When Does It Pass?" In *Citizens as Legislators: Direct Democracy in the United States,* ed. Shaun Bowler, Todd Donovan, and Caroline J. Tolbert, 109–31. Columbus, Ohio: Ohio State University Press.

Barber, Benjamin. 1984. *Strong Democracy: Participatory Politics for a New Age.* Berkeley: University of California Press.

Barry, Jeffrey M. 1997. *The Interest Group Society.* 3d ed. New York: Longman.

Baumgartner, Frank, and Beth Leech. 1998. *Basic Interests: The Importance of Groups in Politics and Political Science.* Princeton: Princeton University Press.

Beck, Deborah, Paul Taylor, Jeffrey Stanger, and Douglas Rivlin. 1997. *Issue Advocacy During the 1996 Campaign.* Philadelphia: Annenberg Public Policy Center.

Bednar, Nancy L., and Allen D. Hertzke. 1995. "Oklahoma: The Christian Right and Republican Realignment." In *God at the Grassroots: The Christian Right and the 1994 Elections,* ed. Mark J. Rozell and Clyde Wilcox, 91–108. Lanham, Maryland: Rowman and Littlefield.

Bergner, Jeffrey M. 1997. Partner, Bergner, Boyette, and Bockorny lobbying firm, Washington, D.C. Interview. 22 October.

Bessette, Joseph M. 1994. *The Mild Voice of Reason: Deliberative Democracy and American National Government.* Chicago: University of Chicago Press.

Bibby, John F. 1994. "State Party Organizations: Coping and Adapting." In *The Parties Respond: Changes in American Parties and Campaigns,* ed. L. Sandy Maisel, 21–44. Second edition. Boulder, Colorado: Westview Press.

Birnbaum, Jeffrey. 1997. "Washington's Power 25." *Fortune* (December 8): 63.

Blumenthal, Sidney. 1980. *The Permanent Campaign: Inside the World of Elite Political Operatives.* Boston: Beacon Press.

Board of Aldermen. 1878. *Report of a Special Committee of the Board of Aldermen Appointed to Investigate the Ring Frauds, Together with the Testimony Elicited During Their Investigation.* New York.

Bonner, Jack. 1998. "Comments on the Congressional Connection." In *The Interest Group Connection: Electioneering, Lobbying and Policymaking in Washington,* ed. Paul S. Herrnson, Ronald G. Shaiko, and Clyde Wilcox, 196–98. Chatham, New Jersey: Chatham House.

Bowler, Shaun, Todd Donovan, and Caroline J. Tolbert. 1998. *Citizens as Legislators: Direct Democracy in the United States.* Columbus, Ohio: Ohio State University Press.

Bradshaw, Joel. 1995. "Who Will Vote for You and Why: Designing Strategy and Theme." In *Parties and Elections American Style,* ed. James A. Thurber and Candice J. Nelson, 30–46. Boulder, Colorado: Westview Press.

Broder, David S. 1998. "Taking the Initiative on Petitions: Signatures for a Price." *Washington Post National Weekly Edition* (April 20): 11.

———. 1997. "Catatonic Politics." *Washington Post* (November 11): A19.

———. 1972. *The Party's Over: The Failure of Politics in America.* New York: Harper and Row.

Broder, David S., and Thomas B. Edsall. 1998. "Amid Election Apathy, Parties Bet on Core Voters." *Washington Post* (September 7): A1.

Browne, William P. 1998. *Groups, Interests and U.S. Public Policy.* Washington: Georgetown University Press.

Brownstein, Ronald. 1998. "Clintonism." *U.S. News and World Report* (January 22): 23.

Bryce, James. 1909. *The American Commonwealth*. Vol. 2. 3d ed., two volumes. New York: Macmillan.

Budge, Ian. 1996. *The New Challenge of Direct Democracy*. Cambridge: Polity Press.

Burnham, Walter Dean. 1982. *The Current Crisis in American Politics*. Oxford: Oxford University Press.

Burstein, Paul. 1998. "Interest Organizations, Political Parties, and the Study of Democratic Politics." In *Social Movements and American Political Institutions*, ed. Anne N. Costain and Andrew S. McFarland, 39–58. Boulder, Colorado: Rowman and Littlefield.

"C&E Survey of America's Political Consultants and Party Leaders." 1994. *Campaigns and Elections* 15, no. 3 (March): 58–59.

Campbell, Angus, Philip E. Converse, Warren E. Miller, and Donald E. Stokes. 1960. *The American Voter*. New York: John Wiley.

Center for Political Studies. 1996. *National Election Studies 1952–1996*. Ann Arbor: University of Michigan Press.

"Citizen Initiatives." 1994. *Campaigns and Elections* 15, no. 5 (May): 33–37.

Coleman, John J. 1996a. *Party Decline in America: Policy, Politics and the Fiscal State*. Princeton: Princeton University Press.

———. 1996b. "Resurgent or Just Busy? Party Organizations in Contemporary America." In *The State of the Parties: The Changing Role of Contemporary American Politics*, ed. John C. Green and Daniel M. Shea, 367–84. Lanham, Maryland: Rowman and Littlefield.

Coleman, John J., and David B. Yoffe. 1990. "Institutional Incentives for Protection: The American Use of Voluntary Export Restraints." In *International Trade: The Changing Role of the United States*, ed. Frank J. Machiarola, 29–57. New York: Academy of Political Science.

Corrado, Anthony. 1997. "Party Soft Money." In *Campaign Finance Reform: A Sourcebook*, ed. Anthony Corrado, Thomas E. Mann, Daniel R. Ortiz, Trevor Potter, and Frank J. Sorauf, 167–77. Washington: Brookings Institution.

Costain, Anne N. 1992. *Inviting Women's Rebellion: A Political Process Interpretation of the Women's Movement*. Baltimore: Johns Hopkins University Press.

Cotter, Cornelius P., James L. Gibson, John F. Bibby, and Robert J. Huckshorn. 1984. *Party Organizations in American Politics*. New York: Praeger.

Crewe, Ivor. 1981. "Electoral Participation." In *Democracy at the Polls: A Comparative Study of Competitive National Elections*, ed. David Butler, Howard R. Penniman, and Austin Ranney, 216–63. Washington: American Enterprise Institute.

Crone, Brad. 1997. "Finding Priority Voters with Database Overlays." *Campaigns and Elections* 18, no. 10 (December): 9–51.

Cronin, Thomas A. 1989. *Direct Democracy: The Politics of Initiative, Referendum, and Recall.* Cambridge: Harvard University Press.

Crotty, William. 1984. *American Political Parties in Decline.* Second edition. Boston: Little, Brown.

Dahl, Robert A. 1994. *The New American Political (Dis)order.* Berkeley: Institute of Governmental Studies Press.

Danner, Dan. 1997. Vice president for federal relations, National Federation of Independent Business, Washington, D.C. Interview. 29 September.

Delli Carpini, Michael X., and Scott Keeter. 1996. *What Americans Know About Politics and Why It Matters.* New Haven: Yale University Press.

De Witt, Benjamin Parke. 1915. *The Progressive Movement.* New York: Macmillan.

Donnellan, Kevin. 1997. Assistant director, Legislation and Public Policy Division, American Association of Retired Persons, Washington, D.C. Interview. 24 October.

Donovan, Todd, Shaun Bowler, David McCuan, and Ken Fernandez. 1998. "Contending Players and Strategies: Opposition Advantages in Initiative Elections." In *Citizens as Legislators: Direct Democracy in the United States,* ed. Shaun Bowler, Todd Donovan, and Caroline J. Tolbert, 80–108. Columbus, Ohio: Ohio State University Press.

Dwyre, Diana. 1993. "The Complete Congressional Party, Governing and Electing: The Congressional Campaign Committees and Responsible Party Government During Realignments." Paper presented at the annual meetings of the American Political Science Association, Washington, D.C., August 31–September 3.

———. 1992. "Is Winning Everything? Party Strategies for the U.S. House of Representatives." Paper presented at the annual meetings of the American Political Science Association, Chicago, September 2–6.

"Early Returns." 1996. *Society* 33, no. 4 (May/June): 5.

Edsall, Thomas Byrne. 1984. *The New Politics of Inequality.* New York: W. W. Norton.

Emery, Michael, and Edwin Emery. 1988. *The Press and America.* Sixth edition. Englewood Cliffs, New Jersey: Prentice-Hall.

Epstein, Leon D. 1986. *Political Parties in the American Mode.* Madison: University of Wisconsin Press.

Erie, Steven P. 1988. *Rainbow's End: Irish-Americans and the Dilemmas of Urban Machine Politics, 1840–1985.* Berkeley: University of California Press.

Faucheux, Ron. 1994. "The Grassroots Explosion." *Campaigns and Elections* 15, no. 1 (December/January): 20–32.

Fenno, Richard F. 1973. *Congressmen in Committees.* Boston: Little, Brown.

Finer, Herman. 1932. *The Theory and Practice of Modern Government.* London: Meuthen and Company.

Fiske, Susan T. 1980. "Attention and Weight in Person Perception and Attitude-Behavior Relations: An Investigation of the 1984 Presidential Election." *Journal of Personality and Social Psychology* 38, no. 6: 889–906.

Fowler, Linda L. 1994. "Political Entrepreneurs, Governing Processes and Political Change." In *New Perspectives on American Politics,* ed. Lawrence C. Dodd and Calvin Jillson. Washington: Congressional Quarterly Press.

Frendreis, John. 1996. "Voters, Government Officials and Party Organizations: Connections and Distinctions." In *The State of the Parties,* ed. John C. Green and Daniel M. Shea, 385–96. Lanham, Maryland: Rowman and Littlefield.

Friedenberg, Robert V. 1997. *Communication Consultants in Political Campaigns.* Westport, Connecticut: Praeger.

Gerber, Elisabeth R. 1998. "Pressuring Legislatures Through the Use of Initiatives: Two Forms of Indirect Influence." In *Citizens as Legislators: Direct Democracy in the United States,* ed. Shaun Bowler, Todd Donovan, and Caroline J. Tolbert, 191–208. Columbus, Ohio: Ohio State University Press.

Ginsberg, Benjamin, and Martin Shefter. 1990. *Politics by Other Means: The Declining Importance of Elections in America.* New York: Basic Books.

Godwin, R. Kenneth. 1988. *One Billion Dollars of Influence: The Direct Marketing of Politics.* Chatham, New Jersey: Chatham House.

Goldman, Ralph M. 1996. "Who Speaks for the Political Parties or, Martin Van Buren, Where Are You When We Need You?" In *The State of the Parties: The Changing Role of Contemporary American Politics,* ed. John C. Green and Daniel M. Shea, 25–41. Lanham, Maryland: Rowman and Littlefield.

Gordon, Stacy B., and Gary M. Segura. 1997. "Cross-National Variation in the Political Sophistication of Individuals: Capability or Choice?" *Journal of Politics* 59, no. 1: 126–47.

Green, John C. 1995. "The Christian Right and the 1994 Elections: An Overview." In *God at the Grass Roots: The Christian Right in the 1994 Elections,* ed. Mark J. Rozell and Clyde Wilcox, 1–18. Lanham, Maryland: Rowman and Littlefield.

Gugliotta, Guy. 1998. "Going Where the Money Is." *Washington Post National Weekly Edition* (July 6): 12–13.

Guth, James L. 1996. "The Bully Pulpit: Southern Baptist Clergy and Political Activism 1980–92." In *Religion and the Culture Wars: Dispatches from the Front,* ed. John C. Green, James L. Guth, Corwin E. Smidt, and Lyman A. Kellstedt, 146–73. Lanham, Maryland: Rowman and Littlefield.

Halpert, Melinda. 1997. Associate director of membership development, American Association of Retired Persons, Washington, D.C. Interview. 23 September.

Hamilton, Bruce. 1997. Membership director, Sierra Club, San Francisco, California. Interview. 6 October.

Hamilton, David L., and Mark P. Zanna. 1971. "Differential Weighting of Favorable and Unfavorable Attributes in Impression Formation." *Journal of Experiential Research in Personality* 20 (nos. 2–3): 204–12.

Hamilton, William R. 1995. "Political Polling: From the Beginning to the Center." In *Campaigns and Elections American Style,* ed. James A. Thurber and Candice J. Nelson, 161–80. Boulder, Colorado: Westview Press.

Hansen, Orval, Robert J. Blendon, Mollyann Brodie, Jonathan Ortmans, Matt James, Christopher Norton, and Tana Rosenblatt. 1996. "Lawmakers' Views on the Future of Health Reform: A Survey of Members of Congress and Staff." *Journal of Health Policy, Politics and Law* 21 (spring): 138–52.

Hartwig, Frederick. 1995. Senior vice president of Garin-Hart Research, Washington, D.C. Interview. 22 September.

Hazelwood, Dan N. 1995. "Targeting Persuasion Mail." *Campaigns and Elections* 16, no. 9 (September): 33.

Heberlig, Eric S. 1996. "The Bias of Mobilization." Paper delivered at the annual meetings of the Southern Political Science Association, Atlanta, November 9–11.

Heclo, Hugh. 1978. "Issue Networks and the Executive Establishment." In *The New American Political System,* ed. Anthony King, 87–124. Washington: American Enterprise Institute.

Heinz, John P., Edward O. Laumann, Robert L. Nelson, and Robert H. Salisbury. 1993. *The Hollow Core: Private Interests in National Policy Making.* Cambridge: Harvard University Press.

Herrnson, Paul S. 1998a. "National Party Organizations at the Century's End." In *The Parties Respond: Changes in American Parties and Campaigns,* ed. L. Sandy Masiel. Third edition. Boulder, Colorado: Westview Press.

———. 1998b. "Interest Groups, PACs and Campaigns." In *The Interest Group Connection: Electioneering, Lobbying and Policymaking in Washington,* ed. Paul S. Herrnson, Ronald G. Shaiko, and Clyde Wilcox, 37–51. Chatham, New Jersey: Chatham House.

———. 1994. "The Revitalization of National Party Organizations." In *The Parties Respond: Changes in American Parties and Campaigns,* ed. L. Sandy Maisel. Second edition. Boulder, Colorado: Westview Press.

———. 1988. *Party Campaigning in the 1980s.* Cambridge: Harvard University Press.

Hill, David. 1995. "Wording Ballot Issues." *Campaigns and Elections* 16, no. 8 (August): 28–29.

Himes, David. 1995. "Strategy and Tactics for Campaign Fundraising." In *Campaigns and Elections American Style,* ed. James A. Thurber and Candice J. Nelson, 62–77. Boulder, Colorado: Westview Press.

Hirczy, Wolfgang. 1995. "Explaining Near-Universal Turnout: The Case of Malta." *European Journal of Political Research* 27, no. 2: 255–72.

Hrebnar, Ronald J. 1997. *Interest Group Politics in America.* 3d ed. Armonk, New York: M. E. Sharpe.

Hrebnar, Ronald J., and Clive S. Thomas. 1993. *Interest Group Politics in the Midwestern States.* Ames: Iowa State University Press.

Imig, Douglas R. 1998. "American Social Movements and Presidential Administrations." In *Social Movements and American Political Institutions,* ed. Anne N. Costain and Andrew S. McFarland, 159–70. Lanham, Maryland: Rowman and Littlefield.

Inglehart, Ronald. 1997a. "Postmaterialist Values and the Decline of Institutional Authority." In *Why People Don't Trust Government,* ed. Joseph S. Nye, Phillip D. Zelikow, and David C. King, 217–36. Cambridge: Harvard University Press.

———. 1997b. *Modernization and Postmodernization: Cultural, Economic and Political Change in 43 Societies.* Princeton: Princeton University Press.

Jackman, Robert W., and Ross A. Miller. 1995. "Voter Turnout in the Industrial Democracies During the 1980s." *Comparative Political Studies* 27, no. 4: 467–92.

Jensen, Richard. 1971. *The Winning of the Midwest.* Chicago: University of Chicago Press.

Johnson, Paul E. 1998. "Interest Group Recruiting: Finding Members and Keeping Them." In *Interest Group Politics,* ed. Allan J. Cigler and Burdett A. Loomis, 35–62. Fifth edition. Washington: Congressional Quarterly Press.

Johnson-Cartee, Karen S., and Gary A. Copeland. 1997. *Inside Political Campaigns: Theory and Practice.* Westport, Connecticut: Praeger.

Katz, Richard S. 1997. *Democracy and Elections.* New York: Oxford University Press.

Key, V. O. 1961. *Public Opinion and American Democracy.* New York: Knopf.

King, Anthony. 1997. *Running Scared: Why America's Politicians Campaign Too Much and Govern Too Little.* New York: Free Press.

———. 1978. *The New American Political System.* Washington: American Enterprise Institute.

King, David C. 1997. "The Polarization of Political Parties and the Mistrust of Government." In *Why People Don't Trust Government,* ed. Joseph S. Nye, Philip D. Zelikow, and David C. King, 155–78. Cambridge: Harvard University Press.

Kirkpatrick, Jeane J. 1976. *The New Presidential Elite: Men and Women in National Politics.* New York: Russell Sage Foundation.

Kleppner, Paul. 1982. *Who Voted? The Dynamics of Electoral Turnout 1879–1900.* New York: Praeger.

Kollman, Ken. 1998. *Outside Lobbying: Public Opinion and Interest Group Strategies.* Princeton: Princeton University Press.

Kuklinski, James H., Ellen Riggle, Victor Ottati, Norbert Schwarz, and Robert S. Wyer, Jr. 1993. "Thinking About Political Tolerance, More or Less, with More or Less Information." In *Reconsidering the Democratic Public,* ed. George E. Marcus and Russell L. Hanson, 225–247. University Park: Pennsylvania State University Press.

Ladd, Everett Carl. 1978. *Transformations of the American Party System.* 2d ed. New York: W. W. Norton.

Lau, Richard A. 1985. "Two Explanations for Negativity Effects in Political Behavior." *American Journal of Political Science* 29 (April): 283–87.

———. 1982. "Negativity in Political Perception." *Political Behavior* 4 (December): 353–77.

Lee, Eugene C., and Larry L. Berg. 1976. *The Challenge of California.* Second edition. Boston: Little, Brown.

Lesperance, John. 1871. "American Journalism." *Lippincott's Magazine* 8 (August): 176.

Lewis, Neil A. 1994. "Lobby for Small Business Owners Puts Big Dent in Health Care Bill." *New York Times* (July 6): A1.

Leyden, Kevin M., and Stephen A. Borrelli. 1990. "Party Contributions and Party Unity: Can Loyalty Be Bought?" *Western Political Quarterly* 43 (winter): 343–65.

Lindblom, Charles E. 1959. "The Science of 'Muddling Through.'" *Public Administration Review* 19 (spring): 79–88.

Link, Arthur S., and Richard L. McCormick. 1983. *Progressivism.* Arlington Heights, Illinois: Harlan Davidson.

Lovejoy, Allen Fraser. 1941. *La Follette and the Establishment of the Direct Primary in Wisconsin.* New Haven: Yale University Press.

"Low Voter Turnout Expected." 1996. *Daily Oklahoman* (November 3): 5.

Lowi, Theodore J., and Benjamin Ginsberg. 1998. *American Government: Freedom and Power.* Fifth brief edition. New York: W. W. Norton.

Luntz, Frank I. 1988. *Candidates, Consultants and Campaigns: The Style and Substance of American Electioneering.* New York: Basil Blackwell.

Mackenzie, G. Calvin. 1996. *The Irony of Reform: Roots of American Disenchantment.* Boulder, Colorado: Westview Press.

Madison, James. 1961. "Federalist #10." In *The Federalist Papers,* by Alexander Hamilton, James Madison, and John Jay, 77–84. New York: New American Library.

Magleby, David B. 1984. *Direct Legislation: Voting on Ballot Propositions in the United States.* Baltimore: Johns Hopkins University Press.

Magleby, David B., and Kelly D. Patterson. 1998. "Consultants and Direct Democracy." *PS: Political Science and Politics* 31 (June): 160–62.

Maisel, L. Sandy. 1993. *Parties and Elections in America: The Electoral Process.* Second edition. New York: McGraw-Hill, 1993.

Mandabach, Paul. 1995. "Strategic Nuances." *Campaigns and Elections* 16, no. 9 (September): 19.

Marcus, Ruth. 1998. "Off the Ballot, but in the Contest." *Washington Post National Weekly Edition* (July 6): 13–14.

Martinez, Michael J. 1998. "Who are Internet Users?" 1998. *abcnews.com* (abcnews.go.com/sections/tech/DailyNews/wwwsurvey980714.html; July 14): 1–3.

Maullin, Richard, and Christine Quirk. 1995. "Audience Response Systems." *Campaigns and Elections* 16, no. 8 (August): 27–28.

McAllister, Bill. 1998. "Pressure's Up to $100 Million a Month." *Washington Post* (March 12): A13.

McCarthy, John D., and Clark McPhail. 1998. "The Institutionalization of Protest in the United States." In *The Social Movement Society: Contentious Politics for a New Century,* ed. David S. Meyer and Sidney Tarrow, 83–110. Lanham, Maryland: Rowman and Littlefield.

McCormick, Richard L. 1986. *The Party Period and Public Policy: American Politics from the Age of Jackson to the Progressive Era.* New York: Oxford University Press.

McCuan, David, Shaun Bowler, Todd Donovan, and Ken Fernandez. 1998. "California's Political Warriors: Campaign Professionals and the Initiative Process." In *Citizens as Legislators: Direct Democracy in the United States,* ed. Shaun Bowler, Todd Donovan, and Caroline J. Tolbert, 55–79. Columbus, Ohio: Ohio State University Press.

McGerr, Michael E. 1986. *The Decline of Popular Politics: The American North 1865–1928.* New York: Oxford University Press.

McKigney, Daryl. 1997. Former state director for Minnesota, the Christian Coalition, Saint Paul, Minnesota. Interview. 12 December.

Milkis, Sidney M. 1993. *The President and the Parties: The Transformation of the American Party System since the New Deal.* New York: Oxford University Press.

Mill, John Stuart. 1910. *Representative Government.* London: Everyman.

Miller, Bill and Susan B. Glasser. 1999. "A Victory for Christian Coalition." *Washington Post* (August 3): A1.

Montgomery, Peter. 1997. Communications director, People for the American Way, Washington, D.C. Interview. 15 September.

Morris, Dick. 1997. *Behind the Oval Office: Winning the Presidency in the Nineties.* New York: Random House.

Neuman, W. Russell. 1986. *The Paradox of Mass Politics: Knowledge and Opinion in the American Electorate.* Cambridge: Harvard University Press.

Neustadt, Richard E. 1997. "The Politics of Mistrust." In *Why People Don't Trust Government,* ed. Joseph S. Nye, Philip D. Zelikow, and David C. King, 179–202. Cambridge: Harvard University Press.

Nie, Norman H., Jane Junn, and Kenneth Stehlik-Barry. 1996. *Education and Democratic Citizenship in America.* Chicago: University of Chicago Press.

Nie, Norman H., Sidney Verba, and John R. Petrocik. 1976. *The Changing American Voter.* Cambridge: Harvard University Press.

Nye, Joseph H. 1997. "Introduction: The Decline of Confidence in Government." In *Why People Don't Trust Government,* ed. Joseph H. Nye, Phillip D. Zelikow, and David C. King, 1–18. Cambridge: Harvard University Press.

Nye, Joseph H., Philip D. Zelikow, and David C. King, eds. 1997. *Why People Don't Trust Government.* Cambridge: Harvard University Press.

Olson, Mancur. 1965. *The Logic of Collective Action: Public Goods and the Theory of Groups.* Cambridge: Harvard University Press.

Parkman, Francis. 1878. "The Failure of Universal Suffrage." *North American Review* 127 (July-August): 3–7.

Pateman, Carol. 1970. *Participation and Democratic Theory.* Cambridge: Cambridge University Press.

Penn, Mark, and Doug Schoen. 1997a. "The New Democrat Agenda." In *Back from the Dead: How Clinton Survived the Republican Revolution,* by Evan Thomas, Karen Breslau, Debra Rosenberg, Leslie Kaufman, and Andrew Murr, 220–221. New York: Atlantic Monthly Press.

———. 1997b. "Neuro-Personality Poll." In *Back From the Dead: How Clinton Survived the Republican Revolution,* by Evan Thomas, Karen Breslau, Debra Rosenberg, Leslis Kaufman, and Andrew Murr, 231–36. New York: Atlantic Monthly Press.

People for the American Way. 1990–1991. Library files on the Christian Coalition. Washington, D.C.

Persinos, John F. 1994. "Has the Christian Right Taken Over the Republican Party?" *Campaigns and Elections* 15, no. 9 (September): 21–24.

Peterson, Paul E. 1985. "The New Politics of Deficits." In *The New Direction in American Politics,* ed. John E. Chubb and Paul E. Peterson, 365–397. Washington: Brookings Institution.

Petrocik, John R. 1981. *Party Coalitions: Realignments and the Decline of the New Deal Party System.* Chicago: University of Chicago Press.

Phillips, Kevin. 1994. *Arrogant Capital: Washington, Wall Street and the Frustration of American Politics.* Boston: Little, Brown.

Plebani, John. 1997. Lawyer, Arter and Hadden, Washington, D.C. Interview. October 3.

Polsby, Nelson W. 1983. *Consequences of Party Reform.* New York: Oxford University Press.

Pomper, Gerald M. 1997. "Campaign Finance." E-mail message on H-Net forum on Antipartyism and Campaign Finance (October 8): 1.

———. 1992. *Passions and Interests: Political Party Concepts of American Democracy.* Lawrence, Kansas: University Press of Kansas.

Potter, Trevor. 1997. "Issue Advocacy and Express Advocacy." In *Campaign Finance Reform: A Sourcebook,* ed. Anthony Corrado, Thomas E. Mann, Daniel R. Ortiz, Trevor Potter, and Frank J. Sorauf, 225–74. Washington: Brookings Institution.

Powell, G. Bingham, Jr. 1986. "American Voter Turnout in Comparative Perspective." *American Political Science Review* 89 (March): 19–43.

Price, David E. 1992. "The Party Connection." In *Challenges to Party Government,* ed. John Kenneth White and Jerome M. Mileur, 133–53. Carbondale, Illinois: Southern Illinois University Press.

———. 1984. *Bringing Back the Parties.* Washington: Congressional Quarterly Press.

Rauch, Jonathan. 1994. *Demosclerosis: The Silent Killer of American Government.* New York: Times Books.

Rehr, David K. 1997. Vice president for government affairs, National Beer Wholesalers Association, Washington, D.C. Interview. 30 October.

Richardson, Jeremy. 1995. "The Market for Political Activism: Interest Groups as a Challenge to Political Parties." *West European Politics* 18 (January): 116–40.

Robinson, Michael J. 1975. "American Political Legitimacy in an Era of Electronic Journalism." In *Television as a Social Force,* ed. Douglas Cater and Richard Adler, 49–67. New York: Praeger.

Robinson, Will. 1995. "Organizing the Field." In *Campaigns and Elections American Style,* ed. James A. Thurber and Candice J. Nelson, 138–51. Boulder, Colorado: Westview Press.

Rose, Gary L. 1997. *The American Presidency Under Siege.* Albany: State University of New York Press.

Rosenstone, Steven J., and John Mark Hansen. 1993. *Mobilization, Participation and Democracy in America.* New York: Macmillan.

Rousseau, Jean Jacques. 1978. *On the Social Contract.* New York: St. Martin's Press.

Rubin, Barry R. 1997. *A Citizen's Guide to Politics in America: How the System Works and How to Work the System.* Armonk, New York: M. E. Sharpe.

Ryden, David K. 1996. *Representation in Crisis: The Constitution, Interest Groups and Political Parties.* Albany, New York: State University of New York Press.

Sabato, Larry J. 1989. *Paying for Elections: The Campaign Finance Thicket.* New York: Twentieth Century Fund.

————. 1984. *The Rise of Political Consultants: New Ways of Winning Elections.* New York: Basic Books.

Sabato, Larry J., and Glenn R. Simpson. 1996. *Dirty Little Secrets: The Persistence of Corruption in American Politics.* New York: Times Books.

Salisbury, Robert J. 1990. "The Paradox of Interest Groups in Washington—More Groups, Less Clout." In *The New American Political System,* ed. Anthony King, 203–30. Second version. Washington: American Enterprise Institute, 1990.

————. 1984. "Interest Representation: The Dominance of Institutions." *American Political Science Review* 78 (March): 64–76.

————. 1969. "An Exchange Theory of Interest Groups." *Midwest Journal of Political Science* 13 (February): 1–32.

Salmore, Barbara G., and Stephen A. Salmore. 1989. *Candidates, Parties and Campaigns: Electoral Politics in America.* Second edition. Washington: Congressional Quarterly Press.

Sartori, Giovanni. 1987. *The Theory of Democracy Revisited.* Chatham, New Jersey: Chatham House.

Schattschneider, Elmer Eric. 1977. *Party Government.* Westport, Connecticut: Greenwood Press.

Schelling, Thomas C. 1978. *Micromotives and Macrobehavior.* New York: W. W. Norton.

Schier, Mary Lahr, ed. 1998. *Take Your Victories as They Come: The Carlson Years in Minnesota Politics.* Minneapolis: MSP Business Books.

Schlozman, Kay Lehman, and John T. Tierney. 1986. *Organized Interests and American Democracy.* New York: Harper and Row.

Schoenfield, Michael A. 1998. "A Cost Effective Vote Maximizing Strategy." Memorandum.

Schrag, Peter. 1998. *Paradise Lost: California's Experience, America's Future.* New York: New Press.

Schudson, Michael. 1998. *The Good Citizen: A History of American Civic Life.* New York: Free Press.

Sease, Debbie. 1997. Legislative director, Sierra Club, Washington, D.C. Interview. 30 September.

Shafer, Byron E. 1983. *Quiet Revolution: The Struggle for the Democratic Party and the Shaping of Post-Reform Politics.* New York: Russell Sage Foundation.

Shaiko, Ronald G. 1998. "Reverse Lobbying: Interest Group Mobilization from the White House and the Hill." In *Interest Group Politics,* ed. Allan J. Cigler and Burdett A. Loomis. Fifth edition. Washington: Congressional Quarterly Press.

Shea, Daniel M. 1996. *Campaign Craft: The Strategies, Tactics and Art of Political Campaign Management.* New York: Praeger.

Shefter, Martin. 1994. *Political Parties and the State: The American Historical Experience.* Princeton: Princeton University Press.

Silbey, Joel H. 1998. "From 'Essential to the Existence of our Institutions' to 'Rapacious Enemies of Honest and Responsible Government': The Rise and Fall of American Parties." In *The Parties Respond: Changes in American Parties and Campaigns,* ed. L. Sandy Maisel. Third Edition. Boulder, Colorado: Westview Press.

Skocpol, Theda. 1996. "Unravelling from Above." *American Prospect* 25 (March/April): 20–25.

Skowronek, Stephen. 1982. *Building a New American State: The Expansion of National Administrative Capacities, 1877–1920.* Cambridge: Cambridge University Press.

Smith, Hedrick. 1988. *The Power Game: How Washington Works.* New York: Ballantine Books.

Sonis, Larry. 1994. "Understanding Direct Democracy." *Campaigns and Elections* 15, no. 1 (December-January): 63.

Soper, J. Christopher. 1996. "The Politics of Pragmatism: The Christian Right and the 1994 Elections." In *Midterm: The Elections of 1994 in Context,* ed. Philip A. Klinkner. Boulder, Colorado: Westview Press.

Souraf, Frank J. 1998. "Political Parties and the New World of Campaign Finance." In *The Parties Respond: Changes in American Parties and Campaigns,* ed. L. Sandy Maisel. Third Edition. Boulder, Colorado: Westview Press.

———. 1992. *Inside Campaign Finance: Myths and Realities.* New Haven: Yale University Press.

———. 1988. "Parties and Political Action Committees in American Politics." In *When Parties Fail: Emerging Alternative Organizations,* ed. Kay Lawson and Peter H. Merkl, 282–308. Princeton: Princeton University Press.

Squire, Peverill, Raymond E. Wolfinger, and David P. Glass. 1987. "Residential Mobility and Voter Turnout." *American Political Science Review* 81 (March): 56–61.

Stengel, Richard, and Eric Pooley. 1996. "Masters of the Message." *Time* magazine, Internet edition (November 6): 1–28.

Straub, Terry. 1998. Vice president for public affairs, USX Corporation, Washington, D.C. Presentation on lobbying, C-SPAN. 11 January.

Thomas, Evan, Karen Breslau, Debra Rosenberg, Leslie Kaufman, and Andrew Murr. 1997. *Back from the Dead: How Clinton Survived the Republican Revolution.* New York: Atlantic Monthly Press.

Thurber, James A. 1995. "The Transformation of American Campaigns." In *Campaigns and Elections American Style,* ed. James A. Thurber and Candice J. Nelson, 1–13. Boulder, Colorado: Westview Press.

Verba, Sidney, Kay Lehman Schlozman, and Henry E. Brady. 1997. "The Big Tilt: Participatory Inequality in America." *American Prospect* 32 (May/June): 74–80.

——. 1995. *Voice and Equality: Civic Voluntarism in American Politics.* Cambridge: Harvard University Press.

Wade, Kim. 1997. Deputy legal counsel, Children's Defense Fund, Washington, D.C. Interview. 11 November.

Walker, Jack L. 1991. *Mobilizing Interest Groups in America: Patrons, Professions and Social Movements.* Ann Arbor: University of Michigan Press.

——. 1970. "Normative Consequences of 'Democratic' Theory." In *Frontiers of Democratic Theory,* ed. Henry Kariel, 227–47. New York: Random House.

Ware, Alan. 1988. *The Breakdown of Democratic Party Organization, 1940–1980.* New York: Oxford University Press.

——. 1987. *Citizens, Parties and the State: A Reappraisal.* Princeton: Princeton University Press.

Watson, Justin. 1997. *The Christian Coalition: Dreams of Restoration, Demands for Recognition.* New York: St. Martin's Press.

Wattenberg, Marvin P. 1996. *The Decline of American Political Parties 1952–1994.* Cambridge: Harvard University Press.

Wayne, Stephen J. 1998. "Interest Groups on the Road to the White House: Traveling the Hard and Soft Routes." In *The Interest Group Connection: Electioneering, Lobbying, and Policymaking in Washington,* ed. Paul S. Herrnson, Ronald G. Shaiko, and Clyde Wilcox, 65–79. Chatham, New Jersey: Chatham House.

——. 1996. *The Road to the White House 1996: The Politics of Presidential Elections.* New York: St. Martin's Press.

West, Darrell M., and Burdett A. Loomis. 1998. *The Sound of Money: How Political Interests Get What They Want.* New York: Norton.

White, John Kenneth. 1995. "Reviving the Political Parties: What Must Be Done?" In *The Politics of Ideas: Intellectual Challenges to Party After 1992,* ed. John K. White and John C. Green, 4–27. Lanham, Maryland: Rowman and Littlefield.

Wiebe, Robert H. 1967. *The Search for Order 1877–1920*. New York: Hill and Wang.

Wilcox, Clyde. 1996. *Onward Christian Soldiers? The Religious Right in American Politics*. Boulder, Colorado: Westview Press.

Wilson, Alita. 1997. Outreach director, Sierra Club, San Francisco, California. Interview. 6 October.

Wilson, Graham K. 1990. *Interest Groups*. Cambridge, Massachusetts: Basil Blackwell.

Wilson, James Q. 1995. *Political Organizations*. Princeton: Princeton University Press.

Wolfinger, Raymond E., David P. Glass, and Peverill Squire. "Predictors of Electoral Turnout: An International Comparison." *Policy Studies Review* 9 (spring 1990): 551–73.

Wolpe, Bruce C., and Bertram J. Levine. 1996. *Lobbying Congress: How the System Works*. Second edition. Washington: Congressional Quarterly Press.

Wright, Gerald C. 1994. "The Meaning of 'Party' in Congressional Roll-Call Voting." Paper delivered at the annual meetings of the Midwest Political Science Association, Chicago, March 22–24.

Zisk, Betty H. 1987. *Money, Media and the Grass Roots: State Ballot Issues and the Electoral Process*. Newbury Park, California: Sage.

Index

Page references in italics are to figures and tables in the text.

Abrams, Robert, 106
Activation strategies: compared with mobilization, 7–9, 14–15, 18*n*1, 43–44, 193; consequences of, 35–39, 192, 199–203; cost of, 30, 163; responders to, 15–18, 27, 32, 133, 163, 169; rise of, 7–41
Activist elites. *See* Party elites; Political elites
Advertising: and 1996 presidential election, 118–20; and advocacy ads, 177–78; assessment by dial groups, 98; as campaign expense, 29–30, 100–101; candidate web pages and, 102; as means of activation, 199. *See also* Issue advocacy advertising; Negative advertising
Advisory initiatives, 142
Advocacy ads, 177–78
"Advocacy" groups, 157
AFL-CIO, 64, 70, 128, 132
Agendas: policy, 143, 194, 196–98, 202–3; political, 23, 47, 71, 165
Aldrich, John H., 48–52, 71, 76, 87, 91–93
Alienation, 11–13, 33–34, 37, 38
American Association of Retired Persons (AARP), 11, 183–85
American Federation of Labor. *See* AFL-CIO
American Medical Association (AMA), 157, 191
Ansolabehere, Stephen, 107
Aristotle Industries, 96–97
Arnold, R. Douglas, 36

"Astroturf" lobbying, 174
"Attentive publics," 36
Australian electoral system, 213
Automatic spending programs, 196–98

Ballots: partisan, 217–18, 221; party-column, 20, 199; printed by political parties, 57, 58; secret, 20, 67; single transferable vote (STV), 211–12, 213
Barber, Benjamin, 21–22, 153
Bauer, Gary, 135
Belgian electoral system, 213
Benchmark polls, 97, 104
Blumenthal, Sidney, 95, 117
Boggs, Tommy, 160
Bonner, Jack, 170–71, 190–91
Bradshaw, Joel, 104–5
Brady, Henry, 17, 202, 204
Broder, David S., 83, 201–2
Brushfire polls, 97
Bryan, William Jennings, 66
Bryce, James, 38–39
Buckley v. Valeo, 210
Budde, Bernadette, 128
Bureaucracies. *See* Executive agencies
Burnham, Walter Dean, 196, 198
Burstein, Paul, 125–26
Bush, George, 106
Bush, Jeb, 99
Business groups, 11, 28, 125, 130, 157. *See also* Trade organizations
Business-Industry Political Action Committee (BIPAC), 128
"Byproduct" theory, 165, 184

Cable television, 102, 163, 200

California initiatives, 145–54

Campaign consultants: and 1996 presidential election, 118–21; role of, 94–95, 103, 104, 143–44, 205; types of firms serving as, 96, 146; view of political parties, 109–10

Campaign finance reforms, 25, 68, 81–83, 84, 108, 205–6, 208–10

Campaigns: candidate-centered, 81–82, 90, 206, 218; and electoral activation, 89–124; financing of, 99–100, 103; messages of, 31–35, 44, 194, 195; party workers in, 44, 77; presidential (1876), 55; presidential (1892), 66; presidential (1896), 66; presidential (1992), 106; presidential (1996), 34–35, 98, 117–23; strategies of, 14, 103–7

Candidates: advertising expenses of, 29–30, 100–101; and campaign finance, 81–83, 92–93, 99, 210; and direct primary elections, 24–25, 69, 199; and electoral activation, 89–124; interest organizations' impact on, 127; messages of, 31–35, 93, 102, 107, 194, 195, 218; political parties as service providers for, 25, 108–10; political parties' benefits for, 48–51; political parties' control over, 24, 47–48, 87; and presidential nomination process, 80; recruitment of, 92, 138; relationship to electorates of, 91–93

Carter, Jimmy, 79

"Cause" groups, 157

Cerrell, Joe, 146

Children's Defense Fund, 157, 167–68

Christian Coalition, 134–35, 166, 168, 169, 187–89; and "Contract with America," 137, 139–40; and "Contract with the American Family," 140; voter guides, distribution by, 138–39

Christian conservatives, 133–41

Citizen Participation Survey, 113n2

Civil rights groups, 157

Civil service reforms, 20, 24, 69, 199

Class bias, 68–69, 74, 133, 196–97

Clergy, 135–36

Clinton, Bill: 1992 election campaign of, 106; 1994 congressional elections and, 137; 1996 reelection campaign of, 34–35, 98, 117–23; Christian con-

servatives' reaction to, 134; health care reform groups and, 176; permanent campaign of, 95

"Coalition" advocacy, 163

Coleman, John J., 47–48, 59, 197

Collective good, 26, 50, 107, 164–65

Committee for Party Renewal, 205

Common Cause, 166, 210

Common good. *See* Collective good

The Commons, 22, 39–40, 107

Communication technologies, 200; impact on targeting of, 8, 27, 195; and outside lobbying, 171; and partisan mobilization, 44. *See also* Technological changes

Community homogeneity, 77, 220

Compulsory voting laws, 214–15, 216, 221

Computer services firms, 99

Concerned Women of America (CWA), 135, 137

Congressional elections, 82, 133–41, 180, 210

Constitutional initiatives, 141

"Contagion" effect, 28

"Contract with America," 118, 137, 139–40, 181, 189

"Contract with the American Family," 140

Corrupt practices acts, 68

Counterinitiatives, ballot, 148–49

Court system, 159

Craver, Roger, 100

Currency standard, 66–67

Dahl, Robert A., 37–38

D'Amato, Alfonse, 106

Danner, Dan, 171, 180

Database management firms, 96

Debates, campaign, 98, 206

DeCourcy, Robert, 66

Delli Carpini, Michael X., 112

Democratic party: and 1996 presidential election, 118–19; and currency standard issue, 66; New Deal coalition of, 74; origin of, 52; and patronage, 74; presidential nomination process reforms of, 78–80; and slavery issue, 53; soft money fund-raising of, 84, 122, 131; and tariff issue, 59–60; Vietnam War protests' impact on, 78

Democratic-Republicans party, 52

De Witt, Benjamin Parke, 67

Dial groups, 97, 104

Direct democracy. *See* Participatory democracy

Direct initiatives, 141

Direct mail communications: consultant services for, 29, 99; effectiveness of, 101, 105; and fund-raising letters, 100; as means of activation, 8, 93, 129–30, 150, 163, 168–70, 199

Direct primary elections, 199, 221; abolishment of, 216; adoption of, 68; candidates' use of, 69; and decline of political party influence, 20, 24–25, 47

Disclosure, financial, 82, 205, 207–8, 218, 220

Dobson, James, 135, 141

Dole, Bob, 121–22, 141

Duberstein Group, 160

Economic policies, 75–76, 196–98

Edelman, Marian Wright, 167

Educational level: and formation of entrepreneurial groups, 27; impact on political participation of, 12–13, 22, 31–32, 43, 111–14, *115–16*, 151, 201; and negative advertising, 34, 35

Efficacy: personal, 201; political, 31, 110–11, *113–14*, 212, 214

Elected representatives. *See* Officeholders

Electoral activation, 89–124, 125–54

"Electoral activists," 16

Electoral College reform, 10, 218–19

Electoral system: non-U.S. examples of, 210–15; progressive movement reforms of, 43, 67–69, 221; reforms of, 204, 215–19; rules' impact on political parties, 52; shortcomings of, 212

Electorates, 91–92, 195*n1*

Elites. *See* Party elites; Policy-type benefit seeking elites; Political elites

Emily's List, 128

Entitlement programs, 196–98

Entrepreneurial groups, 23, 27–28, 71, 166–68. *See also* Interest organizations

Environmental groups, 11. *See also* Sierra Club; Friends of the Earth

Evangelicals, 136. *See also* Christian Coalition

Executive agencies, 70, 75, 159, 199

Expressive benefits, 26–27, 166, 190; and Christian Coalition, 187; and

National Federation of Independent Business, 180; and People for the American Way, 186; and Sierra Club, 182

Family Research Council (FRC), 135, 137

Farm groups, 11, 28, 157

Fazio, Vic, 137

Federal Election Campaign Finance Act (1971), 81

Federal Election Commission (FEC), 82, 84, 132

Federalist party, 52

Federal Reserve Board, 70

Federal Trade Commission, 70

Female suffrage, 68*n4*

Finer, Herman, 69, 226

First Amendment, 207

First National Bank of Boston v. Bellotti, 142–43

Focus groups, 8, 97, 104, 144, 163, 173

Focus on the Family, 135, 141

Forbes, Steve, 121

Ford, Gerald, 79

Fraser, Don, 79

"Free rider" problem, 26, 164–65

French electoral system, 213

Frendreis, John, 47

Friends of the Earth, 11, 157, 166

Fund-raising: consultant services for, 99–100; and initiative campaigns, 142–43; by interest organizations, 129; and soft money, 84, 108, 131, 209

General electorates, 91–92

Geographic mobility of Americans, 77–78

Glass, David, 213–14

Goddard, Ben, 178

Gold standard, 66–67

Gompers, Samuel, 64

Gordon, Stacy B., 214–15, 216

Gore, Al, 183

Government: business influence on state and local, 67; disaffection with, 10–12; and hyperpluralism, 36; impact of, on entrepreneurial groups, 168; interest organizations' impact on, 155–93; political parties' impact on, 50–51, 69

"Governmental activists," 16

Grassroots political activity: by Christian conservatives, 133–41, 208; by lobbyists, 161–62, 170–77, 208; as means of activation, 32, 34; and participatory democracy, 19

"Grasstops" lobbying, 175, 179

Great Depression, 73

Greek electoral system, 213

Guth, James L., 135

Hamilton, Alexander, 51–52

Hamilton, William R., 103

Hansen, John Mark, 9, 16–18, 112

Hard money contributions, 84, 85, 108, 206. *See also* Political contributions

Harmon, Shawn, 97

"Harry and Louise" ads, 177–78

Health Insurance Association of America (HIAA), 178, 180, 191

Heinz, John P., 28

Herrnson, Paul S., 47, 83–84, 85

Hill and Knowlton (firm), 160

House of Representatives, U.S.: funding campaigns for, 103; political parties' role in election of, 25, 58, 108; ratings of members by interest organizations, 128–29; recruitment of candidates for, 138

Huddleston, Walter, 106

Huffington, Michael, 139

Humphrey, Hubert H., 78

Hyperpluralism, 36–37

Immigrants, 63–64, 65

Income level, 111, *114–16*

Independents, 25, 78

Indirect initiatives, 141–42

Individualistic democracy, 200, 221

Information costs, 173, 214; government policy impact on, 167–68; impact of education on, 22, 31–32; political parties' impact on, 15, 52

Inglehart, Ronald, 33–34

Inhofe, Jim, 138

Initiatives, referenda, and recalls, 10, 18, 20, 68, 141–54, 221

"Inside" lobbying strategies, 127, 156, 158–62

"Institutional" lobbies, 157–58, 171

Interest organizations: case studies of, 179–89; coalitions of, 158, 162, 163, 176; compared with political parties,

8, 126; and electoral activation, 125–54; fragmentation of, 28; goals of, 156, 162–63; and government, 155–93; incentives to join, 164–66; and initiatives, 141–54; messages of, 31–35, 44, 195, 200, 219; and PACs, 82, 93; proliferation of, 10–11, *12,* 26–29, 38, 70–71, 199, 203; strategies of, 14, 127–33, 156, 160–61, 173–75. *See also* Lobbying

Internet, 8, 102, 163

Irish electoral system, 213

"Iron triangles," 28–29

Issue advocacy advertising, 84–85, 109, 118–19, 132, 209, 220. *See also* Advertising

Issue-based membership groups, 166

"Issue networks," 191

Iyengar, Shanto, 107

Jackman, Robert W., 213–14

Jackson, Andrew, 53

Jarvis, Howard, 146

Jefferson, Thomas, 52

Johnson, Hiram, 20

Junn, Jane, 32, 45

Keeter, Scott, 112

Key, V. O., 167

Kimball, Kelly, 146

King, David C., 33, 117

Kleppner, Paul, 68–69, 71

Knapp, Bill, 118

Knowledge firms, 96, 97

Kollman, Ken, 172–73, 176–77

Labor, campaign, 44, 77

Labor organizations, 11, 157; and Democratic party, 73–74; membership in, 165; membership response to activation strategies, 133; policy goals of, 130–31; and political machines, 64

La Follette, Robert M., 20, 68

Lahaye, Beverly, 135

Largent, Steve, 138

Laumann, Edward O., 28

Law firms as lobbyists, 160

Lear, Norman, 185

"Legislative champions," 162

Legislatures: initiative politics' impact on, 20, 152; nonpartisan election of, 68; political parties' impact on, 50–51,

69–70; role of, in participatory democracy, 37; as targets of "inside" strategies, 159, 161–62
Lindblom, Charles E., 11
List management firms, 99
Literacy tests, 68
Lobbying: case studies of organizations, 179–89; firms, types of, 160; new techniques of, 170–77; proliferation of lobbyists, 156; reform of, 207–8, 219–20; traditional techniques of, 30, 158–62. *See also* Interest organizations
Lobbying Disclosure Act (1995), 207, 220
Local political party organizations, 57–58
The Logic of Collective Action (Olson), 26, 164
Luntz, Frank I., 89–90

Mackenzie, G. Calvin, 27
Madison, James, 10, 52, 207, 219
Majority rule: and activation strategies, 9, 18*n*1, 36, 195; inclusiveness in, 23; and individualistic democracy, 200; influence on policy agendas, 194, 202–3; and interest organizations, 126, 192; minority influence on, 15
Mall groups, 98, 119
Maltese electoral system, 211–13
Mandatory voting laws. *See* Compulsory voting laws
Marginalized groups, 20–21, 28, 125
Market specialization, 22–23
"Mass issue marketing," 173, 175, 177–78
"Mass public," 16
Material benefits, 26, 164, 180, 183–84, 186
Maullin, Richard, 98, 231
McCain-Feingold Bill, 208–9, 218, 220
McConnell, Mitch, 106
McCormick, Richard L., 56
McGerr, Michael E., 54–55
McGovern, George, 78–79
McKinley, William, 66
Media firms, 96, 99, 100
Membership groups, 26, 157, 164–70. *See also* Interest organizations
Mill, John Stuart, 21
Miller, Ross, 213–14
Mobilization, partisan: and class, 74, 196–97; compared with activation strategies, 7–9, 14–15, 18*n*1, 43–44, 193; decline of, 15, 39, 42–88, 215;

and franchise expansion, 52; techniques of, 53, 55, 56
Money firms, 96
Morris, Dick, 118, 119, 120, 121, 231
"Motor voter" registration, 214
Movements, 11, 20–21, 28, 125
Mugwumps, 65–66

Nader, Ralph, 167
Narrowcasting, 15, 163
National Association of Manufacturers, 70
National Civic Federation, 70–71
National Coalition to Ban Handguns, 166
National Committee for an Effective Congress (NCEC), 129–30
National Conservative Political Action Committee (NCPAC), 130
National Election Studies, 111*m*, 112, *115*, 139
National Farm Bureau, 165
National Federation of Independent Business (NFIB), 170, 179–81, 191
Negative advertising: direct mail as medium for, 102; and fund-raising letters, 100; impact of, 77, 105–7; and issue advocacy, 132; as means of activation, 34, 35; and post-materialist values, 33; radio as medium for, 101. *See also* Advertising
Nelson, Robert L., 28
"Network centrality," 32
Neuman, W. Russell, 16
"Neuro-personality profile," 120
Neustadt, Richard E., 14
New Deal, 73–76
New institutionalism, 2, 220–21
Newspapers: and ballot printing, 58; increasing independence of, 71–72; as means of partisan mobilization, 8, 53, 56, 63, 71–72, 220
"Niche marketing," 14
Nie, Norman H., 32, 45
Nonrival and nonexcludable benefits, 50, 148, 164
Nonvoters, 68*n*4, 195
Nye, Joseph H., 33

Officeholders: corrupt behavior of, 19; interest organizations' impact on, 127, 130, 171–73; lobbying efforts of, 176; political parties' benefits for, 48–49,

50–51; political parties' control over, 47–48

Olson, Mancur, 26, 50*n*1, 164, 184

"Outside" lobbying strategies, 5, 156, 161, 170–77

PACs. *See* Political action committees

Parkman, Francis, 65

Participatory democracy, 10, 18–23, 39, 141–54, 164, 201–3

Partisan activists. *See* Party elites

Partisan ballots, 57, 217–18, 221

Partisan press. *See* Newspapers

Party-column ballots, 20, 199

Party elites: impact on candidates, 92, 93; impact on political parties, 217; and majority rule, 15, 194; polarization of, 33. *See also* Policy-type benefit seeking elites; Political elites

"Party of nonvoters," 195

Party workers, 44, 77

The Party's Over (Broder), 83

Pateman, Carol, 21

Patronage: decline in party influence on, 20, 47, 69, 205; Democratic party use of, 74; election officials chosen through, 59; and government appointments, 63; as means of partisan mobilization, 24, 53, 57, 77

Patrons' funding of interest organizations, 168

Patton, Boggs, and Blow (firm), 160

Pendelton Act (1883), 24, 69

Penn, Mark, 98, 118–21

People for the American Way (PFAW), 169, 185–87, 191

"Permanent campaigns," 95, 117

Personal contacts: consultant services for, 99; and "grasstops" lobbying, 175; as means of partisan mobilization, 8, 44–45, 53, 56, 57, 77

"Persuadables," 104

Petrocik, John R., 78

Policy agendas. *See* Agendas: policy

Policy environment: changes in, 70–71, 75, 196–98, 205, 207; political parties' influence on, 47–48, 59–60, 85

"Policy-type benefit seeking" elites, 87, 92, 110

Political action committees (PACs), 82, 93, 128, 129, 130–32

Political activists, 13–14, 16–18, 117, 135–36

Political agendas. *See* Agendas: political

Political contributions, 84–85; in 1996 presidential campaign, 122; and PACs, 82, 93, 130–32; reform of, 205–6, 209, 218; use by political parties, 108

Political elites, 2, 14, 39; impact on candidates, 92, 100; and outside lobbying, 170; and progressive movement reforms, 221; and the public, 7–8, 10. *See also* Party elites; Policy-type benefit seeking elites

Political environment, 24, 33

Political participation: and Citizen Participation Survey, 113*n*2; and educational level, 12–13, 22, 31–32, 43, 111–12, *113*, *115–16*, 151, 201; and low voter turnout, 201–2; and partisan mobilization, 44–45, 194; reforms to enhance, 196–98, 215–17

Political parties: compared with interest organizations, 8, 126; comparison of national and local organizations, 57–58; corrupt behavior of, 20, 59, 67; decentralized character of, 52–53, 57–58; decline in influence of, 24–26, 27, 42–88, 109–10, 151–52, 167, 196, 199, 209; and electoral activation, 89–124; electoral rules' impact on, 52; functions of, 25, 46, 50–51, 108–10, 128; and immigrants, 63–64, 65; impact on government, 50–51; messages of, 44, 194, 195, 200, 203–4; and the New Deal, 73–76; and nominating conventions, 80–81; and party machines, 19, 57, 62–63, 64; and party workers in campaigns, 44, 77; and political contributions, 82, 84–85, 108, 209, 218; and primary elections, 24–26; regional dominance of, 66–67; renewal of, 204–7, 217–18; role of, in political socialization, 55; strength of, defined, 46–48, 53, 86, 204. *See also* Mobilization, partisan

Political socialization, 55

Politicians. *See* Candidates; Officeholders

Polling, 8, 97–99, 104, 120–21, 144

Pomper, Gerald M., 208

"Post-materialist" values, 33–34, 43

Powell, G. Bingham, Jr., 214

Presidential elections: 1876, 55; 1892, 66; 1896, 43, 66; 1936, 73; 1992, 106; 1996, 117–23; financing of, 81–82; nomination process for, 80; and voter contacts, 112
Pressure groups. *See* Interest organizations
Price, David E., 79
Primaries. *See* Direct primary elections
Primary electorates, 91–92
Professional associations, 157
Progressive movement, 19–20, 43, 65–73, 95, 199, 221
Propositions, 10 (Calif.), 150
Proposition 11 (Calif.), 150
Proposition 13 (Calif.), 146, 150–51
Proposition 187 (Calif.), 149
Proposition 209 (Calif.), 149, 151
Protests, public, 175–76
Public Citizen, 210
Public good. *See* Collective good
Public interest groups, 11
Public relations firms as lobbyists, 160
Purposive benefits, 166
Push polls, 98–99, 102, 104

Quirk, Christine, 98
Quick-response polls, 97

Racial conflicts, 78
Radio, 100–101, 150
Rallies, 55, 57, 220
Ratings by interest organizations, 128–29
Rauch, Jonathan, 36–37
Recalls. *See* Initiatives, referenda, and recalls
Reed, Ralph, 134–35, 137–38, 167, 168, 187
Referenda. *See* Initiatives, referenda, and recalls
Reforms, 194–222; campaign finance, 25, 68, 81–83, 84, 108, 205–6, 208–10; civil service, 20, 24, 69, 199; Committee for Party Renewal, 205–6; compulsory voting laws, 214–15, 216, 221; electoral system, 43, 67–69, 204, 215–19, 221; lobbying, 207–8, 219–20; and the progressive movement, 20, 43, 65–73, 199, 221; resulting in more participation, 18–19; and "strong democracy," 21–22; voter registration laws, 216, 221

Regulatory agencies. *See* Executive agencies
Rehr, David K., 161–62
Republican party: and Christian Coalition, 134–35; and Christian conservatives, 140–41; and "Contract with America," 118, 137, 139–40; and currency standard issue, 66; and slavery issue, 53; soft money fund-raising of, 84, 131; and tariff issue, 59–60
"Reverse" lobbying, 176
Richardson, Jeremy, 22–23
"Rifled" messages, 90, 123, 195
Robertson, Pat, 134, 168, 187
Roosevelt, Franklin Delano, 73–76
Rosenstone, Steven J., 9, 16–18, 112
Rousseau, Jean Jacques, 19
Rubin, Barry R., 177

Salisbury, Robert H., 28, 157, 167
Salmore, Barbara G., 105–6
Salmore, Stephen A., 105–6
Satellite technology, 102, 163
Schattschneider, E. E., 46, 192–93, 201, 219–20
Schelling, Thomas C., 107
Schier, Stephen E. (great-grandfather of author), 60–61, 77
Schlozman, Kay Lehman, 17, 157, 202, 204
Schoen, Doug, 98, 118, 120
Scientific Games of Atlanta, 147
Secret ballots, 20, 67
Segura, Gary M., 214–15, 216
Senate, U.S.: funding campaigns for, 103; political parties' role in election of, 25, 58n2, 108; ratings of members by interest organizations, 128–29; recruitment of candidates for, 138
Shaiko, Ronald G., 176
Shays-Meehan Bill, 208–9, 218, 220
Shea, Daniel M., 90
Shefter, Martin, 199
"Shotgun" messages, 90, 123, 194, 218
Sierra Club, 11, 170, 181–83, 191
Signature solicitation firms, 146
Silver standard, 66–67
Single transferable vote (STV) ballots, 211–12, 213
Skocpol, Theda, 203
Slavery, 53
"Soccer moms," 105

Social Contract (Rousseau), 19
Social justice groups, 11
Social networks: church-based, 134, 136; and educational level, 32, 112; role of, 17; and voting norms, 45, 56, 57
Social welfare groups, 157
Socialists, 64
Soft money contributions, 84, 108, 122, 131; reform of, 206, 209, 218
Solidary incentives, 165–66; and Christian Coalition, 188; and People for the American Way, 186; and Sierra Club, 182
Speeches, 98
Split ticket voting, 25, 33, 85
"Spoils system." *See* Patronage
Squier, Bob, 118
Squire, Peverill, 213–14
Stehlik-Barry, Kenneth, 32, 45, 163
Stratification, political, 18, 31, 35–36, 72, 200–201
Straub, Terry, 192
"Strong democracy," 21–22
Suffrage, female, 68n4
Supreme Court, U.S., 85, 142–43, 210
Survey research, 97, 163, 173
Swing voters, 92, 93, 106; and 1996 presidential election, 34–35, 117–23; candidate traits important to, 105; focus group participation of, 97; mall group participation of, 98; role in majority rule, 36; and television advertising, 30

Tammany Hall, 62
"Targeted issue marketing," 173
Targeting: of advantaged individuals, 17; as campaign strategy, 90; choice of targets for, 91, 112, 133, 163; of direct solicitation targets, 100; and educational level, 111–12, *113–15;* and income level, 111, *114–16;* of the public, 30–31, 32, 220; technology's impact on, 8, 27, 102, 163; of white evangelical Protestants, 136
Tariffs, 47, 59–60, 75
Technological changes: impact on lobbying by interest organizations, 163, 171; impact on political participation, 27, 29–31, 44, 200; targeting techniques created by, 102. *See also* Communication technologies
Teeter, Robert, 101

Telephone contact firms, 99
Telephone contacts, 8, 102, 133, 163
Television advertising: in 1996 presidential election, 118–20; candidate marketing through, 29–30, 100–101, 102; effects on declining partisanship, 33; free time for political parties, 205–6, 218; and initiatives, 144, 150; and issue advocacy, 109; and negative advertising, 106–7; by PACs, 131–32; postwar impact of, 76–77
"Thin democracy," 21
Tierney, John T., 157
Tracking polls, 97, 104
Trade organizations, 11, 157. *See also* Business groups
"Tweed Ring," 57, 62
Two-party system, 52

Verba, Sidney, 17, 202, 204
Veterans' organizations, 11
Vietnam War protests, 78
Voters: attitudes and behavior of, 25, 33, 68n4, 107, 114–17, 132, 150; and increase in "party of nonvoters," 195; and initiatives, 151; "neuro-personality profile" of, 120; "persuadables" as targeted, 104; and voter research, 97. *See also* Electorates; Political participation; Swing voters
Voter turnout: in nineteenth-century elections, 56; in 1936 presidential election, 73; in 1994 congressional election, 139; and corruption, 59; decline in, 26, 44–45, 68–69, 200, 213–14; and educational level, 12–13; and female suffrage, 68n4; impact on political participation, 201–2; and initiatives, 142; in non-U.S. democracies, 196, 210
Voting: and class bias, 68–69; compulsory voting laws, 214–15, 216, 221; and corruption, 59, 62, 68; as indicator of public will, 17; and literacy tests, 68; payments for, 62; secret ballots, 20, 67; and single transferable vote (STV) ballots, 211–12, 213; and voter guides, 138–39, 144; and voter registration laws, 20, 67–68, 199, 214, 216. *See also* Political participation; Split ticket voting

Walker, Jack L., 21, 127
Walsh, Tom, 129
Ward, Doug, 122
Ware, Alan, 46, 48, 53, 86, 199–200, 204
"Warm transfers," 163
Washington operatives, 15
Watergate scandal, 78, 82–83
Web pages, 102
Whig party, 52, 53
Whitaker and Baxter (firm), 146

White House. *See* Executive agencies
Why Parties? (Aldrich), 48
Wilson, James Q., 165–66
Wilson, Pete, 139
Wolfinger, Raymond, 214
Wolpe, Bruce C., 160–61, 174
Woman suffrage, 68n4
World Wide Web, 102

Zelikow, Philip D., 33